All the Essential Half-Truths about Higher Education

George Dennis O'Brien

THE UNIVERSI.

CHICAGO PRESS

CHICAGO AND LONDON

The University of Chicago Press gratefully acknowledges the
assistance of the Exxon Foundation in the publication of this book.

The University of Chicago Press, Chicago 60637
The University of Chicago Press, Ltd., London
© 1998 by The University of Chicago
All rights reserved. Published 1998
Paperback edition 2000
Printed in the United States of America
07 06 05 04 03 02 01 00   2 3 4 5

ISBN: 0-226-61654-1 (cloth)
ISBN: 0-226-61657-6 (paperback)

Library of Congress Cataloging-in-Publication Data

O'Brien, Dennis, 1931–
    All the essential half-truths about higher education / George
Dennis O'Brien.
        p.   cm.
    Includes bibliographical references (p.   ) and index.
    ISBN 0-226-61654-1(cloth : alk. paper)
    1. Education, Higher—United States.   2. Universities and
colleges—United States.   I. Title.
    LA228.037   1998
    378.73—dc21   97-14479
                                                                  CIP

To David T. Kearns

friend of education, excellence, and economy
humane executive
friend

It is often deemed sufficient to have a philosopher-statesman re-state the ideals of higher education, with all those warmed by affect rather than informed by analysis. There is typically less there than meets the eye.

Burton Clark, *Perspectives on Higher Education*

Contents

Full-Face Preface

In a book that takes as its subject *half*-truths, it would seem advisable to have a whole-truth, full-face preface. The central question of this essay could be stated as follows: *who* will decide the future of higher education in the United States? Or: *what* principles will govern such decisions? I emphasize "*who* will decide" because the "*what*" has lots of commentators. Discussing the (to the author's mind) proper aims for higher education is stock and trade for pundits within and without the academic community. In the 1960s and their aftermath, radical-left critics envisioned various egalitarian, experiential ends to be realized by universities. More recently, neoconservative critics have declared for meritocracy and "traditional" values. In the meantime, a significant proportion of students probably drifted through higher education as an escape from home, a place for adolescent pleasures, or a preparation for a job. There is much food for thought in all these meditations on higher learning—and the fact of student drift—but it remains only mental victuals unless one believes that there is somebody *who* can actually effect change. The *who* of educational change is, however, obscure.

Who has authority in the contemporary university? It may appear that the decision structure in colleges and universities is perfectly obvious: the president and board of trustees (or equivalent) are positioned on any available organizational chart as the supreme authorities in institutions of higher learning. Fortunately (mostly) the organizational charts are historical anachronisms. There was a day when presidents and boards decided for higher education, but something radical happened about a century past that altered all that: the rise of the research university. Before that educational revolution, American higher education was dominantly religious and denominational. Colleges were the creatures of the various sects; the minister-presidents presided and decided in the light of denominational dogma and decree. The Christian aims were clear—at least to the specific founding congregation—and no one doubted the authority of the president (minister) and board (elders).

The research university revolution caused a tectonic shift in authority away from the president to the faculty. In the old-style denominational colleges, the Truth was already known (at least the faithful so believed); one needed only to preach and practice the known. The research universities proclaimed that *the* truth is yet to be discovered. Faculty with their specialized skills are the designated discoverers. In an institution-of-discovery, the discoverers achieve authority. Old-style presidents ministered to the Truth; modern presidents *ad*minister unto the truth seekers.

Simply denominating "the faculty" as primary decision makers within the university would be most uninformative. It is necessary to understand the philosophical assumptions that define a modern faculty *post* the research revolution. After all, there have been "faculty" ever since the Middle Ages, but the modern, federally funded researcher is not to be confused with the mendicant monk of medieval Paris (although it is true that both do a fair amount of "begging"). Much of the analysis in this book is devoted to understanding the species of faculty created by the research university, and the assumptions thereof. It is from the view of a *research university faculty* that the principles that do and will govern higher education must be understood and evaluated.

But I have already perpetrated a half-truth. The organizational charts with the president at the top of the higher education heap reflect not only a charming past but also a significant present reality. Henry Rosovsky, the distinguished former dean of the faculty at Harvard, has commented that American higher education is unlike higher education elsewhere in the world because of the presence of both strong faculties *and* strong administrations. On the world scene, faculties have traditionally dominated, while nominal "leaders," rectors and chancellors, have been little more than ceremonial figures. The American situation of dual authority of faculty and administration, Rosovsky believes, is one of the reasons why the great majority of the world-class universities are in the United States. European universities, dominated by one "faction" (faculty and its fashions), have usually been "reformed" from outside by acts of parliament or the ministry of higher education. American higher education has an inner dynamic; it reforms itself—at least in some aspects—through the pull and tug between faculty and administrators.

Dual authority within the contemporary American university is a product of the specific history already noted. When the research university revolution occurred in the United States, it was built on an existing model of plenipotentiary ministerial presidencies. While faculty gained decision power in the new establishment, they did not become the university whole and entire, as had been the tradition in Europe. The rise of faculty authority within the research university context was as inevitable as it has been desirable. On the other hand, the persistence of presidents in the American experience has given a certain managerial sophistication to these complex organizations while, at the same time, acting as something of a goad and check on faculty single-mindedness.

What is more surprising than the managerial transmutation

is the persistence of moral mission in the modern university. If the minister-president became the administrator-manager in the research university, the spirit of denominationalism continues to hover over the presidential office—and the institution overall. American universities not only preserved presidents but also continued to house the ghostly presence of their former moral mission. It is this continuing presence (or pretense) of moral mission in the modern university that gives license to its contemporary moral critics. Because Allan Bloom assumed that there was a moralizing mission for higher education, he could decry the "closing of the American mind" in the modern open curriculum. Advocates of diversity argue, on the other hand, that the curriculum is too closed and should be opened to the farther ranges of human experience. The rights and lefts and wrongs of the argument are not as important as the persistent American belief that there should be a "moral" content for university study.

European universities again offer a contrast to the moral fervor of American higher education. In the standard European model, "freshmen" enter into a more or less fixed professional program. One matriculates in the faculty of medicine or law, not in the "liberal arts" pattern typical in the American experience. It is the "liberal arts" claim that enshrines the moral interest of American higher education. The contrasting European sense of "liberal arts" was expressed in a comment made to me several years ago by the minister of higher education in Sweden. The minister noted that the government restricted the number of students studying "liberal arts" (his characterization) because Sweden already had "too many museum directors." "Liberal arts" designated a profession, not moral uplift. The American sense that higher education has a direct moralizing function (however vaguely expressed in the admission brochure and the president's convocation address) is a wraith of the religious past.

I happen to believe in the moral mission of higher education—particularly in the American context—but to what extent is the modern university living off the moral capital of the older denominational college? The modern university certainly espouses no given tradition or fixed creed, yet the notion persists that university education somehow contributes to moral and political wisdom. The problem with living on yesterday's moral capital is that the inner principles of the research revolution are so sharply divergent from what could plausibly pass as "moral" education. The spiritual division between the older denominational college and the modern research university is profound. Much of the detailed analysis of this book is intended to understand the nature of that conflict for good and for ill.

Moral arguments about the nature of higher education might be regarded as an interesting diversion, but there is a more pressing issue for contemporary higher education: not morals, but money. The rise of the research university has truly been a *rise*. For almost the entire twentieth century, universities and colleges in the United States have expanded. In 1900, less than 5 percent of the eligible population attended colleges; by the end of the century, more than 50 percent of that population was in some form of "postsecondary" education. The rise in attendance has been more than matched by a rise in the funding of universities and colleges. The old-style college, if it taught science at all, could get by with a Bunsen burner and a set of stuffed birds. The modern research university requires vastly intricate and enormously expensive instrumentation. The faculty who attend the machines justly demand more than the minister's mite for their expertise. Any reasonable forecast for higher education in the twenty-first century projects not only an end to expansive funding but also a significant decline in financial support for higher education. Critics and funders currently demand that higher education be more "productive," more efficient, and more effective.

Restriction or retraction is a new phenomenon for American

higher education—particularly for academics whose experience was shaped during the years since World War II. The financial crisis of higher education places an enormous strain on
the dual decision structure of the American university. Faculty
interests can be as unlimited as the great scope of knowledge.
There are never enough physicists! The president is the ultimate
financial manager and so must seek some boundaries. But what
boundaries? How many physicists are enough? These are not
questions for which the president has any special expertise.
Physicists know the needs of physics, historians history, and so
on. If the budget is to be balanced, there will be limitations, but
they are as likely to be political as philosophical, market driven
as moral. The inherent expansiveness of knowledge has been
matched for a century by financial expansiveness. When the
coffers close, who will decide on the intellectual survivors?

The research revolution, as it has developed institutionally
over the last century and a half, left two fundamental issues unsettled and unclear: what are the inherent aims of this new educational enterprise, and/or who will decide those aims? Because
the rise of the modern university is also the rise of faculties from
subservience to authority, it would seem that it is faculty aims
and faculty authority that will resolve the unsettled state of affairs. Yet, while faculty gained authority, they did not *quite* become the university whole and entire. Presidents persisted, and
the moral aims of denominational education (however vaguely
proclaimed) were somehow grafted onto a new set of research
aims, with which they are scarcely compatible. Thus, when it
becomes necessary to discern the *essential* university tasks for
either monetary or moral reasons, neither the faculty nor the
president is well equipped by experience or principle to locate
the core in more than an ad hoc manner. And if either party discovered an essence, it is not clear that the lucky party would
have authority to act on such a wonderful insight.

Higher education is therefore vulnerable to both internal and
external critics who will (and do) claim that there is no guiding

vision. In a time of financial stringency, internal critics among the faculty can legitimately ask why there must be these financial cuts and not others—is the administration only concerned with a balanced budget? Educational planning driven by dollars appears ad hoc and irrational—particularly if it is *my* department that has been deleted, demoted, or diminished. External critics of the university may criticize its lack of fiscal discipline. Boards of trustees cannot understand why expensive Department A cannot be shut down like an unprofitable production line. The president and faculty offer pious rejoinders about the large mission of higher education. It is not a balanced budget but a balanced curriculum that guides decisions. Philosophical critics counter that the mess of the modern permissive curriculum shows that the university really has no sense of mission. One defends against mere budget balancing by developing a balanced philosophy of education whole and entire, but the moral critics claim that there is no such philosophy at play in the faculty senate, the president's office, the board room, or the fraternity quad.

Before concluding these prefatory comments, some clarifications and disclaimers: I have singled out the revolution of the research university as the pivotal event in understanding modern higher education in America. One might believe that the focus of this discussion is on the 50 to 100 *universities* that can justly claim to pursue advanced research and produce graduate students. Not so. I intend these remarks to cover almost all of the 3,000 and more colleges and universities in the land. In the text, I use the terms "college" and "university" almost interchangeably, if for no other reason than verbal variability. When I mean to single out some different sort of institution—PhD-granting institution, liberal arts college, community college—I hope to make that apparent in the text. Obviously most American higher educational institutions are not research universities by any stretch of the local propaganda. Nevertheless, the basic sense of higher education (and, I suspect, of *all* education from K–12 to graduate school) was radically redefined by the research university, and that sense pervades almost every institution from the great Harvards down to the junior colleges. There are a few interesting exceptions (largely religious colleges), and the problems of these institutions vis-à-vis the "mainstream" will be used to illustrate the character and dimension of the research revolution.

A significant part of this book questions certain assumptions that faculty in the modern university hold as absolutes—in particular, the assumption is that "the faculty *is* absolutely the university." Because the author is a former university president, one could regard these criticisms as traditional administration-versus-faculty tussling. Although any president must have a list of faculty he or she would gladly tussle away in fact or in reflection, it is not my intent to undermine the ascendency of faculty. Far from wishing to return to presidential denominational dictatorship (Presbyterian, Catholic, Jungian, Marxist, Radical Right, Radical Chic, etc.), I believe that the future will require new structures of faculty responsibility *for the institution*. The research revolution placed faculty in charge of their disciplines, but there is more to the *institution* than individual disciplines singly or collectively. To bring faculty into larger institutional accountability and constructive decision making is no small task, and it involves changing many of the fundamentals of current faculty self-understanding, status, and the present governance structures. If the understandings of current faculty status and structure are *absolute,* no such changes can be expected—thus, my intent to convert absolute truths into half-truths.

A central thesis of this book is that discussions of higher education are anywhere from misplaced to mistaken because they address the *idea* of higher education, not the *institution* of higher education. *The* American institution of higher education at the end of the twentieth century is the *research university.* The character of the American research university rests on certain fundamental "scientific" assumptions *and* a historical "hangover" of moral mission. Failure to address *institution* is subtly distorting. An *idea* that has absolute validity in its own right becomes subtly changed when it becomes institutionalized—in the language of this treatment, an absolute truth becomes a half-truth. If the institutionalized idea continues to be asserted as an absolute, all manner of confusion and mayhem may result. A potent and crucial example is "academic freedom." On its own grounds, free inquiry is a virtual absolute. However, when it becomes *institutionalized* as academic tenure, the notion is fundamentally qualified—or should be qualified in terms of the financial and/or philosophical state of the institution granting tenure. It is institutionalization, from absolute ideal to concrete reality, from the *idea* of a university to the historical reality of our present university *institutions,* that is the theme of this analysis.

Because I am interested in *institutions,* I am necessarily interested in *history.* Institutions are historical entities: if one studies government, it is best to address the history of the British Parliament or the Constitutional Convention of 1789. Interest in history is grounded on the belief that we learn about the value of anything—including the value of higher education—from its history, its "tradition." "Tradition" is a key element missing in the philosophy of the research enterprise, and it is the concept needed if the moral hangover of higher education is to be something more than a historical headache. To many readers, a claim for tradition may imply something darkly "conservative," rigid, and reactionary. I do not mind being thought "conservative"; indeed, it is universities that I very much wish to conserve against both external threat and their own internal incoherence. What I would wish to dispel, however, is the linkage of tradition with "rigid" or "reactionary." I believe that tradition, properly understood, is exactly the opposite of "rigid." The ideology of the modern university has its own curious "rigidity," which I hope to reveal, if not repeal.

A philosophy mentor of mine told a story about being interviewed on French radio. Although he had studied in Paris and was fluent in the language, he found himself baffled trying to find the French equivalent for "muddling through." The radio interviewer was of no assistance and asked what the phrase meant. "It is what the British do in politics," my mentor replied. "Ah, in that case," the interviewer replied, "there is no such word in French!" This book may make the mistake of being too French. I am particularly conscious of this French failing in describing the historical change from the denominational college to the research university. The actual course of events requires a "thick description"; it is certain that the various actors, then and now, would insist that it is all much more complicated. So be it. Nevertheless, I am content to cut through the bushes in the manner of a French formal garden, creating straight pathways bounded by overtrimmed trees, with the hope of bringing clarity to what is inevitably a historical tangle.

I will in the course of the treatment offer recommendations that might remedy both the moral and the monetary dilemmas of the day. But, after all, American higher education may simply "muddle through." The emergent muddle would not be without merit. The modern American university is a treasure trove of excellences, which, even in a reduced and ill-shaped form, would have much to commend to the eager student and affluent donor. Nevertheless, I believe that clarity about fundamentals could make American higher education both more effective and more economical. I also believe that it might resuscitate the moral mission.

"Muddling through" may also explain the "tone" of this treatment. Higher education is a serious subject, but it does not profit from ponderous profundity. Ponderosity suggests that the author speaks the whole and absolute truth, and that will not do for a book of and about half-truths. If I am critical of the modern university, I would be chiding, not churlish. My criticisms are themselves half-truths if looked at in the light of the extraordinary accomplishments of the university revolution. Even as a muddle, American higher education remains the world leader—far eclipsing other distinguished and ancient university systems. That it suffers from serious financial and philosophical problems is the price paid for its virtue. Still, I think one could lower the price and enhance the virtue.

1 Anyone for Higher Education?

I generally write books and articles by first finding a proper title. The title then becomes a leitmotif for the content and tone of the presentation. A "witty" (perhaps) book on theology was entitled *God and the New Haven Railway: And Why Neither One Is Doing Very Well.* As is appropriate to a religious work, the title came to me in a dream. I have been hoping for a similar divine titular inspiration for a book on higher education, but I doubt that the deity is all that interested in the subject. Worse yet, I suspect that readers are even less interested in another book on higher education, regardless of the title—divinely inspired or not. So uninteresting did the prospect of a book on higher education seem that I was tempted toward the title *Why Are Books on Higher Education So Boring?* Why *are* books on higher education so boring? This presentation is intended to answer the question while attempting to avoid the fault.

It is, alas, true that most books on higher education are boring. An immediate explanation can be found in the epigraph from Burton Clark. Books on higher education seem to range between two extremes. "Philosopher-statesmen" like to discuss "the aims of education" at some level of transcendent cliché, which warms the affect while lulling the mind. At the other end are "exposé" books—for example, Charles Sykes's *ProfScam*—which, while they are rather entertaining, inhabit the same clichéd precincts as the works of the high-minded philosophers. It is always amusing to show that the transcendent pundit presides over a congregation dotted with fools and failures. If the philosopher neglects the comedic realities, the critic has nothing to contribute beyond finger pointing. The critique books are boring, therefore, by sheer repetition of anecdote, until the reader says, "Enough, already!" and lays the book aside.

This current book (boring or not) sets out to discover why books on higher education are so unsatisfactory. I offer two hypotheses: first, most books about higher education are not about higher education at all—and thus are boring because they are words searching for a subject; second, the "philosophic" claims made about higher education are at best half-truths—sometimes sheer mythology on the pathway to fairy tale. The two faults are related, and, under either hypothesis, the real subject of higher education can be gracefully avoided.

Books about Higher Education
Are Not about Higher Education

The noblest of the misdirected descriptions of higher education turn out to be encomiums on culture, the intellectual life, high science, or some equally great worthy. How many commencement sermons have extolled Socrates and the Socratic method as the heart of the university? But Socrates carried on his incisive dialogues in the public market quite without any need for a university. Associate Professor Socrates? The man never published a thing—and he would have thought an intellectual-compound-for-philosophers directly counter to his "prophetic" mission.

Another case in point. Nothing so defines the culture of the modern university as the centrality of natural science. Thus, it seems easy enough to extol the importance of the university as the locus of great science. But a glance at history should give pause. As one commentator notes, "Experimental science . . . evolved basically outside and in opposition to the traditional universities." The Royal Society was the locus of Newton's scientific activity; it was historical accident that he was domiciled at Trinity College, Cambridge. In short, activities that are claimed as the essential stuff of the higher education enterprise—philosophy, art, science, and the lot—have all enjoyed a boisterous life not only far from academic halls but also far from even the idea of a university.

The fault in so many high-minded presentations of the university is that they forget that the university is not an *idea;* it is an *institution*. Intellectual conversation has had most of its history outside things called "universities" or "colleges," so that defending elegant intellectuality quite bypasses the fact that in Europe somewhere in the twelfth century, a peculiar institution was created that has endured and come to be known as the "university." (It was not originally called a "university." *Universitas* was a term that applied to formal associations of like-minded folk. There would be "universities" of goldsmiths, weavers, and logicians. Our "university" was called a *studium generale* and only later took on its current appellation by borrowing from the *universitas* formed by the "guilds" of the professors.)

There is nothing essentially boring about discussing the development of philosophy or physics, but since that conversation is elevated so far above the nuts and bolts of the *institutions* of higher education, it opens the door to the Charles Sykeses of this world to describe the nuts and dolts that slip in under the transcendental veil. Discussing the intellect and not the institution misses the mark and leaves the reader who is genuinely interested in *universities* unilluminated.

Neglect of the *institution* of the university may seem no great fault. There they are in all their pseudo-Gothic halls and laboratories. True, science and philosophy may have had a youthful career in the shops and streets, but they have now found lodgement on a long lease in "universities." The physicist knows that plumbing is part of the institutional architecture, but "it goes without saying" in the life of the mind. The present author, as a former university president, may have had the duty of worrying about budgets and bathrooms, but that is all rather trivial. (And thus is the presidential office oft regarded.)

Neglect of the *institution* leads, however, to critical practical and philosophical problems. Practical first: universities in the United States (and worldwide) are under enormous financial pressures. It is clear that the percentage of national income expended on the growth of higher education during the roughly twenty years from 1960 to 1980 will not be expanded or even sustained. Financial crisis raises *institutional* issues. Will there be a Department of Greek? Can one afford high-level specialties? Can one afford liberal arts? The financial constraints of higher education may suggest not only minor trimming but also total institutional restructuring. The British Open University, with instruction to home viewers by television, has been a significant success. You *can* have higher education without plumbing.

Radical economic reconstruction of the institutional framework for higher education could simply eliminate many current institutional understandings of the "university." Students would not attend Old Siwash; they would channel surf through higher learning. Faculty would forgo tenure for a share of the residuals. The "university" is one historically developed medium for carrying forward science, culture—and, lately, art. It has not always been the institution for learning and may cease to exist in anything like its current form. The philosophical issue is whether a radical change in the institutional setting for higher education would inevitably change its meaning and function, both for society and in itself. Socrates saw "philosophy" as an engaged critique of the public pieties of his day. Philosophizing off the streets and in the study room would have been for Socrates a wholly different—and not very useful—endeavor.

If the historical entity "university" is to have a future, it will need to examine its *institutional* assumptions. Academics are enamored of Socrates' Delphic injunction: *Know thyself.* It is nowhere more honored in the breach than on the home campus in regard to the institution in virtue of which there are "academics." Institutional assumptions, such as academic freedom, the liberal arts, and collegial governance, are all part of the taken-for-granted ideological furniture of the modern university; they are likely to receive as little analytical examination as the already noted notably ignored plumbing. The outcome of this charming neglect is that most of the dogmas of academic life function as half-truths. Like shamans and scarecrows, these deep notions can be used to spook one's enemies: "We must defend the liberal arts tradition at Siwash State!" But they deserve better treatment.

Discussions of Higher Education Rest on Essential Half-Truths

Higher education is addicted to highly valuable and essential half-truths. Another putative title for this treatise was *From Myth to Cliché in Higher Education.* I rejected that title as misleading. "Myth" suggests to the ordinary reader "falsehood," and the pronouncements with which I am concerned are not finally out-and-out wrong. What is claimed is *essential* but not *absolute.* When these "half-truths" are uttered with appropriate *brio,* they become the clichés of the day for both academic defense and critique. I devote one chapter to each of these essential half-truths.

The Faculty Is the University

An exemplary half-truth. As a pious cliché, it is frequently uttered—mostly by faculty who believe it. (Board chairs and university presidents also find the proclamation a vital part of their defensive arsenal.) It is an essential half-truth about higher education. It is true enough that higher learning rests on the skills of the highly learned; absent a faculty, there is no university worth discussion. But a collection of highly learneds is not a university, as the crowds around Socrates or Sir Isaac Newton would attest.

Various contemporary critics of universities have suggested the radical notion that it is the presence of *students* that converts a collection of high skills into a higher school. A research institute may be only the collection of the scientifically capable, but a college or university requires attention to some sort of interchange between those with faculties and those who would acquire same: individuals with faculties are not *a faculty*. And there is even more to "university" than teacher-student, as the Socratic counterexample indicates. Socrates did not give letter grades.

Having noted that "the faculty *is* the university" just will not do, it is important to emphasize that it is a half-*truth*. It was the construction of guilds of officially accredited scholars in the medieval universities that became the *institutional* structure for the special type of intellectual endeavor and tutorial effort that we know as "the university." Just being wise and having "students" do not count for university status until there is a guild of Socrateses dispensing credits and diplomas.

In the Middle Ages, "the faculty *is* the university" was at least a three-quarters-truth (and has remained the dominant European tradition). The formal institutional structure quickly developed after the model of Paris, where faculty reigned—in contrast to Bologna, where students were in charge. Medieval universities had rather modest laboratory and plumbing needs, so that when a faculty member was sufficiently annoyed with the local scene, he would simply pick up and relocate to a more favorable site. Oxford was populated with faculty refusniks from Paris, and the "wandering scholar" was a commonplace of the times. (The fact that the faculty were often members of the mendicant religious orders lent a certain economic freedom to relocation. Reinstating the vow of poverty, however, is probably not the solution to the contemporary financial crisis.) In the days since—and particularly following the rise of the "research university" at the end of the nineteenth century—"the faculty *is* the university" has retreated toward a half-truth. Vast libraries, complex experimental equipment, football, and fraternities have converted the happy band of wandering scholars into a formidable corporate and material structure quite different from its twelfth-century ancestors. It is this historically, geographically, and ideologically unique structure that should be the focus of discussions about higher education.

By failing to address the institution of the modern university, one misses the substance of the matter in a specifically important manner. When it comes to "substance," it was the inventor of the notion, Aristotle, who criticized previous philosophers for neglecting "the efficient cause" of the thing. Analyzing any old thing at hand, even a university, requires asking what it is good for, what shape it has to take in order to accomplish its purpose, what it should be made of. A knife is for cutting; it should have a sharp edge and not be made of jello. Aristotle thought that his predecessors had done pretty well on aims, forms, and matter, but that they forgot to tell us how the thing got made. To whom was this knife construction project addressed? Knives do not come about by nature, and it is no good talking to a pudding maker about this instrument. A blacksmith seems plausible.

The Aristotelian admonition about "efficient cause" is particularly relevant to discussions of higher education. To discuss the "aims of education," the *idea* of the university, and not indicate who should/could craft the object aimed at seems a peculiarly fruitless—and boring—enterprise. Failure to identify the efficient cause is, however, endemic to the literature of the field. Another title that I contemplated for this presentation underlined the issue of "efficient cause": *Who Will Decide the Future of Higher Education?* In current business school lingo: who has the decision rights in university? I submit that this is perhaps the cloudiest issue of all for the contemporary university—particularly the American university.

The question of who decides is also historically unclear. We have only good guesses about what the circumstances were in the twelfth century that actually created the universities; we are slightly better off when we try to trace the rise of the research universities at the end of the nineteenth century. One can point to the great formative presidential leaders of the nineteenth century—Eliot (Harvard), Gilman (Hopkins), White (Cornell)—but naming those great efficient causers will only heighten the dilemma of the late-twentieth-century university. The great formative or reformative presidents used the authoritarian presidential traditions of older denominational colleges to create research universities, which compromised, though they did not wholly eliminate, presidential authority. No one at Increase Mather's Harvard would have dared to claim that the faculty was the university—after Eliot, it was at least half true. The irony of nineteenth-century presidential authoritarianism is that it was used to shift authority toward the new research faculty without defining a structure of governance that reflected the new reality.

Given the sheer confusion about who manages the modern university, it is no wonder that commentators address the aims of education. Discussing the idea of a university has intrinsic interest, but since one has no notion to whom these lofty aims should be addressed, the issue is left unsaid, and the edifice unconstructed. Cardinal John Henry Newman's *The Idea of a University,* a prospectus for a Catholic university in Dublin, is a case in point. A favorite text for commencement genuflections to ideals, Newman's discourses enjoyed no *institutional* realization. The efficient causers of his Idea were to be the Irish bishops of the day—addressing instructions on knife making to pudding cooks? Lacking a sure sense of "who decides," earnest presidential prose on higher education creates its own indecisiveness. The president proclaiming reform needs to persuade a suspicious faculty, a restive alumni body, a bottom-line board of trustees, and a transient population of adolescents. The president tries to solve the problem and salve the proletariat at the same time. This is an inherently contradictory task, and so ringing calls for reform often prove to be little more than the sounding off of the brass and the tingling of symbols.

Decision rights are an *institutional* issue. The paradigm medieval *universitas* was in one sense the creature of the faculty union: *universitas professorum*. But given the conditions of the early universities, there was little institutional baggage. Medieval monks dissatisfied with the local educational emporium "voted with their feet," so the issue of who governed the campus at Paris or Bologna was of secondary interest. Over the many years since, institutions have elaborated, and decision rights have shifted with the sense of the institutions. In the course of this treatment, I concentrate on the development of American higher education from a period of Protestant denominational colleges—where the minister-president held all the decision authority—to the rise of the modern research university—which seismically shifts authority to the faculty, but in an institution with aims vastly different from those of its denominational predecessor or its medieval ancestor. Understanding the role of faculty in the research university is *the* prime task in clarifying the nature of the modern *institution*.

Tenure Is the Necessary Condition of Academic Freedom

If "the faculty *is* the university" is one of the essential half-truths about the modern university, corollary propositions about faculty define their role and status. One of the achievements of the modern (twentieth-century) professor has been the establishment of "academic freedom." The importance of that notion is seemingly absolute, since it is a necessary concomitant to the development of the various disciplines and studies that constitute the core of the research university. The *institutional* expression of academic freedom became entangled, for good reason, with a rather different concept: academic tenure, that is, a guaranteed contract for employment. In professorial circles, the phrase "academic freedom and tenure" is often regarded as a single notion. The necessary connection between academic freedom, on the one hand, and tenure, on the other, is a worthy half-truth—but no more.

Universities Are Neutral on Moral Value/ Universities Teach Moral Value

These are two half-truths that do not add up to a whole truth. The first half-truth seems to follow from the claim of academic freedom and the second from the denominational origins of American higher education. If one has some designated institutional value, it seems that academic freedom would be compromised. The issue is alive and well on Catholic university campuses. In the celebrated case involving Father Charles Curran at the Catholic University of America, the court decided that the institution would have to decide either for academic freedom, and become a "real" university, or for the dismissal of a dissenting theologian, and be something less than the real thing.

That Catholic University had moral values was certainly clear to me when one of my daughters enrolled there as a freshman and the president used his welcoming remarks to praise chastity—a speech unlikely to be replicated elsewhere in the Association of American Universities (AAU) community. But if the other presidents were not greeting their freshpersons with praise of sexual prudence, one can be certain that they were extolling some special *values* from the Princeton/Haverford/Bryn Mawr/Antioch/Slippery Rock experience. Unhappily, most of these local encomia for values are as vague as the rest of the talk about higher education. There must be some special (even moral) value embedded in the collegiate experience—but it is best not to say where. The value debate for colleges and universities claims both too much and too little, which allows both half-truths to be solemnly affirmed.

The Liberal Arts Curriculum Aims at Distribution/Diversity

"Distribution" is the institutional expression of the goal of a "well-rounded" education. Well-rounded? As has been brightly said, a cue ball is well rounded and rolls wherever it is neatly stroked. Depending on where one emerges on the value-free/value-laden and diversity debates, one could well argue that production of angularity would be a desirable aim. Does circumferential education imply breadth of knowledge (which and how much?), improvement of character (in the university?)? What qualifies as pure-gold half-truth is the illusory realization of well roundedness in the common curriculum. On either score, the practice of distribution requirements is at best a gesture, at worst a futile gesture.

"Diversity" has but recently come into prominence—at least in its present verbal configuration—and it should definitely not be confused with the older cliché of "distribution," though both seem to urge moving around the intellectual landscape. Proclamations of diversity are made on both moral and intellectual grounds, and it is often impossible to tell which is being championed. That is a first confusion. If one can be clear about the moral or intellectual claim, then promoting diversity might qualify as a *whole* truth but for the fact that "diversity" does not mean *diversity.* "Diversity" is often a code word, and when one deciphers the code, it turns out that diversity is not at all the issue, and when it is used as an issue (in its coded form), it often means precisely the opposite of diversity. My conclusion: more diverse higher education (in some sense) must be at least half true. The problem is which half.

Teaching Is the Primary Task of Higher Education

If faculty liberals and cultural conservatives take opposite sides on the matter of value in the curriculum, they are both likely to salute the above statement. It may be the merest piety, but it is difficult to find anyone who will outright deny the claim. I have participated in an untold number of discussions at meetings of research university presidents worrying about the need to reaffirm the transcendence of teaching at their institutions. I am sorry to say that I think that the emphasis on teaching—and the much-publicized conflict between research and teaching—is downright misleading. The terms of the discussion are faculty terms: *faculty* teach, *faculty* do research. The proper issue is not so much the faculty *teaching* as it is the students *learning*. The neglected topic in university assessments is not teaching; it is learning—with or without a (faculty) teacher.

The Problem with Higher Education Is the Administration

This claim is delightfully ambiguous and half false. Intoned by faculty, it clearly means that those meddlers at the middle with their infernal committees and bureaucratic shuffles hinder the natural energies of the mental life. The thesis gained articulation from Paul Goodman in *The Community of Scholars* many years ago, but it is a favorite at any faculty coffee hour. Uttered by senators, talk show hosts, and the occasional exasperated board chair, the proposition has the opposite intent. The problem is that there is not *enough* administration at the old U. What is needed is clear-cut managerial decisiveness, as at General Motors or Trump Enterprises. (I name only corporations that have, within the memory of man, announced spectacular financial losses.) Somebody should be right on the issue of university administration: do we need more or less of it?

But, then, just who or what constitutes *the* administration; that is, who *is* running the show? In a classic study of college management, Professors Michael Cohen and James March concluded that universities were not managed at all: they constituted a unique social entity, which they labeled "organized anarchy." To add legal conviction to confusion, the United States Supreme Court decided (in *NLRB v. Yeshiva University,* discussed later in the text) that *faculty* "substantially and pervasively manage" the university—a splendid, judicially affirmed half-truth.

Low-Cost Public Education Benefits the Least Advantaged

This half-truth moves out of the interior debates of university life into the placement of higher education within the entire social fabric. It is, however, an important *institutional* issue, since it seems to divide higher education into public and private institutions. The actual *difference,* however, is largely in the fantasies about funding, not in the facts about faculty and program. I am inclined to think that the public claim to help the disadvantaged is statistically misleading, if not completely false. If I grant even half-truth status to the claim for low-tuition public education, it is because there is more to the story than mere economics—but not much more.

The University Is the Axial Institution of Modern Society

I save the most macroscopic half-truth for a summative last word. Downgrading the claim to a mere B– is not intended to downgrade the genuine importance of higher education; it is intended to throw some sensible perspective on commencement day oratory. I believe that the moral institutions of society are more crucial than the intellectual ones—and I will expand on why research universities are unlikely repositories of practical wisdom.

So much for my essential half-truths about higher education. Are these *all* the essential half-truths? Not at all; the titular claim must itself be a half-truth, but I emphasize that these se-

lect claims are *essential* half-truths. If we are to preserve the
great cultural accomplishment of the university-as-institution,
each of these weighty statements requires our measured veneration. Veneration is not, however, adoration, and the task of
this book is to supply some counterweights and measures.

2 The Faculty *Is* the University

There is a famous story about General Dwight Eisenhower's introduction as Columbia University's new president. The general was escorted about the campus, met with trustees, greeted administrators, and finally attended a meeting of the faculty. He opened his remarks by saying how pleased he was to meet with the "employees" of Columbia. Professor I. I. Rabi, distinguished senior faculty member and future Nobel Prize winner, rose and said with measured dignity, "Sir, the faculty are not the *employees* of Columbia University, the faculty *is* Columbia University."

Any presentation of the modern university must start with faculty and recognize the force of Rabi's rejoinder. Recognizing faculty as prime actors reflects contemporary perception (and underlying reality), as the Eisenhower anecdote quite properly demonstrates. Contemporary perception and faculty axiom do not, however, conform to historical precedent or philosophical necessity. If "the faculty *is* the university," a prior question might well be this: what is the *university*? Or to turn the question in reverse: what is a university in which the *faculty* is the university? Or even more specifically: what is a university in which the "new" breed of faculty produced by the research university revolution is the university?

Faculty are indeed the repositories and creators of specialized knowledge and skill. But a university is not just a *collection* of learned persons. Trivially, most universities are fixed places needing heat and light. The contemporary mega-university, or even the modest college, possesses a significant infrastructure of facilities and finances whose tending is quite beyond the interest and skill of the collective faculty members. The Nobel physicist expects the lights to work in the lab but probably has no interest in determining whether the power comes from a gas turbine co-generation plant or Consolidated Edison.

If the university is an assemblage of learned persons in a place with central heating, it is also not *any* assemblage of learned folk, but a specific kind and variety of such. The *contemporary* university assemblage will be composed of *specialists* in various academic *disciplines*. The division of knowledge into specialties and disciplines, with specialists gathered in specific bureaucratic entities (departments), is a modern idea—and a virtual signature of the research university culture. William Rainey Harper, founding president of a quintessential research university, the University of Chicago, was puzzled and annoyed by the rise of departments as meaningful divisions of intellectual endeavor. Harper's views did not prevail in the development of the modern universities: institutionally, they are collections of disciplines in bureaucratic departments.

It has not always been so. The old-style collegiate institutions of the nineteenth century were populated with faculty who taught almost everything in the curriculum. There was not much in the curriculum beyond the classics and the Bible—and, from a contemporary perspective, the faculty were at best ardent amateurs. The ascendence of the disciplinary specialist is, then, a twentieth-century notion that contrasts not only with the pious amateurs of yesterday but also with polymaths like Gottfried Leibniz, the co-inventor of the calculus, who wrote on history, law, diplomacy, nature, and grace. But he was, after all, a librarian, not a professor.

As one determines the nature of a proper curriculum, one determines the kind of learned folk on site—or, as one determines which learneds, one will implicitly create the curriculum. St. John's College in Annapolis has a four-year "great books" curriculum in which every faculty member participates. Whether this qualifies the St. John's faculty as geniuses of Leibnizian proportions or not, it emphasizes that curriculum can determine faculty. What is consequential for the research university (and almost every higher education institution with the exception of the few St. John'ses) is that faculty specialists drive the curriculum, not the reverse. If, then, modern universities are specific collections of specific specialties, which specialties and how many of such become issues to be determined.

Deciding what departments to support in the emporium of education is beyond the attested skill of individual disciplines. Generally, the presence of *other* departments makes little difference to individual specialties. Except for areas that are directly supportive (e.g., math for physics, physics for chemistry), the specific collections of departments must be determined by a rationale external to the individual disciplines. Tradition, marketplace, political correctness, political obtuseness, keeping up with the Yales, economic necessity, moral overlay, and administrative whim may be convicted as the culprits in creating the specific collection or rarefied remnant that comprises the faculties of any college or university. There are appeals to "basic" studies, but quarrelling about "basic" may seem to be the basic business of educational commentators inside and outside the academic precincts.

Adding a specific assemblage of specialists to sound plumbing will not yet yield the notion of a university. That would be a reasonable definition of a research institute. A university has students. The presence of students creates an educational mission to the unwashed not present in the research institute. This could be a minor matter if there were no *undergraduate* students. Graduate and professional school students track through the learned disciplines like apprentices in the guild. (This is the dominant pattern in European universities, where students matriculate as "freshmen" in specific faculties, such as law, medicine, or art. In the United States, major research labs, e.g., Bell Labs, actually confer PhD degrees.) In American universities and colleges, for a variety of reasons, the majority of undergraduates are subjected to (or privileged by) some sort of "general education" or "liberal arts curriculum," which makes claims beyond professional skill and accreditation, claims often on morality or citizenship. It is in this "liberal arts" claim or component that the "moral" direction or distraction of contemporary American higher education is most obvious. Deciding the shape of *general* education for moral, political, or aesthetic purpose is again not part of the specialized competencies of the particular disciplines. Deciding what is in or out of the general plan of study is a perennial pedagogical puzzle.

All these issues—lighting the labs, selecting the disciplines, and educating the undergraduates—constitute worthy subjects for innumerable, interminable academic conferences, but the present and future financial crises of higher education bypass philosophical debate in favor of fiscal decision. If dollars are short, decisions will be made—or forced: what needs to be taught (for the good of the undergraduate student? the graduate student? the country? the ecosystem?), and what can we afford? The good and the practical impinge on the learned disciplines with special urgency when social ethics and financial support unravel simultaneously. And so it is at the present moment.

The theme of this book is the university as *institution*. Learning in any field, however arcane, is a good-in-itself, but when one creates an institution of learning with facilities and fees, good-in-itself has to answer this question: good for what? *University* education is not a private hobby personally funded; it is a service "sold" to societies, governments, businesses, and individuals. The buyers demand value for price. Any, all, and every knowledge and truth may be "priceless" as such, but in the institutional budget, every science and every art comes with a dollar sign. Does the individual discipline, does the collection of disciplines, does the university as institution have a moral, political, economic, or other justification for its pursuits? Such a question is likely to lead to considerable sputtering, since it seems—particularly to professional academics—that just these studies and just these institutional configurations are "beyond question." Indeed—yet it is worth noting that most humans throughout history, and most of the current inhabitants of the planet, have managed to get from dawn to dusk without university education. And if that is not enough to give pause, one need only listen to various contemporary American critics who alternately decry the Ivy Tower, advocate the "school of hard knocks," condemn the inherent racism of the standard studies, or find the very attitude of mind inculcated in the university coldly impersonal, inhumane, and ultimately socially destructive. Besides it is too expensive.

Given the twin crises of morals and money, the axiom that "the faculty *is* the university" is plausibly deconstructive. Faculty specialists have neither the taste for nor the training in the problems of the university-as-a-whole. The very purpose of appointing a distinguished chemist is *not* to have him be bothered with the budget and how many courses in French are needed for a proper education. If the university-as-a-whole (heat and curricular light) is at issue, what principles should be appealed to for "rational" decision? Lest anyone immediately assume that someone *else* possesses this remarkable metaphysical talent—deans or presidents, students or trustees—I cheerfully admit that they are probably equally incapable of formulating more than an outline of a sketch of a possible scenario for the university overall. The difference, of course, is that presidents and trustees do make—or try to make—these decisions about the university *institution* under whatever conditions of enlightenment they can muster. (Students are supposed to make some "holistic" sense out of the wandering path through the curriculum, even if their learned masters cannot.)

If "the faculty *is* the university"—and it is facul*ties* as collections of specialists that make up the modern configuration—it is easy enough to discern why overall cohesive planning and decision making seem (are) so difficult in the "multiversity" setting. Clark Kerr invented the notion of *multi*versity as a more adequate description than *uni*versity for the modern academic conglomerate. He noted that "pluralistic" faculties have significant capacity to *veto* institutional direction but find it very difficult to initiate overall direction. (Any change may threaten my department, so better remain with the status quo. If they eliminate Department A, who knows? I may be next!) The more arbitrary the particular collection of studies appears, the more arbitrary and threatening any decision to eliminate any area of study seems.

The President *Is* the University

If the modern axiom affirms that "the faculty *is* the university," the nineteenth-century axiom might well have been "the president *is* the university." In order to comprehend the currency and importance—and the limitations—of the present faculty ascendency, it is necessary to understand the revolution in higher education that occurred at the end of the nineteenth century. This revolution changed the "managerial" assumptions of the university, but that was only a secondary effect of a basic change in the very meaning of higher education.

If one contrasts the collegiate institutions of the nineteenth century with the universities of the twentieth, the underlying *philosophical* change is the move from *denomination* to *discipline*. The old-style college was a Christian denomination writ large, and the denomination was the ministerial president writ large. The curriculum was determined by the moral interests of the church, and the ministerial president was the clear manager of the entire enterprise. The modern governance structure of American colleges and universities, with a board of trustees as the final arbiter, is little more than the Presbyterian style of church governance applied to higher education. As the elders elected the minister and acted as custodians of parish finance (early college trustees were often called "custodians"), so with modern boards—unhappily no longer suffused with the Holy Spirit.

After the American Civil War, a sprinkling of American college graduates drifted to Germany to receive advanced instruction and the PhD degree. While the German example can be overplayed in understanding the origin of American research universities—the Scottish universities were also influential in modes of organization—the sense of research and scholarship fostered in Germany was decisive. Given the Biblicism of the traditional American denominational college, the effect of German Biblical studies was particularly crucial. Where the ministerial president read the Bible for religious inspiration, the German scholars read The Book as a historical document, a gathering of disparate texts and traditions. Critical discipline prevailed over denominational piety. If one could free the Bible from denominationalism through historical discipline, it was relatively easy to free any and all other possible areas of study from religious restriction. The immense controversy over Darwin convulsed American colleges of the late nineteenth century, but in the long run it was clear that Discipline (the science of biology) would prevail over Adam and Eve and their ecclesiastical supporters. Finally, the German university not only put the Bible in its (historical) place but also was the world leader in the development of the natural sciences. The development of advanced technological industry (chemistry in particular) in Germany demonstrated the power of research in creating new products. The university, instead of being a removed religious refuge, became an engine of economic advance.

The shift from denomination to discipline can be further explicated as a shift to *science*. The notion of "science" is the constitutive principle for the claim that "the faculty *is* the university." "Scientific" has its primary focus on the natural sciences, but it is not misleading to claim that the methods and assumptions of the natural sciences are the model for *all* contemporary university studies. While there is obviously a significant difference between the chemist presiding over his test tubes and the historian puttering over his texts, the cast of mind in both cases is "scientific"—"scientific" in the sense of dispassionate scrutiny free from personal, political, patriotic, Protestant, or papal aims. German historian Leopold von Ranke, in many ways the founder of modern "scientific" history, contrasted his own publication with the propagandistic histories of previous monarchic regimes. Ranke's motto for historical writing: *wie es eigentlich gewesen war* (how things actually were). While it is certainly true that not every modern academic reaches the high ascetic demands of the scientific paradigm, the final product is expected to be above party. (It is this impersonal "scientific" paradigm that has been challenged by the various diversity, multicultural, and politically correct movements of the present day. Those who dislike the research paradigm pejoratively label it "scientistic" to indicate an illegitimate encroachment upon "humanistic" study. Much more of that in due course.)

The old-style denominational college had a unified and paramount moral mission, which determined the curriculum and the extra-curriculum. Moral discipline, religious revival, and the college as ethical tutor *in loco parentis* all fit the philosophy of the denominational collegiate institution. Knowing what to do, all that one needed was a presidential enforcer to sustain the Gospel. President Mark Hopkins of Williams College not only battled the evil of the extra-curriculum (fraternities; he lost) but also could set the whole curriculum. He opined that there was only one book needed in the library: the Bible. It was James A. Garfield who commented that all one needed for great education was a student on one end of the log and Mark Hopkins on the other. President Mark Hopkins *was* Williams College.

However it may be explained (denomination, size, rurality), the president was the institution in the earlier years—and presidents have remained more authoritative in American higher education than similar officials (chancellors, rectors) in other countries. But for all the overhang of authority, the modern university president stands in a radically different position than his nineteenth-century precursor. Paradoxically, it was the inherited ministerial tradition of supreme presidential authority that allowed the great reform presidents of the late nineteenth century to revolutionize higher education away from religion to research—and away from presidential autocracy toward faculty governance. Given traditional presidential authority, the Eliots and Gilmans of the period were able to create or recast higher education on a model that gave prominence to discipline over denomination, faculty over founding church.

The Students *Are* the University

If "the president *is* the university" may be a plausible characterization of the past, "the students are the university" also has a past and (perhaps) a prominent—if curious—future. Some of the earliest university institutions were created and managed by students. The students in turn hired the masters they deemed needed for instruction. One of the first "revolutions" in the history of higher education occurred when the faculty guilds wrested control of the institutions from the students.

The modern university faculty may grudgingly admit the continuing presence of the president and his henchpersons for the sake of the physical plant, but that administrative duty is theoretically dispensable. Students, however, are a philosophical and financial necessity. In the earliest universities, the administration was de facto dispensable when medieval masters taught in any room with a roof. The University of Rochester opened (in 1850) without a president in rented hotel rooms and, as Ralph Waldo Emerson commented, went about "improvising education like a picnic." But no matter how meager the facilities (and hence the absence of administration), the essential ingredient for converting assembled learning into educational institution is the presence of students. "Student" is also an institutional concept. This is not any old passing on of skill and wisdom from master to apprentice, from elder to initiate; the university formalizes the relationship in fees and grades and degrees and licenses. If the presence of credit-earning students converts an assemblage of learned folks into a "faculty," could one allege that students *are* the university?

Something like that claim can be heard currently at the extremes of the morals and money demands on higher education. At the "moral" extreme, student-centered education becomes a species of psychotherapy, in which students are encouraged to express themselves, to build self-awareness and a sense of value. A colleague tells of participating in just such an "English lit" seminar during the heyday of student-centered therapy–higher ed. Students were asked to relate painful incidents in their lives, to touch the face of a partner, to feel the sadness or salvation of the other—and that sort of thing. Some of the more ardent multiculturalists of the present day offer variations on the "therapeutic" theme. One must avoid the "hegemonic" ("authoritative" in the dictatorial mode) dominance of the teacher so that the student may come to realize himself/herself. Since the university institution is itself hegemonic (all those "masters") in the style of dead, white, male Europeans, students must be liberated unto themselves as live and other-than-white or female or non-European or [unhappy group to be designated]. The professor-as-therapist is not at all the authoritative faculty specialist of the research revolution. One delves the spiritual resources of the student-patient, not the periodic table or the *Patrologia Latina et Graeca*.

If a "moral" agenda can create the student-centered university, money will do almost as well. The student becomes a *consumer,* and "the customer is always right!" Unlike the self-awareness model, the consumerist view does assume specialized knowledge in the instructor. The teacher has a skill that the student wishes to purchase. While this might give some psychic encouragement to the professorate, it obviously leaves the content of higher education to the urges of the consumer.

Both the morals and the money claims for student "hegemony" are present realities for the university and are no minor challenge. I will expend much ink discussing the complexities of the moral challenge of multicultural self-awareness in the course of this book; the monetary ones are easier to identify. Every time a college or university downsizes, rearranges, reasserts a mission, or defines a new one because of financial crisis—hardly a rare occurrence today and a commonplace for the years to come—the power of the consumer to shape the institution is clear. Traditional faculties bemoan the utter pragmatism of student course choices: not Pascal, the sage, but Pascal, the software. Carried far enough, the consumer may close down ancient product lines—starting with ancient Greeks and moving right on to such antiquities as the history of the New Deal.

These two plausible, present, and powerful interpretations of "the students *are* the university" are important as fundamental challenges to the research university claim that "a *specialist disciplinary* faculty *is* the university." Under either scenario, research faculty are dispensable. In the moral scenario, the student is the source of knowledge, value, insight; the so-called faculty do not dispense knowledge but rather draw value forth from the student. The faculty person is a therapist or facilitator who allows the student to tap deep personal meaning. In the multicultural scenario, the faculty member may seem to be more authoritative. The instructor will have an extensive scenario of the culture at hand, but it seems clear that in the extreme cases the aim is not so much education as *propaganda fidei.* The instructor is attempting to create a sense of moral worth in the student, about the culture, often with the clear intent to protest the injustice of demeaning its cultural claim. There is nothing essentially wicked about propagation of the faith—it was the principal function of the older denominational college—but the culture-therapist-cum-propagandist is hardly "faculty" as that term is defined by the research university model.

The consumerist challenge is more subtle because in some sense "faculty" are still a necessity. Nevertheless, student consumerism is as fundamental a rejection of the research university model as propaganda pedagogy. The research model originated from and is based in disciplines that, because of their complexity and sophistication, make *research* a sensible endeavor. *University* studies are supposedly *fundamental* studies of great scope and importance. While it is true that a "teacher" can instruct "students" in hair styling, it does not appear to be a subject that in itself profits from extensive research. The research assumption claims that the studies fostered in the university have some fundamental and essential (moral, scientific, political, salvational) value that justifies their place in the curriculum—and their funding in the budget. That is the way a learned faculty will justify the assemblage of university subjects, but the student consumer need not be convinced and may choose to spend the tuition dollar elsewhere on more entertaining or economical instruction.

Consumerism requires a faculty, but which faculty is at the whim of the market. The *university faculty* must make a case in the face of consumerism that the subject matters of the university are what the student *really* wants and needs. It is not student choice; it is, at some level, faculty choice that says, "This is worth knowing." If faculties become incapable of making and carrying that argument, the university institution of the present day will evaporate or be metamorphosed into something quite other—even if the name on the memorial gate remains. Physics was not part of colonial Harvard; it might migrate again.

The claim that "the faculty *is* the university" implies deep philosophical assumptions about teachers, students, and subject matter; those assumptions are undergoing a powerful challenge from social values and the economy. If the university as we know it is to survive and maintain the considerable virtues attained, it will have to articulate more effectively its moral case and its management structure—neither of which rises much above muddle or descends much below starry ideal. Since "the faculty *is* the university" in some fundamental sense post the research revolution, presumably it is *faculty* who need to clear the moral muddle and manage the enterprise. The research revolution is not an obvious help on either score.

The Faculty Is *Not* a University: Disciplinary Deconstruction

Nineteenth-century denominational colleges were unitary institutions—unitary with a dogmatic vengeance. The proliferation of colleges in the United States during the nineteenth century is attributable at least in part to the demand for a "unity in faith and morals." If Old-Style Christian College began to backslide into liberalism, a group of true believers would be moved to establish their own collegiate guardian of the Faith. The various Protestant denominations demanded their own colleges and often bitterly opposed the attempts of other sects to establish local institutions.

Denominationalism, dogma, and decision making all fit into a cohesive structure. The Truth being known, all one needed to do was to inculcate it. The Good being known, all one needed to do was to enforce it. The authoritative ministerial president was the symbol of this unitary vision; he was clearly the decision maker because there was no need to deliberate decisions among constituents: faculties were "of the Faith," and students existed to be trained "in the Truth."

One would hardly hold out this vision of the denominational college as the *beau ideal* of higher education. It is not even necessary to animadvert here about the narrowness of the pedagogy and the stultifying air of the old-style college. The numerous student riots of the nineteenth century are testament enough to the failure of the denominational colleges to realize their own dogmatic ends. I present the old-style college, and the figure of its dominating president, as a contrast to the new-style universities, with their dominating faculties. It is more than a half-truth to claim that the move to faculty prominence over presidents has been a development for the good. However, before declaring the arrival of the educational millennium, it is important to note what was *lost* in the transit to the modern dominance of disciplines. Most notably, what was lost was the *uni* in *uni*versity. While there is much to celebrate in the *multi*versity, which replaced the constricted unity of the nineteenth century, the multiversity experiences critical and often paralyzing inability to decide what its size, content, curriculum, or mission should be. The inability to decide is not accidental; it is a plausible by-product of the disciplinary revolution.

Why are disciplines deconstructive of institutional unity and cohesive decision making?

Disciplines Are Indifferent to Moral Ends

The pursuit of truth and knowledge need not—should not—bend to moral ends. (I do not believe that this claim can be wholly substantiated, but it is widely believed. More of that when the moral assumptions of higher education are reviewed in detail.) The controversies about academic freedom that marked the initial decades of the research university arose because faculty perceived that certain "scientific" theories, for example, evolution, ran counter to received moral wisdom of the old denominational colleges. So much the worse for moral concerns if the scientific facts will not support them. Since the old-style college regarded its mission as moral as much as anything, the "neutrality" of the "scientific" disciplines appears to undercut radically any attempt to create a coherent moral direction to the overall enterprise. As noted, the bitter collegiate battles over Darwinism and its eventual triumph over the Book of Genesis symbolize, if nothing else, the dominance of scientific discipline over "moral" dogma. If the unity of the university is to be some moral direction, that unity cannot be created on the base of science.

Disciplines Are Quasi-Independent

While it is the case that some disciplines rely on skills developed in other areas—for example, mathematics as a tool for physics—advanced research in any area of knowledge follows its own logic and interests. The physicist probably has no direct interest in advances in topology—and if he does, he might as well contact the appropriate specialist (who is at Brand X university anyhow) by e-mail. Lacking any practical (moral, religious, political) reason to limit the work of other disciplines, all are cheerfully encouraged to flourish—or to vanish from the budget and the quad. The late twentieth-century issue for colleges and universities challenges the basic assumption of disciplinary diffusion not on moral grounds but on the basis of sheer economics. Since all studies cannot be financed, which ones should be chosen?

Disciplines Are Institution-Independent

If disciplines are at least quasi-independent from one another, they are manifestly *institution*-independent. This assumption is critical—and it is at the heart of the research university revolution. One might invert the normal public perception of multiple university institutions at which there are departments of physics and say that it is more accurate to speak of the International Institute of Physics with a number of local franchises. If this is not exactly how it is in corporate reality, it is how it is in the minds of disciplinary academics. Various sociological studies of faculties have demonstrated that primary loyalty is to the discipline. Loyalty to the specific institution can be very tenuous. Being institution-independent is extremely valuable in maintaining the standards and integrity of disciplinary fields; it can be a significant hindrance to rational planning at the specific institutional level. Problems of *institutional* (economic, educational) integrity may fail to register with a faculty basically concerned with the trans-institutional character of the discipline.

In sum, the rise of the disciplines (a good thing for "science") presents a problem—largely unsolved—when trying to establish a cohesive sense of the very "institution" in which these disciplines find lodging. The denominational college had an ideology that guided decision making and determined the decision makers. The disciplinary university trends toward a geographical location. As Chancellor Robert Hutchins of the University of Chicago commented: "The university is a collection of departments tied together by a common steam plant."

If "the faculty *is* the university," one must understand clearly the changing meaning of "faculty." While there were "professors" in the denominational institutions of the past century, and "professors" stretching back to the cathedral schools of the Middle Ages, the modern "professor" represents a radically different institutional reality. That institutional reality is part and parcel of the research university model currently ascendent. Nothing is a better mark of the new professorate (and the role of faculty within the university) than the concept of academic freedom and tenure, to which I now turn.

3 Tenure Is a Necessary Condition of Academic Freedom

In addressing the university at any time in history, the status of faculty is crucial to understanding the meaning of the higher education at hand. It was the institutionalization of faculties in the *universitas,* or guilds, of the Middle Ages that led to the fundamental institution that goes beyond all the ad hoc congregations of sages gathered then and now for the pursuit of learning. Once there is an *institution* of higher learning, who belongs to that institution, the grounds on which he belongs, and how and by whom he is designated a member become essential issues. No one is appointed to a bull session; not so with university faculties. If "the faculty *is* the university," then one will have to understand what rights and privileges thereunto appertain. The concept of academic-freedom-and-tenure is a focal point for understanding the character of faculty in the modern research institution. Tenure is highly controversial, is subject to great pressure for change, and conceptually enshrines the most important central issue for higher education reform: the nature and role of faculties.

Like almost all the terminological absolutes that define contemporary American higher education, "tenure" is a modern invention. As a historical reality, it stems from the formation of the American Association of University Professors (AAUP) in

1915. This new organization, sponsored by such distinguished intellectuals as John Dewey, had legitimate grounds to be concerned about "academic freedom." The previous decade had seen a number of cases of plain and simple political suppression of distinguished faculty at major university centers. These actions—normally instigated by trustees outraged at the political and economic sentiments of "progressive" faculty—suggested a clear and present danger to advanced scholarship and research. Tenure contracts were to isolate those appointed against such political passions.

As the title of the organization (American Association of *University* Professors) might well indicate, the original scope of tenure included only *university* professors, since they were conceived to be the ones primarily concerned with advanced research. *College* professors, in contrast, were charged with conveying received knowledge to the "immature" (original AAUP language); academic freedom was not necessary or perhaps not desirable in the latter case. (Tenure has, of course, spread like the Gospel or the Plague—depending on one's view of the idea—to almost every collegiate establishment in the land.)

Two Theories of "Academic Freedom"

If "tenure" is not yet a century old, it is not without ancestral roots. Ancient precedent is often cited as an ideological defense of this modern academic assumption. Unfortunately, if one looks at tenure's ancestral line, the case for the modern concept becomes cloudy at best. The lessons of history by no means defend contemporary tenure.

It could be argued that the first plea for tenure was Socrates' recommendation to the court of Athens that he be allowed to continue his critical inquiries—and be provided with free meals for life in the Prytaneum, the traditional reward for Olympic athletes. His suggestion was offered as an alternative to the death penalty. The original AAUP plea for tenure was based on two notions: researchers need freedom to inquire, and since academics are so poorly paid, a career-long contract is a balancing compensation. Freedom and free meals for life have a history.

Socrates' mocking recommendation sealed his fate, and ever since, the shade of Socrates has been evoked when battling with forces of parochialism and oppression. I would be the last one to counter that heroic exemplar, but the lessons of Socrates are never free from irony. Consider the image of Socrates, successful in his plea, sitting with the Olympic wrestlers, munching out his years as the licensed gadfly of Athens. There is something faintly comic about an authorized prophet.

If Associate Professor Socrates with tenure seems odd, his qualifications would appear absolutely outlandish to the AAUP and any academic tenure committee. At most American universities and the leading colleges, tenure is granted after a probationary period, in which the fledgling academic is given an opportunity to test his or her academic skills. It may not be publish or perish, but most tenure committees would worry that candidate Socrates published nothing at all, and what would any learned reviewer make of the claim that the only knowledge the applicant possessed was of his own ignorance?

Although Socratic precedent is universally appealed to in rhetorical defense of academic freedom, it is not the real progenitor of modern academic freedom and tenure. There are really two deep—and in some ways antithetical—traditions behind open inquiry. Confusion between the two background theories can cancel out any coherent understanding. "Academic freedom" then becomes a slogan for the opportunistic, not a sober claim for scholarly probity or prophetic mission.

One can argue for "academic freedom" on the basis of either manifest *ignorance* or attained *knowledge*. Socrates offers a relatively pure case of inquiry from "ignorance." He argues for freedom to continue his task of challenging people in the *agora* (marketplace) because of the virtually inescapable darkness of the human mind. Only the gods are wise, and humans can be wise only in recognizing their own ignorance. Dialectical challenge is eternal because we never fully seize the truth, which lies beyond us in eternal Ideas. It is the quest for truth that counts, not the conquest of truth. Absent the persistent sting of the Socratic gadfly, mankind slumbers in the illusion of truth-at-hand.

What would a claim for *academic* freedom mean on Socratic assumptions? Socrates asks for "security," but he obviously regards it as a jest. It is Plato who creates a special precinct (in the Athenian district of *Academe*) as a gesture of disillusion over the fate of his great teacher. The notion of a removed grove reserved for assembled Socrateses would have seemed absurd to the original. It is not insignificant that Socrates carried on his annoying questioning in the marketplace, in the gymnasium, and at drunken feasts. If the search is for *wisdom,* one must search for it wherever, among the tanners, poets, politicians—and, yes, occasional "professors" (the traveling sophists of the Hellenic world). Freedom to inquire is not the special privilege of the learned (sophists); it is the duty of everyone.

Lest anyone think that these are arguments that would impress only a fifth-century B.C. Greek, consider what happens to professorial tenure if the focus of higher education turns away from such obvious skill subjects as physics to psychic issues like "learning to live." During the wilder days of the 1960s campus riots and protests, radical students were quite willing to abjure the professorial faculty in favor of gurus, urban guerrillas, and all manner of those-who-have-lived rather than those-who-have-learned. *Crescat scientia, vita excolatur:* Let science/knowledge increase, so that life may move to a higher level—the motto of the University of Chicago, a (the) quintessential research university. But does "science" really improve our living—particularly our ethical insight and behavior? Does one go to a *professor* to learn the meaning of life? This remains an issue in bloom.

If one tradition of "academic freedom" originates (ambiguously) in Plato's great teacher, the opposing tradition stems from Plato's great pupil, Aristotle. The first sentence of Aristotle's *Metaphysics* reads: "All men by nature desire to know"; the rest of that formidable treatise is meant to demonstrate that this "natural" desire is not to be defeated. Truth, says Aristotle, is like the proverbial barn door (this is in the Greek!), which no one can entirely fail to hit. Where Socrates draws the sharpest contrast between gods and men in terms of wisdom versus ignorance, Aristotle argues that humans are most *like* the gods in the act of knowing.

The Aristotelian tradition is the mainline AAUP tradition of academic-freedom-and-tenure. Tenure is granted for an attained skill; it is an entitlement based on that proficiency. One has the freedom to search because of some level of truth attained (thus, the initial reservation for *university* professors). Tenure is a freedom-to-search license analogous to the physician's license to practice medicine. The surgeon is "free" to do things to my body that are not open to anyone; he or she has attained this freedom on the basis of demonstrated skills attained from specialized education and training.

In the Middle Ages, when universities were formed, masters literally received a teaching license, the *ius ubique docendi,* which allowed them to practice their craft. (The notion of licensure is dimly echoed in the medieval language of collegiate diplomas, which admit the graduates to the "rights and privileges" that appertain to that degree.) The *licentia docendi* has an obvious relationship to modern tenure. In research universities, tenure is granted on the basis of demonstrated competence in a field after a probationary period (usually attested by peer-reviewed scholarship and publication). At lesser institutions, tenure may be granted on the basis of teaching or years of continued appointment. It is at least implied that if you have not been dismissed over the stated time span, you must be "competent."

For all that the medieval *licentia* and modern tenure are based on attained competence, the institutional reality of these two "licenses" is radically different. Medieval schools and their masters were very poor (if not in fact, in vows of poverty). If a licensed master found himself in conflict with the local institution, he would pack up and take his practice elsewhere. The "wandering scholar" was a medieval fact of life made utterly plausible by the modest equipment needs of the masters. Since the days of the monks, any decent scholar needs access to elaborate libraries, not to mention cyclotrons. Universities own the tools of the trade (the "means of production"), so that modern tenure "license" is not *to the individual* as in the *licentia docendi,* but tenure *to a specific institution:* Prestige U. Failure to attain tenure at some institution or other can be virtual denial of the ability to practice the trade—at least it is for philosophers, since a place for metaphysics in the marketplace has yet to be secured. Back to Socrates!

Academic Freedom versus the Bill of Rights

Common usage in the modern academy speaks of academic-freedom-and-tenure as inextricably fused concepts. Whatever the value of this conjunction, the essential meaning of freedom changes radically depending on which of the background traditions is brought into play. The two basic theories rest on such differing assumptions that a single coherent theory and set of policies and practices on tenure can become virtually impossible to formulate.

If one appeals to the Aristotelian theory that freedom of inquiry (and tenure) is based on competence in place (attained and maintained), then one formulates some set of institutional policies to assess competence. Current tenure reviews, with varying degrees of stringency and success, assess competence. And if continuing appointment rests on competence, it would seem plausible to have continuing review of competence. Loss of competence would mean loss of position or specific function; surgeons who lose competence lose the license to suture. Since modern tenure is not a license to the individual but an "employment" contract, loss of competence would mean termination or alteration of function. It is, however, virtually impossible to find post-tenure review policies in universities—more precisely, post-tenure reviews that alter status for incompetence. The reason for this curious omission is not wholly surprising: it is psychologically difficult to dismiss long-standing members of the community; there are moral compulsions; and—finally and incoherently—whenever competence is in question, one may "retreat" to the alternate Socratic argument: who is competent anyhow?

Review for competence is even more problematic if one considers the original purpose of academic-freedom-and-tenure as a protection of the *university* professor's *research* against the contemporary broad-scale granting of tenure in all sorts of institutional settings. If tenure originated to provide freedom for research and new discovery, what is the point of tenure in a *teaching* college? If the issue remains *competence*, it must be teaching competence that is at issue, but teaching may be even less frequently evaluated than research facility. Teaching is often evaluated via student questionnaires and the grapevine, but abysmal teaching is seldom taken as a cause of dismissal for incompetence. To reiterate: academic *freedom* guaranteed by tenure is ultimately justified by the legitimate needs of open inquiry for advanced research. But in institutions where advanced research is modest at a stretch, "tenure" cannot be a function of *that sort* of academic freedom.

Raising competence questions about either research or teaching can, of course, be a mask for ideological disagreement. The conservative economist may believe that Professor K. Marx is not just different but also incompetent. Radical new theories may be excluded because a traditional paradigm prevails in departmental politics. Niels Bohr once said to a col-

league: "That theory is crazy, but not crazy enough to be true."
One may decide that the crazy-true theory is just crazy—and
exclude it.

A competence-based test can be circumvented by shifting the
argument to manifest political issues. I may suspect that a subject proclaiming the newest "-ism" is merely grievance with a
technical vocabulary, but who knows the truth about such matters? One shifts into a Socratic theory of academic freedom, for
which demonstrated competence is not required. The Socratic
shift, subtle as it is, fundamentally reorients the issue of "freedom of inquiry." Under Socratic assumptions, there is properly
no *academic* freedom because there is no *academy*, no place of
sure-fire established competencies—frail as they may be. The
Socratic theory is really an argument for something like the *civil
right of free speech*, which is quite different from academic freedom, despite the amiable confusion of the courts and public
opinion on the issue. (Socratic searching is not the civil right of
modern liberalism, which seeks a society permissive of multiple
private goals in life. Socrates thought there was *the* good society—note *The Republic*—but given the darkness of the human
psyche, it required continual prodding and investigation—free
inquiry—to catch a glimmer of the Good.)

I illustrate the difference in the two notions of freedom with
an actual case. During my presidential days, the administration
had to decide whether a particular faculty member could teach
a course on creationism. We decided that since he was not
trained at all in biology, he could not. The criterion was clearly
Aristotelian competence. (One might deny Professor Shockley
the classroom to discuss racial differences on the grounds that a
Nobel Prize in physics does not make one an anthropologist.)
On the other hand, had the professor in question wanted to rent
a hall at the university to profess his beliefs about creationism,
we would certainly have permitted him to do so under the
rubric of First Amendment rights of free speech and assembly.
The ability to express opinions in the public marketplace of

ideas—Socrates' turf, not the academy—is not at all based on prior demonstrated competence. If it were, the political process might be much improved.

The Socratic-cum-civil-rights notion is infinitely broader than the notion of academic freedom, since it has no limitation on who may enter the discussion. Socrates practiced so; anyone from slave to sophist could enter into the discussion and might well be a source of illumination. Poets and prophets were particularly interesting, since they did seem to get things right from time to time but simply had no interest in reviewing, reflecting, and evaluating their plausible revelations.

Given the confusion between licensed competence and free speech, it is manifestly practical for anyone denied tenure on supposed grounds of competence to shift the argument to the Bill of Rights. One sues in the courts to attain tenure on the grounds that one has been denied a property right without "due process." The review was prejudiced at the source because the plaintiff was the wrong sex or sexual orientation, or the dismissal abrogated a constitutional right of free speech in the public marketplace. Mary McCarthy wrote a novel during the Joe McCarthy period in which an incompetent assistant professor pursues tenure by falsely claiming to be a Communist. Lest anyone suspect that he was denied tenure because of his political views, he is duly promoted by his liberal institution.

It would be misleading to suggest that tenure reviews on the basis of competence have disappeared or that they are routinely defeated by civil action. Not at all. Competence reviews proceed with care, and in most cases, they are accepted, even when the results are negative. What is important, however, is that the historic AAUP argument for tenure has been largely eroded by court actions in the past half-century. The classic case for academic freedom was to protect the political or religious "radical" from the ire of conservative university authorities. Individuals were dismissed for reasons having nothing at all to do with their disciplinary skills. The Angela Davis case at the

University of California would seem to be the precedent to set that fear to rest. Ms. Davis, a supposed Communist, was dismissed for radical comments in the public arena. She sued on the grounds that her free speech had been infringed and that she had been denied a property right without due process, and she won the case clear and simple. The issue of academic freedom as protection from political and religious repression has been largely incorporated into the broader notion of free speech.

Academic Freedom: Internal and External

I would submit that the problem of "academic freedom" as a check on external pressure has essentially been resolved by the steadfast action of the United States courts—as well as the general liberalism of most university cultures and customs. The real dilemmas for "free inquiry" are internal and involve disentangling institutional mission and academic freedom. Does a determined institutional mission and philosophy compromise academic freedom, as seems to have been the case with the old denominational colleges (and perhaps with contemporary religious institutions)?

Contemporary checks on freedom of inquiry are much less likely to come from crusty trustees, who, though they may fume, have largely been tamed by the times, than from the prevailing methods or fashions within departments and fields of study. This is notably the case in the humanities and the "soft" social sciences, where academic competence often becomes bound up with passionate contradictory claims about the nature of the human race. I recall trying to chide a chairman into hiring a non-Marxist (or was it a non-Maoist?) as a member of his departmental faculty. (This is ancient history.) I was told that it would not do because it would break up "the sense of community" in the department. Conservatives cluster with as much conviction as Communists. (Not such ancient history.)

Political ideology may be too controversial, too reminiscent of the repressive actions that engendered tenure in the first place, but consider a current controversy over mission, academic freedom, and tenure where there is no such overtone. As I write this piece, high up in a tower in Vermont, I read that my neighbors to the south at Bennington College have just made two stunning announcements: the college intends to *lower* its tuition, and it is immediately dismissing some twenty faculty, several of them tenured. It is hard to decide which is the more surprising turn.

The rationale for lowering tuition and downsizing the faculty is, of course, strictly economic—or, more precisely in this case, an educational change of "product" for the sake of better economic prospects. Bennington is hardly singular in facing such economic stringency. Even the most well-endowed institutions have been forced by restrictive finances to dwindle faculty size by non-replacement and early retirement. In order to understand the significance of the Bennington case, one must understand the technical notion of "financial exigency" as it is used to abrogate tenure contracts.

Abrogating tenure contracts for purely financial reasons is something that is within the current set of institutional understandings of higher education. The American Association of University Professors is as smart as anyone; it recognizes that since tenure is to the institution, if there is no institution there is no tenure. Thus, a college that is threatened with financial extinction may declare "financial exigency" and, under that special condition, dismiss even tenured faculty.

Bennington, however, did *not* declare financial exigency; it claims to be engaged in rational planning. The college's board of trustees has decided to return to an earlier mission, pursued when the faculty was heavily populated with performing artists and creative folk rather than more "conventional" professors. To be sure, the change in mission was prompted by economic considerations, but they were not judged to be so dire as to constitute financial exigency. The economic strategy may not work, and the educational program may be flawed, but it would seem to be within the scope of an institution to decide on a mission and a market strategy. Unless, of course, "the faculty-as-now-constituted *is* the university," in which case one should expect no change of mission short of foreclosure.

I am compelled to believe that Bennington's abrogation of tenure to alter mission will prevail as precedent. It would be an absurd outcome for American higher education if colleges and universities were not allowed to recast themselves—even if some dismissal of current tenured faculty must be endured. In the long run—and there is not much of a run at that—the general economic distress of higher education may well force significant changes of mission.

Mission Maintenance and Morality

Academic-freedom-and-tenure is more than an economic problem for schools with a dominant sense of "moral" mission—just as it was in the nineteenth century. Catholic colleges and universities are currently struggling to discover in what way they can be first-rate, fully accepted members of the new world of major research universities and yet preserve a sense of religious mission. Father Charles Curran at the Catholic University of America, having been "de-licensed" by the Vatican as an official teacher of theology, sued the university for violation of tenure. The court failed to reinstate Father Curran, noting that Catholic University had the option of either being a real university with full academic freedom *or* dismissing Father Curran because his views clashed with church dogma.

While the court's opinion sounds sweet to defenders of academic freedom (real university = academic freedom), the consequences of this equation are not by all means positive. Why can't an institution define a certain educational mission—maybe even with moral interests—and then confine its faculty to that mission? One would not wish the college to be on a perpetual nervous hunt for heresy, but casting out the egregious opponent to the basic mission seems within reason. (For the record, my sympathies were with Father Curran, whose views on moral theology conform to majority Catholic opinion in the United States, even if they aggravate the Roman curia. Far from being a harassing heretic, Father Curran argued from the mainline of standard Catholic moral reasoning, albeit reaching some mildly novel conclusions.) As Professor Fred Crosson of Notre Dame has pointed out, mindlessly applying academic-freedom-at-all-costs, rather than fostering a diversity of educational aims and styles in American higher education, eventually homogenizes all institutions. If one may use a religious figure without offending academic freedom, it is the Noah's ark principle for faculty building: two of each—two Catholics, two Muslims, two Darwinists, two creationists, two Marxists, two Friedmanites, and so on and so off. One might well conclude that academic freedom is an inherent barrier against a college or university claiming any consistent and coherent philosophy.

Less controversial than the religious mission would be "scholarly philosophy." The University of Rochester is one of the smallest of the major research universities, yet several of its academic departments have been consistently ranked among the leading graduate departments in the nation. The secret of success was avoidance of Noah's ark. By concentrating on "rational decision theory," the departments of economics and political science were able to create colleagueship and a fertile atmosphere for advanced research. There is an obvious risk in establishing a philosophy—moral, religious, artistic, scholarly—because it may be utterly wrongheaded or out of fashion. A scholastic supermarket seems safer—mindless as it may be.

There are, then, in my judgment two arguments for attenuating tenure: economic and educational—even a moral educational mission (of which more in the next chapter). In a time of economic distress, it may be necessary either to change the mission of the institution *or* to retain the saving remnant. Bennington believes that it must change the mission to remain economically viable; this should be a legitimate reason for dismissing tenured faculty who, unhappily, are incapable of serving the new mission. A different case is the institution that retains its mission but needs to downsize its faculty. The rational course of action would be to preserve the *best* faculty, the saving remnant, who can rebuild the teaching strength or the research reputation of the institution. Tenure artificially constrains the choice for the saving remnant. It may well be that a senior faculty member is the leading light and should be retained under whatever conditions of restriction apply, but it may also be that the three-year assistant professor is a brilliant wave of the future, while Dodderer is hopelessly out of touch. Most current tenure rules demand Dodderer's retention.

I am persuaded that some combination of economics, legality, and rational common sense will eliminate, or at least seriously qualify, current tenure practices and assumptions. The important thing about such a sea change will lie not so much in the increased flexibility of planning or the ability to eliminate "deadwood"—a problem much exaggerated anyhow—as in a subtly changed view of faculty, the nature of the institutional integrity, and the role of faculty and other constituencies in university management and governance.

Free Meals in the Prytaneum, That Is, Salaries

The second classic argument for tenure was based on economic considerations. Since faculty were modestly paid in 1916 (to say the least), continued assurance of employment was appropriate. The argument cannot be, however, that low pay per se establishes any claim for tenure. Claims for continued employment, if they exist at all, are based on competence. John Silber has pointed out the importance of "moral tenure" based on competence. Employers have a moral obligation to continue their employees' appointments after a certain period—the period to be based on levels of expected competence. Thus, a building custodian (formerly "janitor") has a claim on continued appointment after a relatively short probationary period. A surgeon in the same building has a longer probationary period before establishing a claim for continuance. At universities, the standard probationary period is set at seven years before continued employment is guaranteed in the formal tenure contract.

The notion of "moral tenure" is important as a counter to the illusion of the "hardheaded" economist, who sees employees as so many interchangeable expense items. (There is at least one such "hardhead" on every board of trustees.) "Tenure" as "moral" claim is not, then, the wicked invention of the American Association of University Professors. Even if there were no de jure tenure contracts, faculty would have a moral claim for employment just from hanging around. (This is the assumption behind the less stringent tenure contracts that are granted after time served. If you have been at the place for five years and they have not fired you, they have evidently decided you can do the job.) A "moral" claim for continuance is weighty. As Willy Loman says, "A man isn't an orange. You can't eat the fruit and throw the peel away." But weighty claims have to be measured against other weighty claims—not the least being the welfare of the ultimate beneficiaries (students) and the mission and viability of the entire enterprise.

The early AAUP claim for tenure because of low pay cannot, then, stand of itself. There may be a larger social argument that since the competencies of university professors are so valuable and since normal market mechanisms (high salaries) are not sufficient to attract a sufficient supply, some "fringe" benefit will have to be added, that is, guaranteed employment. Unfortunately, the argument has two further problems. First, economic conditions for faculties in the 1990s are not what they were in 1916; second, the AAUP argument for tenure cuts both ways: if you have low wages, you deserve tenure, but if you have tenure, you should expect your wages to be moderate.

It is difficult to get an exact fix on whether faculties are "fairly" compensated. I once did an accreditation review at Amherst College. When the president left the room, the faculty present complained bitterly about low salaries. As dean of the faculty at a rival institution, I considered myself something of a student of the subject of faculty salaries. I was amazed at these complaints, since the Amherst salaries seemed most generous in comparison to the ones that I administered. However, as one of the company explained, an Amherst trustee (in a moment of unbridled boosterism, no doubt) had declared that Amherst College faculty salaries should be "second to none." If you are Amherst College in Massachusetts, you really do not have to look beyond the state borders to find higher faculty salaries.

Faculty salaries, like everything else in the modern university, have to be understood in the context of the research university revolution. My grandfather joined the faculty of Ripon College in Wisconsin in 1914 for economic reasons. He was at the time a minister serving a congregation in Lakota, North Dakota. With five children, he calculated that the only way he could give them a college education was through the fringe benefit of free tuition offered to college staff. Ripon in 1914 was, however, a denominational college in the old-style mode. Grandfather's credentials for appointment were denominational; as a minister, it was easy enough to move to a denominational faculty, where he taught economics and sociology—in neither of which developing discipline did he have an advanced degree. Grandfather could not be appointed to contemporary Ripon—not to mention Research U. Grandfather had a *vocation;* modern faculty have a *profession.* The Christian "calling" that led Grandfather to a pastorate was only marginally different from the calling to the professorate.

The research university changes all that. Faculty see themselves as professionals with highly specialized training similar to doctors and engineers. Salary expectations are set by professional models, not divine calling. I am certain that faculties— even Amherst's—are not paid a "just wage" commensurate with the burden of their education and preparation or with their inherent value to society (the professional comparison). However, the "just wage" is, at best, a useful moral fiction for tempering the market, not for setting it. The connection between tenure and "low" pay may prove a useful device in the long run for abolishing the practice. It would seem more than plausible for an institution to offer faculty the option of the tenure track or the money track. The tenure track would be lower paying as a recognition of the university's long-term "reward" to the individual; the money track would offer significantly higher salary because of the risk to the faculty member and the value to the institution of flexibility in appointments. Unfortunately, one suspects that given the choice, the best faculty would choose the money track—calculating that they were good enough to be appointed elsewhere or anywhere if the occasion arose. Lesser lights would choose the security of tenure. Under such a scheme, anyone who opted for tenure should be dismissed!

Tenure and Sinecure

If the courts (and internal collegiate custom) have largely removed the notable political atrocity case from the threats to academic freedom, the Congress in its benevolence has created a situation that theoretically undermines the practice of academic tenure: elimination of mandatory retirement. It has been a specific assumption of AAUP statements regarding tenure that it is *not* a sinecure, a lifetime guarantee of employment. Tenure was a contract that guaranteed academic freedom to the recipient as long as he or she was employed—and that meant until a stated retirement age. Absent any retirement age, tenure would appear de facto to guarantee continual employment.

One might suppose that the effect of lifting mandatory retirement was to create every job in the country as a sinecure, in which case the academy is no worse off than the steel plant.

There are specific problems in higher education, however, that steel puddlers are unlikely to face. Three very specific problems for higher education are the lack of post-tenure competency reviews, the presence of students, and the effect on the very ideal that tenure was originated to protect: research.

One *positive* effect of non-mandatory retirement is that it focuses the question of tenure back on the idea of competence. If senior faculty are to be compelled to retire, the only legitimate ground for such action should be failure of competence. Unfortunately, as noted above, few universities and colleges have established programs for post-tenure competency reviews. This is, of course, theoretically remediable. However, if there are to be post-tenure reviews, presumably they could not be *only* for the over-70 faculty. I assume that the first faculty member dismissed via an over-70 review process will sue for redress on the grounds of age discrimination. Why should only senior citizens be reviewed for competence?

If competence is an issue, it applies to all faculty. Of course, it always has applied to all faculty, but I know of no case where it has actually ever been undertaken and carried through. Individuals who are incompetent, obnoxious, or minor scoundrels may be persuaded to retire or simply "bought out," but a review on competency grounds at most universities is virtually unheard of. (I know of one difficult instance, a classroom disaster where the faculty member in question was translated into the university archivist. It was then opined that what the institution needed was "more archivists.") Given the rarity of current post-tenure competency reviews, any attempt to review *systematically* the over-70 cadre would have to result in a practice of reviews for all tenured faculty to avoid the charge of discrimination. But if all faculty are periodically and systematically reviewed for competence, the de facto reality of tenure at colleges and universities will be fundamentally eroded, whatever remains of the formal concept. At the present time, an individual granted tenure is for all practical purposes secured employment *usque ad terminum*—however one may define *terminum,* from "my personal decision" to "my personal death." A second issue for colleges in the lifting of mandatory retirement has to do with the presence of students. Recall that tenure is in its origin a protection for faculty *research;* it does not relate at all to teaching students. It may be an unfortunate fact, but universities are largely in the youth business because of the presence of "students." The spectacle of an ever-aging faculty instructing an ever-young student body does leave something to be desired. I am certainly not opposed to the idea of callow youth benefiting from the wisdom of graybeards, but the age gap cannot be judged to be the perfection of educational context.

Finally, the facts of current academic life suggest that, if tenure becomes a lifetime contract, the very notion it was meant to protect, research, will be compromised—not for individuals, but as a collective and ongoing enterprise. Although there have been several scrupulous studies about an impending faculty shortage, one could hardly prove that thesis from the difficulty graduate PhDs have in securing employment. One must conjecture that non-retirement of current faculty will further reduce job openings. The situation is paradoxical: universities produce PhD graduates to continue the enterprise of scholarship and research (which tenure protects), but the faculty who produce that research, by virtue of their tenured-in status, block possibilities for the young scientists or scholars pursuing research. Of course, eventually, all the current faculty will die off, and there will be lots of openings—but by that time, all the actual and potential PhDs will be working on Wall Street as brokers or taxi drivers.

The institutionalization of free inquiry through the device of tenure at an institution occurred within a set of historical, legal, and institutional assumptions that have changed markedly over the past century. Tenure was first for *university* professors because they were doing research; tenure was not for college teachers charged with conveying an established culture. Now almost any faculty member, from the community college on, may hold a tenure appointment and demand "academic freedom." If academic freedom is no longer a special prerogative of the most advanced scholars, forceful intervention of the courts on the side of free speech has also broadened the protection of faculty at all levels from arbitrary dismissal. Tenure grew as a practice while institutions prospered financially, adding departments and faculty. The faculty as an aggregate somehow constituted the reality of the university cum multiversity. What happens to expansive tenure in a contracting institution, an institution focusing its mission (what is the focus?) or changing its mission (who determines mission?)?

Since academic freedom and tenure arose in protest over denominational (moral) restriction, it is appropriate to move now to examine the status of "moral" mission(s) in the research university context. To what extent do current moral complaints about the college curriculum compromise academic freedom? Does academic freedom bar universities from adopting overall "moral" goals? What capacity, if any, does the research model have for pursuing "moral wisdom"? Does the research model simply fail to create moral wisdom by sheer omission, or is the very character of the institution antithetical to moral judgment—serving as the unconscious purveyor of relativistic, if not nihilistic, ways of life (Allan Bloom's specific charge)? If the twin crises of the modern university are morals and money, is the public paying a lot for the demoralization of the young?

4 Universities Are Neutral on Moral Value/Universities Teach Moral Value

"For God, for country, and for Yale"—the greatest anticlimax in the history of civilization according to Harvard types. An anticlimax, indeed, but so it was with the original American collegiate universities. Modern Harvard may sniff at the pretension of its Connecticut cousin, but Harvard itself was formed with clear ecclesiastical intent. The Puritan founders of Harvard imitated the "school of the prophets": Emmanuel College at Cambridge. Emmanuel was a place to educate preachers "at once learned and zealous, instructed in all that scholars should know, but trained to use their learning in the service of the reformed faith." The problem of a "reformed faith" was that it seemed to be *semper reformanda,* and each new reform created a new collegiate calling. When Harvard became too "liberal," there was created Yale, and so with a series of parochial fissiparations and enthusiasms. But no matter how far this collegiate division extended, each and every college was likely to proclaim a true faith and a moral mission. The measure of the early moral mission can be gathered from a student comment on a founding faculty member of Harvard, Nathaniel Eaton. The student opined that he would have been "fitter [as] . . . an officer of the Inquisition or master of a house of correction."

The previous chapter noted a collision course between a

broad interpretation of academic freedom and dedicated moral mission. One might allow Bennington to populate its faculty with potters—not professors—because that is within the prerogatives of a "specialized" school; engineering schools do not have to hire poets. It is the moral, political, or religious views of the institution that are not to enter into hiring and firing decisions. For God and country, but not in the job description. Given the religious ancestry of the present research university, nothing is more radical and revolutionary than the apparent abandonment of "moral" mission in higher education. The nature and scope of this change and the place of moral mission (if any) in the modern setting are the subjects of this chapter.

One could regard "God and country" as an archaic curiosity and ancient custom, but the history is much more complex. In 1937, Charles Seymour was installed as president of Yale, and he included the following injunction in his inaugural address: "I call on all members of the faculty, as members of a thinking body, freely to recognize the tremendous validity and the power of the teaching of Christ in our life-and-death struggle against the forces of selfish materialism." (Since Seymour was president of Yale in my undergraduate years, I like to think collegiate moral mission is not sheer archaeology.) I am certain that the current president of Yale, Richard Levin, would omit the denominational turn, but though he is an economist, he is likely to echo the university's moral mission against "selfish materialism" (a moral position that has utilitarian value during a major fund drive).

Denominationalism has surely faded from most of the leading American colleges and universities. (Catholic universities are an exception, along with a scattering of evangelical or fundamentalist institutions.) *God* may have held out at Yale until Charles Seymour, but His or Her star seems also to have faded as the Protestant Establishment institutions have drifted into "Established Nonbelief" (to quote from the title of George Marsden's recent account of this slide from grace). *Country* held up somewhat longer as a moral ideal, but it is not clear that it survived the

1960s. As for *Yale,* what is the university's moral purpose absent God and nation? It might appear that the collegiate establishment has finally and utterly abandoned the moral urge. Liberal faculty may applaud this advance toward academic freedom, while conservative moral critics without will bemoan the betrayal of a cultural duty. (I was an undergraduate at Yale when William Buckley so bemoaned in *God and Man at Yale.*)

I do not believe that the universities can eliminate moral assumptions. There are at least three places where ethics lurks about the quad. First, moral intent—broad and vague—is often proclaimed in the institution's official prose. It is the perennial theme of commencement oratory as properly educated graduates are sent forth to reform a tired old world. Second, whatever the cloudy cultural hope of commencement oratory, there is a highly specific and rigid ethic implicit in the institutional research ideology, which defines the contemporary university. This *internal research university ethic* is as powerful as it is often unacknowledged and underdeveloped. When the research ethic is fully comprehended, however, it may well become the focus of a powerful moral counterattack. This is precisely what has happened in the current and bitter multicultural debates on and off campus. Finally, no matter how cloudy the cultural agenda or how restricted the research morality, contemporary students abound in ethical enthusiasms for various liberations—the more notable the research institution, the more notable the crusade. Leaving commencement oratory aside for the moment (the reader may hope "forever"), in this chapter I will examine the connection between the inherent ethic of the research academy and the moral enthusiasms of the young.

Values Strictly Academic

In examining the moral assumptions of the contemporary university, one should begin with the most purist of positions: the modern university has no moral task at all. The argument is straightforward. Universities are interested in theory, not practice; they teach science, not virtue. The only coin of value at a university is verified truth. Whether the truth is put forward by a saint or a scoundrel is no business of the university. Every institution endures rascally faculty whose intellectual contributions are beyond reproach, and what the students do on the weekend is not within the proper purview of the faculty, who, after all, are "scientists," not moralists. During my early days in administration at Princeton, it was the custom of the assembled faculty in formal session to vote to suspend students for "violation of the rule regarding women in the dormitory" (as the dean delicately phrased this offense at a then all-male institution). Such votes are no longer recorded in Nassau Hall not only because undergraduate women reside by right in all the dormitories, but also because Nobel physicists finally decided it is none of their business who is in whose room for what purpose whenever.

There is, of course, common civic morality even in the university. Academic life does not run well in times of mayhem. It is assumed that as a geographically dense community, individuals will not rape, pillage, and plunder, but those are matters for the criminal law, not for strict academic concern. Just as there must be plumbing, there has to be some means of flushing out conduct that disrupts the basic order that any community can legitimately demand. Universities are no different from the local fire brigade in expecting civility from the members.

Morality, then, exists in a different realm from intellectual search, and though common decency demands common courtesy and non-criminality for the college, it is not the special business of the academy to enforce moral codes. So runs the position of the intellectual purist. I disagree: intellectual Puritanism is as mistaken as Nathaniel Eaton's Puritan theology when it comes to understanding the "moral" dimensions of the university. Moral values are inherent in the ethos of the research university, and these values have a wider scope in governing campus behavior than the disciple of pure theory may wish to acknowledge—and, if given ultimate scope as a "philosophy of life," may merit ultimate rejection.

A Community Search for Truth

A moral value essential to the academic enterprise is truth-telling. The moral ascendency of truth-telling emerges in such special academic sins as research fraud and plagiarism. Fraud is a straightforward offense in the palace of truth: it is publishing falsehood. Plagiarism is more complex: it is telling a truth *not your own*. The simplest explanation for the offense of plagiarism is that it makes grading difficult. I cannot give Sam or Sarah an A+ for the work of Susan Sontag. But the offense of plagiarism is deeper than interference with grading practices; it offends the *learning assumption,* which is inherent in the modern university's search for truth. A university is not a collection of wildcatters drilling for the oil of knowledge. The learning assumption holds that truth can best be approached by organized communal effort, in which individuals learn from the insights and discoveries of their fellow workers. Fraud passes off falsity as a discovery; plagiarism is a refusal to play the cooperative game. You have been counting on my effort and insight, but in plagiarism, I make no effort and offer no new insight. (American universities have institutionalized the assumption of "cooperative" learning by following the eighteenth-century Scottish university model of departments that cluster colleagues of similar rank. The German university model, with a single professor in an institute surrounded by docents, expresses the triumph of genius over cooperation. However, geniuses must not plagiarize; it would be a denial of geniushood!)

Plagiarism is a special sin defined by the philosophical assumptions of the modern academic community. It is because of an overall commitment to research and discovery that plagiarism is so fundamentally offensive. In the world of entertainment, plagiarism is the sincerest form of flattery as individual entertainers mimic the style and fashion of the day. Elvis Presley "plagiarists" proliferate without offense. Plagiarism has a conceptual and institutional importance for the modern university in contrast to earlier schools and academies. The conceptual notion that truth-is-to-be-discovered makes plagiarism an acute fault. If truth has already been fully revealed ("There is no King but Elvis!"), then "plagiarism" is ethically appropriate. Lest this example be regarded as too frivolous, consider that the "imitation of Christ" has been recommended in the church community since the time of the Desert Fathers. If one knows the truth, imitation can be a virtue. Such was an assumption of the imitative "recitation" pedagogy of the nineteenth-century classical colleges. In short, the offense of plagiarism reveals the "moral" dimension of the research university's search for truth, in contrast to the denominational colleges' moral training in the light of Truth revealed.

Plagiarism is a moral fault within the special community of learning that constitutes the research university. What is not so immediately perceived is the extension of the "morality" of this academic community into areas that might appear at first glance to be merely personal choice or life style, quite external to the special demands of higher education. I choose two aggravated examples: drugs and sex.

Drugs

If the pursuit of truth implies putting your *own* mind to work on the task rather than cadging off someone else, there is the implication that one will *have* a mind at work. Why should there be any more concern about what students smoke in their rooms than there is about other entertainment practices common to coeducational dormitories? To the extent that drugs (alcohol included) are a health hazard or lead to boisterous behavior dangerous to lounge furniture, there is a simple social concern, but nothing strictly academic. As a policy for incidents, relegating drug problems to medical or criminal jurisdiction may be quite sufficient, but the philosophy of drug use—if one may use such an exalted notion—would seem to call for a sterner stance from universities.

Freud summed up the aim of his psychiatric practice: where *id* is, there *ego* shall be. In more scholastic terminology, common reason should reign over idiosyncratic passion. The function of drugs is the reverse of the Freudian dictum. The specific function of drug use is to put *id* where *ego* has been, to seek intoxication and the elimination of "rational" ego function. At its farthest reaches, drug use clearly replaces reality testing with fantasy. Because the university is dedicated to common reason, it has every right to censure drug use on strictly "academic" grounds. When one adds to the philosophy of drug usage the biological possibility of habitual or addictive use, then the habit of mind of the university is determinedly in opposition to "the habit."

Objecting to drugs is not the same as being a grouch about fantasy. Physicists as well as poets are encouraged to "fantasize" in the hope that scaling off present truth and reality will reveal new and surprising vistas. But the difference between the physicist's fantasy and the addict's is that the physicist is able to reconnect fantasy with fact, reality, and common reason. One dreams about unheard-of structures of the universe and then seeks to see how these could be revealed in the waking life of reason. It is said that nineteenth-century chemist Friedrich Kekulé discovered the structure of organic compounds in a dream. Hardly. Lots of folks dream of geometrical shapes (Kekulé's dream); it takes a worried waking chemist to connect the dream shape with carbon bonding—and then to demonstrate the efficacy of the model as an explanation of fact. Similarly with the poet: the fine eye of fancy must be converted into the crafted shape of meter, rhyme, and sense. Despite the romantic claim that drugs and madness are a key to deeper reality, the empirical record for the claim is bleak. Pop culture likes to suggest the "madness" of genius. But if one takes a peculiarly odd lot, composers of classical music, there seem to be only two who were certifiably insane: Robert Schumann and Hugo Wolf. As both composers descended into madness, their musical gifts disintegrated concomitantly.

Sex

When Princeton's Nobelists gave up disciplining violations of the rules regarding women in the dormitories, they reflected the obvious fact that sexual rompings as such seem to have little effect on the pursuit of truth. Satyromania may devour the time needed for research and blunt a career, but it is not necessarily a hindrance when and if Professor X shows up at the lab bench. Unlike drug addiction, sexual interest has no inherent coercive effect on the brain other than distraction. So far so good, and if the matter can be left at just plain sex—if that is conceivable— the Nobelists have again shown the way. But if the fundamental academic principle is mutual dialogue toward common truth, one needs sexual warning signs and sanctions.

Sex can be just sex, but it rarely is. Generally, the partners have some personal interest in one another, and that can be a problem in the academic arena. The "ideal" of the modern academy is a grand "impersonality" about truth and reality. When the academic dialogue becomes a personal combination, confrontation, or cohabitation, truth is a ready casualty. Sex is, of course, only one of the more obvious ways in which personal affection (or hostility) compromises the austere commands of reason. One of the more difficult moments for a dedicated faculty member involves the refutation of a friend's pet theory. Flunking one's own kin in calculus or savaging a lover's term paper strains the possibilities of academic dedication. As drugs substitute private fantasy for public argument, so having a sexual fancy for X or Y may breach the ethical fault line that divides what is common, universal, "impersonal," and rational from what is private, personal, and subjective.

Sex, love, and friendship present complex and unavoidable ethical problems to a community of scholars. One hardly demands a community of ascetic monks eschewing "particular friendships." Having friends in the department may encourage me to show my shaky results before braving the impersonal world of the learned journals. Faculty fall in love with graduate students, graduate students with undergraduates, and vice versa—and up and down the hierarchy of position. No one need object to these nice human traits, even among college faculty. But the warning sign and sanction remain: personal connection cannot be allowed to replace professional distance and dialogue. If you marry your student, he or she should not be your student; husband and wife colleagues do not formally review one another's research. Of course, one might "rise above" personal affection—some faculty might even relish flunking slothful kin—but the appearance is all against it. Appearance is, in this case, no mere appearance; perhaps the most corrosive threat to the proper austerity of truth is concealed relationship. If a faculty member *marries* a student, then the relationship is in the public domain, and in almost every case, some public adjustment will be made: your spousal oboe student switches to another studio. However, if this is a clandestine relationship, the same personal dynamic will be at work wreaking whatever havoc may ensue on the professional relationship, but no public or institutional pressure will occur to adjust to altered circumstance.

I offer this sketch of a slightly extended morality strictly academic for several reasons. First, there is a surprising lack of articulated statements about proper conduct for members of the community: students and faculty. The student code, once as elaborate as Deuteronomy (well, it was Deuteronomy) has largely been shredded by courts and the liberal urges of the community. Faculty ethical codes are only at the very edge of visibility. Real estate agents and lawyers are infinitely more articulate on ethical standards for their professions. The AAUP statements on academic freedom contain some cautionary language about proper professional conduct from faculty. These injunctions are so general that they would certainly not stand any legal test, falling under the same vagueness test that abolished codes of *student* ethics that forbade actions "unbecoming to a gentleman."

One may detect from my discussion why it is that the professorate has not sought an ethical statement for itself or the community at large: the assumption is that pure theory lives in a world removed from direct ethical consideration. If one is intoxicated by the notion of "pure theory," one might well draw the mistaken conclusion that morality is another country altogether. Absence of an academic code of ethics does not suggest that faculty are any more wayward than lawyers. An elaborate code of ethics will not prevent shysters, quacks, and charlatans in any trade.

A second reason for sketching the ethical traits of the trade is the peculiar persistence of the belief that higher education also has a moral effect on its clients. Just how could a palace of theory have such a "moral" effect? Moral critics, such as William Bennett, Allan Bloom, Lynn Cheney, Charles Sykes, and Dinesh D'Souza, are not speaking to a vacuum; it is because a moral aura lingers on in the modern university that critics fulminate about the results.

The moral criticism of universities falls under two quite different heads. On the one hand, there are those who suspect that the university has some specific moral agenda that the critic finds unacceptable; for example, that the economics faculty preaches Marxism *or* unbridled capitalism. More interesting because more fundamental is the suspicion that the essential, inner "morality" of the "scientific" university is amoral, relativistic, nihilistic, and inhumane. Multiculturalists, deconstructionists, diversity advocates, some feminists, and so on find the impersonal ideal of a research university downright immoral. It sounds very grand to talk about "impersonal" reason, but if we think that is a way to live, we are issuing a pernicious moral injunction.

In the wilder reaches of the sixties counterculture, even (especially) sex and drugs were somehow keys to the true insight that higher learning denied. It is precisely because sex *is* personal that "knowing Eve or Adam" (biblical language) was judged to be vastly more instructive than scholastic Biology 101. I attended a conference at Harvard during the sixties at which the president of one of the most countercultural colleges of the day—and days past—boasted that his institution was the first to put "f——ing" into the curriculum. (I thought the portrait of Increase Mather on the wall behind the speaker might fall to the ground.) I will examine this "multiculturalist" challenge in some detail later, not only because it is so fundamental but also because it is a criticism largely from within the academy, as opposed to the Marxist and free-market critics, who are generally without, writing screeds about the betrayal of the clerks.

Moral Habits and University Teaching

The research university may have an explicit code-for-truth—with some interesting extensions into matters of sex and drugs—but the curriculum also contains courses in moral philosophy. I have actually taught some, so I know that they exist. All sorts of university courses abound in general moral and religious values explicit and implicit. It was said of Charles Eliot Norton's lectures on art at Harvard that they were lectures "on modern morals, illustrated with ancient art." Just what do these dollops of moral tutelage do and fail to do in the overall ethical enhancement of the young?

The relationship of universities to moral value can best be approached by noting an ancient distinction. Contemporary discussions of morality—particularly in academic arenas—tend to be discussions about moral *judgment;* for example, is abortion an ethical choice? While discerning right and wrong is no mean task, it is interesting that the most ancient tradition of morality seemed to regard discernment as a secondary concern—or a late development dependent on the *prior* acquisition of virtue. The first concern was moral *habit;* for example, does the individual have the habit of courage or temperance? The distinction is crucial for both morality and university pedagogy. Habits come about by *training,* repeated performance; moral discernment is more an "intellectual" capacity and comes about by *teaching.* One learns to be courageous by performing "courageous" acts until the ability to withstand fear and pain is "habitual"; then we say that the person is courageous, has the habit or virtue of courage. Deciding whether euthanasia should be legally permitted is an "intellectual" task that involves assembling a variety of insights and observations about what is generally regarded as moral and legitimate conduct and then seeing whether this case fits the pattern. One might conclude that euthanasia is a moral act and yet lack the habit of courage necessary to carry it through. The ancient Greeks were interested first in the matter of moral habits because they believed that morality was first of all, and above all, a matter of *doing* something, not just drawing conclusions.

If one contrasts old-style colleges with new-style universities, the distinction between morality as *doing* and morality as *thinking* (drawing ethical arguments) is striking. Nathaniel Eaton's "house of correction," a.k.a. Harvard College, knew what was right and what was wrong; the problem was to *train* the wretches in moral habits. The meager rations served to the first Harvard students by Mrs. Nathaniel Eaton were probably as much a part of the spiritual formation as the bread and water of Trappist monks. On the whole, modern universities avoid saying that they *know* what is right and what is wrong (fraud and plagiarism excepted); classes in moral philosophy wrestle toward conclusions that are, of course, always subject to further debate. Unsurety about right and wrong obviously precludes training in moral habits. What morality should be habituated?

The problem for the modern university is not only that there is no substitute at hand for the Book of Deuteronomy, but also that the *mode of instruction* is unfit for habituation. The modern university teaches; it does not train. The strength and feebleness of the old denominational colleges lay in the fact that they were involved in training at the expense of teaching. The dominance of training fit the character of the students, who were often of an age with contemporary high school students. (The violence rampant in nineteenth-century colleges can be attributed in part to the collection of juveniles cooped up in these pious "houses of correction.")

The "intellectual" part of the nineteenth-century college conformed to its correctional mode. Moral habits were sternly pressed in everyday life, and the mode of instruction was recitation of classic texts. These cullings from ancient authors served two purposes: they were set as exemplars of proper literary style *and* depictions of good republican habits. One learned Cicero's periodic style and also admired his opposition to antirepublican conspiracy. While literacy habits are not the same as moral habits, the aim of instruction was habit. Recitation and continual practice produce habits of performance, whether in morals, manuscripts, or music. Musical pedagogy, in fact, retains the older pedagogy of repeated practice of classical masters leading to recital because it is a *performing* art. Insofar as morality is also a *performing* art, the moral purpose of the older colleges was well served by its repetitive classical curriculum.

"For God, for country, and for Yale" is the motto of an old-style denominational college, which was sure about God's moral stance (the Bible) and the country's (republican virtue in the Roman sense was the standard depicted in Latin classics). Knowing the moral code, President Timothy Dwight (circa 1800) could oversee an institution of moral habituation (and have the Christian student society at Yale named for his efforts: Dwight Hall). What is President Levin to do with the motto, given the withering of codes and the death of a recitational pedagogy? William F. Buckley's condemnation of modern Yale for abandoning its Christian commitment should have been expected, given the fundamental change in the nature of the universities that had occurred since God and man had collegiate currency.

Absent the possibility of adopting a definite moral code, absent habituation in the absent code, absent the recitational and practice pedagogy for moral habituation, what, if anything, can be made of the university's proclaimed, though vague, commitment to lead students (and society?) to a better life?

Choice and Chance in Campus Morals

Whatever the pretense emblazoned on the university shield and banner, there would appear to be a two-pronged skepticism about the institution's capacity as moral tutor. Intellectual purists would avoid inherently unscientific moral claims; practical thinkers would recognize that morality is a matter of doing, not thinking, and abandon the austere tower of theory as a place for ethical training.

While it may appear that the university is not a proponent of any fixed moral attitude (beyond plagiarism and fraud), a closer look at the contemporary campus would reveal that despite all the intellectual disclaimers, the place is overwhelmed with moral urgencies. In its way, the modern campus can be as prudish as its pious predecessors. Elaine May used to do a comedy routine in which a harassed housewife in the midst of cooking dinner is asked by her six-year-old how babies are made. The mother, without missing a beat of her souffle, gives the youngster a fully explicit depiction of the sexual process. The child then asks, "Why are there white people and black people?" The mother lays aside her task, turns gently to the child, and starts to explain about the many colored flowers of the field.

Contemporary colleges have become more or less indifferent to the "facts of life" (as they used to be called), but very sensitive to a whole new range of issues in the area of minority concerns—women and those of various sexual orientations included. I do not mention this change to demean this new sensitivity—far from it; it was a long time coming, and the previous concern with sexuality was obsessively paternalistic. The point is that on any college campus, one will discover exquisite moral sensitivities put forward as *essential* university concerns. Speech codes, guarding against offensive racial or sexual comments, have the whiff of Puritan censorship for all that they rest on benign motives. In a recent issue of the Stanford University official newspaper, there was a report of the University Grape Committee. This committee, which reports directly to the president and provost, was suggesting a *change* (yet!) in the official university grape policy. Is there any inherent connection between a grape crusade and the ascetic morality of research?

If, as suggested, the modern university still harbors the ghost of its Puritan ancestors, it may not be surprising that moral causes, far from being expunged by high science, are bursting out all over the quad. But the new moral crusades are certainly not echoes of the Ten Commandments (particularly number VI). Biblical codes and classical exemplars as sources of morality were, like everything else, put to question by the research impulse of the new university ethos. Academic freedom asserts independence of fixed authority lest the search for truth be hindered. Given the centrality of "freedom" in the new university dispensation, it is to that great concept that one may look for grounding the ethical wars of the contemporary campus.

The denominational college was, as noted, concerned with moral *habits* and *training*. Talk about *habits/training* is off-putting not only in the modern university but also in any complete view of morality. We do not think that the moral automaton is the model to be pursued. The fault of the classical college curriculum was that it seemed to be nothing more than *indoctrination* via rote and repetition. Not a thinking woman's curriculum at all—and bound to produce morally rigid personalities. Historical evidence suggests that it often accomplished just such a result. While it is clear that we want people to have good moral habits, we want these to be thoughtful habits. Aristotle, who seems to have gotten most of this stuff correct, defined true virtue as a habit of *choice* as a person of *practical wisdom* would determine. It is not just doing the deed, but also *choosing* the deed that implies something more than rote reaction. Further, one should choose *as the person of practical wisdom* would choose. The modern university is fully enamored with choice; it is in the pedagogy of practical wisdom that it is befuddled.

The modern educator, in reaction to rote, recital, and repetition, is very much into *choice*. The pervasive "values clarification" (VC) curriculum of the lower schools is based on the notion that real morality cannot be imposed, but must be an individual choice. By presenting different situations of choice, the educator in a VC program forces the student to decide something rather than react on impulse or mere routine. The university offers advanced VC. Read almost any college prospectus, and you will see praise for the variety of the curriculum, the student body, the faculty; all this is a means for broadening the individual by expanding the range of value alternatives. The outcome is the deparochialization of the student toward broader sympathies and a sense that values (including his or her own) must be chosen, not simply recited from Sunday school.

All that is a good start. One is unlikely to have a sense of choice if value alternatives are never known. The student taught to fear blacks or dismiss Jews learns a mighty lesson from roommates of that race or persuasion. Riffling through the variegated course choices in the catalogue will certainly broaden any student's sense of value range. *But*—an all-important "but"—when it becomes painfully clear that there are values to be chosen, what resources will be brought to bear to justify these choices? The great sociologist Talcott Parsons opined that individuals "construct pseudo-rational mythologies to justify inscrutable choices." (The entire advertising industry rests on the truth of that comment.) Having been thoroughly deparochialized, will the student exercise choice based on practical wisdom, Parsons's "pseudo-rational mythologies," or something even more pseudo yet?

The notion that the university has done its duty to morality by offering an emporium of value choices qualifies as a definitive half-truth. As against the narrow and mechanical curricula of the past, it certainly is a step in the right direction, but only a half-step/truth. The fault with this value prospectus lies in two dimensions: assumptions about the student and assumptions about the course of study.

The modern "moral" curriculum is a sort of value jumble sale; it is a reaction against the older curriculum, and the student product of those religious academies. But there are few academy students anymore. David Riesman once said to me that he thought the only student who would really benefit from a Harvard undergraduate education was a Roman Catholic from upstate New York. (When I quoted this back to Riesman several years later, he did not believe that he had actually said any such thing. Since I consider the statement to be at least half-true—and thus worth including in the current account—I will attribute it to a researcher who has uttered more whole truths about American higher education than anyone else. He is entitled to the better part of my half-truth.) My interpretation of the pseudo-Riesmanian claim is that, *if* one comes with a solid dogmatic background and is well trained in the moral habits of, say, the Jesuit persuasion, then the wide, wide world of the Harvard curriculum could be a genuinely broadening and sophisticating experience. Presumably, our upstate Catholic would continually be bringing his or her dogmas and moral behaviors to bear on the delirious diversity of the curriculum and the life in Harvard Square.

Aristotle's theory about the moral life assumed that one had to *acquire* moral virtues before one could philosophize about them. Virtues are not just lying about like moles and mountains; they are special aptitudes that we "learn," like a critical ear for music or the ability to identify good cheese. One cannot *discern* the proper application of courage (discernment being the activity of practical wisdom) if one does not know courage already (the virtue). If one has not already *experienced* the value of courage, there will be no great motivation to discover whether the experience has some deeper philosophical justification. Presumably, our Jesuit graduate (or Yeshiva product) has been "habituated" in certain types of conduct and associated beliefs about their meaning and importance. But what if our student is a product not of the S.J.s but the VCs? I fear that our freshman's values have been clarified like butter: melted down and transparent to the point of invisibility.

I do know from long experience in the dean's office that young people do not come to college these days with a big brace of moral dogmas. When Freud was creating psychiatry in turn-of-the-century Vienna, the dominant psychic problem seems to have been repression of emotional needs (sexual in Freud's view) by a rigid external social code and ingrained habits. The inner conflict between dogmatic conscience and sexual demands resulted in severe neurotic symptoms. The sense I receive from college psychiatrists is that contemporary students suffer from identity *diffusion,* not an overdetermined, dogmatic identity. Sophisticating the diffuse through a jumble sale of values does not sound like a promising pattern of moral education. Our Jesuit product fits the standard pattern for sophisticating the dogmatic, but he or she is an endangered species. Fixating on the failure of routine habit reveals the importance of *choice* in the moral realm. But while choice is a condition of moral worth, it is not itself the content of moral worth. A course of action is morally worthy not because it is chosen but because it is morally worthy. Dictators and old-time college tutors may be faulted for denying free choice as a *general policy,* but the fact remains that choice itself is only a half-truth of the moral life. By all means, one should be placed in a position of choice (morally important), but without some principle of choice, the path taken owes more to chance or pseudo-rational mythology than to moral wisdom. And a decision founded on chance (fashion's current myth or a coin flip) is not even worthy of being denominated a *choice.*

I opined that the average freshman does not come to campus with a dogmatic set of beliefs and behaviors—with one notable exception: free choice (i.e., Don't Bug Me!). If our freshman is a proper product of VC High, he or she regards *choice* as the very essence, form, and content of moral action.

It would be a gross oversimplification to say that all the moral crusades pursued on the contemporary campus are based on a claim to freedom and choice, but when push cometh to shove, one can be reasonably certain that the freedom to "choose" a life style and stance will overcome any qualms about the moral worth of the claim. In an academic arena—particularly the modern university—the claim for free assertion is a virtual absolute. The *moral* position has a positive resemblance to the *free speech* theory of academic freedom discussed previously. Once one comes to doubt that there is any established intellectual or moral *competence,* then one might as well let anything be said or done with the hope that out of the melee, some light might emerge. It may not be accidental that the era of "revolution" in universities began with a free speech movement at Berkeley—only to be followed by the "filthy speech" movement. The current fad of speech codes, while they seem to deny free (or filthy) speech, is based not so much on some positive morality as on the notion that obnoxious speech is actually a means of *silencing* the other. Calling my opponent a "feminazi" excludes her from any dialogue—and that is the cardinal (maybe the only) sin.

Choice *as* moral content is a splendid philosophy for identity diffusion. Dogmatists have a strong, sometimes rigid, sense of self-identity; "diffusionists" exist in a state of continuous possibilities/choices. This is not a pleasant state, made all the worse by the urge to morality, which happily persists in the family, the nation, and even the university. In order to anchor the self, one makes a choice. In some sense, it does not make any difference what choice; the fact of choice establishes my Self. One of the baffled characters in a Sartre short story chooses to be an anti-Semite; it makes him *somebody*. "One can't invite Jules to the party with the Levinsons, he is very anti-semitic." Fortunately for our diffused frosh, there are lots of excellent moral causes floating about the campus with which he or she may ground a sense of Self. One may hope for the best from this solution by choice, but the foundations of moral action are like unto the biblical story of the man who builded his house on sand. Having chosen, one is bound to defend one's choice, but it turns out that it was the choice that counted, not the cause.

The problem with grounding one's position on freedom/choice is that it undercuts moral discussion. To be sure, you have chosen that view, but why? Yet the fact of choice is the value, not the why. The passion and posturing of various campus crusades often rest on the irrationality of sheer choice absent the foundation of practical wisdom. This is not to say that the cause may not be unimpeachable, but the protester is deflected from the rationality of the cause by the excitement of choice.

As an antidote to the censored curricula of the past, there is much to be said for the cornucopia of values available and asserted in the contemporary academic community. The issue that remains is whether simply offering an emporium of assorted values in all sizes, shapes, and personal embodiments constitutes the limits of the university's capacity and responsibility. Given the recoil from denominational dogma, the university may well say that its task is fulfilled by presenting options. One believes that sorting through the possibilities will somehow sieve out the gold and leave the dross behind. Perhaps like Adam Smith's "invisible hand," which guides the market, the whole messy interchange somehow comes to an acceptable ethical equilibrium.

Having been corrupted by Plato and Aristotle at an early age, I think that the jumble sale approach to value is insufficient. Difficult as it may be to attain, there is "practical wisdom," and *if* (a big *if*) the university is to muddle in moral issues, attention should be paid to a curriculum of such wisdom. The failure of the modern university in this arena is difficult to evaluate because it depends on evaluating the university as a general social institution among other social institutions, with their values and social beliefs—God and country, for instance. While I believe that practical wisdom is a goal to be pursued, it is not clear that the modern university is, can be, or should be the place of such a pursuit. Socrates certainly believed that practical wisdom was a life task—the only important life task—but he thought it could be found in the marketplace, not with the "professors," the learned sophists whose approach to value bears an uncanny resemblance to the ideology of the modern university. The responsibility of the university to develop "practical wisdom" may be proportional to the perceived viability of other social vehicles for attaining such insight. Plato depicts Socrates as a powerful external critic of the "professorial" approach to morality. If there are powerful external "teachers" of moral wisdom, the university's jumble sale can be incorporated in a larger ethical dialogue.

The "danger" for the modern university as a place of practical wisdom may come from the very prestige of the enterprise. The modern university is a powerful and vastly important social construction. Because of its importance and power, one may come to believe—and the university may come to believe—that it is as puissant in matters of morals as in the physics of matter. Maybe so, but the inner logic of the research enterprise and the practice of the modern curriculum do not make that equation obvious.

Later I will deal with the claim that the university is the "axial" (central) institution of modern society. It is in the context of that discussion that I want to draw some conclusions about the role of the university in developing practical wisdom. It may well be that the university is the axial institution in society. Given the general withering away of religion, the dismay about political institutions, and even the breakdown of the family institution, the university has been turned to as the final repository of social value and validation. The university not only is an instrument for developing special skills, but also becomes the validator of morals and the vehicle of salvation. The problem with designating the university as the axial institution for society—above and beyond religion, politics, family, or whatever—is, as stated, that the inner rationale of the research university does not seem congruent with the task proposed. In the next chapter, I want to consider two current "curricular" patterns that can lay claim to producing "moral" results—well-rounded education and multiculturalism—as these are expressed in curricular distribution and "diversity."

While I would opt for "practical wisdom" within higher education, I want to close this chapter with an example of the hazards of such a claim. One of the more comical conflicts between wisdom and modern academia is a legal case: *Columbia University v. Jacobsen.* Jacobsen was a student at Columbia University. He failed to pay tuition, and the institution sued. Jacobsen countersued on the grounds that the university had not provided him with "wisdom." University officials argued in the New Jersey courts that wisdom was an elusive quality and that no one had ever promised to deliver the product. Jacobsen, acting as his own lawyer, countered by citing numerous inscriptions on the facades of buildings at Morningside Heights that alluded to *"Sophia"* and *"Sapientia."* Why, if wisdom was not in the curriculum, was it advertised on every wall? I am sorry to say that Jacobsen lost the case.

5 The Liberal Arts Curriculum Aims at Distribution/Diversity

It might appear at first glance that distribution *is* diversity or vice versa. However, as these notions are developed in contemporary academia, they are actually antagonistic. What they have in common is that they both make moral claims on the university, but the moral ideals behind the curricular proscriptions are radically different. I start with "distribution," since it has a longer history.

Distribution and Drudgery

Distribution requirements are the curricular means to the traditional aim of a "well rounded" education. "Well rounded" is one of those deceased metaphors resurrected as literal truth that abound in educational rhetoric. A mite of thought suggests some serious need to understand what sort of "roundedness" is hoped for. "Roundedness" is by no means equivalent to "interesting" or "creative." Clearly, many of the world's most interesting and creative people have been highly skewed or notably angular—if one must adhere to geometrical metaphor. It is no fault that Shakespeare probably did not know the physics of his day or that Einstein may have had a low/no opinion of Tennyson.

On its own spherical ground, it is not easy to ascertain the exact virtue of "well roundedness." Chicago's Robert Maynard Hutchins regarded the Ivy League universities of his day as "men's finishing schools." A modern educational theorist, Arthur Chickering, thought the Ivy League offers "touring car education." MIT offers a "rocket curriculum": here is what you want to know, for example, nuclear physics, and this is the straight shot to that goal (a line, not a sphere). The Ivies and elegant liberal arts places offer, in Chickering's view, a leisurely tour in an air-conditioned car through the cultural landscape.

The well-roundedness of a finishing school or an air-conditioned tour allows the product to make bright remarks on almost any subject in any company, but it seems rather anemic as an educational goal. At a cocktail party, it would be more interesting to corner the nerdy fellow who knows only about Madagascar than to endure clever quips about everything from cabbages to kings delivered by one's well-rounded and thoroughly finished host. (I do not endorse Hutchins's critique of the Ivies as such, though one can certainly find just such well-polished alumni. The Ivies certainly have higher aspirations for their graduates than elegance.)

Sticking to geometrical tropes: distribution aims at "breadth" (liberal arts, general education) in contrast to "depth" (the departmental major). These are dangerous metaphors. If general education is broad, does that imply that general education is not deep, that is, it is shallow or superficial? If so, why is a brush with "the philosophical tradition," "world literature," or "Eastern religions" a desirable educational goal? If a little knowledge is a dangerous thing, once over lightly with Hinduism seems ill considered—particularly when the average American student, having grown up in a country deeply influenced by Protestant religious values and structures, may already know more about the Mahareshi than John Calvin.

Of course, the point of general education is *not* once-over-lightly with the Pali Canon or St. Paul; these are merely *introductions* to the whole vast field of the subject being taught. You have to start somewhere. Agreed. But does the actual practice of general education in the distribution requirement mode suggest that there is life after a 100-level course? To be broadly educated is an instance of an intellectual *ideal* that is wholly valid, but when institutionalized at the 100 level, it can become even less than a half-truth. Rather than being an introduction to something yet to come, all too often it is a termination devoutly to be wished.

There are at least three major fault lines running across the pursuit of wholeness and breadth in the modern university: faith, faculty, and freshmen.

Faith

No one believes today in "the Renaissance man (or woman)." Maybe Leonardo could know everything that was worth knowing, but with the vast explosion of knowledge since the Cinquecento, the omni-competent savant is no longer a possibility. As a collection of specialists, the clear message of the university itself is anti-Leonardo. Knowledge is properly divided into specialties and subspecialties because it is only possible to master the most limited area of the vast acreage of knowledge. Does the university, having firmly committed to the reality of specialization, urge undergraduates to be bogus Leonardos?

Faculty

The university holds out to the undergraduate an educational ideal that it does not itself visibly practice. If broad education is good for undergraduates, it would seem to be good for faculty as well. There are many faculty who are broadly educated beyond their professorial expertise, but that remains largely a private matter, not something visible in the instructional practices of the institution. Recruiting faculty to participate in courses outside their special fields of interest is one of the most difficult tasks that any "breadth" educator is likely to face.

A case in point is the history of the Harvard Red-Book curriculum. The Red-Book curriculum was a worthwhile case of general education: a coherent, intensive, and extensive analysis of crucial ideas in the history of thought. (Notwithstanding the discussion so far, I am actually in favor of "broad" education.) The Red-Book curriculum vanished, however, to be replaced by a set of distribution requirements in various topical fields. This new curriculum was much touted—as any Harvard jiggle is likely to be hailed as cataclysmic—but close examination of cause and effect suggests only a ripple effect. The Red-Book curriculum was a post–World War II phenomenon originating in the fervor of "democratic culture victorious." As years went by, the fervor died, and so did the instructors. A Harvard dean of faculty confessed to me that one simply could not get new faculty to teach the Red-Book. The road to honor and tenure at Harvard lies not through the bogs of *general* education, but through deep pursuit and publication within a specialty. Harvard, as it always does, made the best of it, and the resulting "new" curriculum allowed students to be *broadly* educated by taking *narrow* courses, albeit in broadly grouped "fields." Nineteenth-century naval history is, after all, *history,* and history is, after all, a humanistic study (or is it a social science?), so Trafalgar is indeed some sort of exemplar of the eternal struggle between the Children of Light and the Children of Darkness—or something like that.

In sum, modern faculty in proper self-understanding pursue specialized research—and this has produced magnificent results. If this is the faculty thinking clearly about themselves, the reality and organization of the knowledge, and their institutional establishment, that is, the university, what authority can be given to *general* education? Not much.

Freshmen

General education toward well-roundedness is in most institutions spelled out in a set of required courses, usually called "distribution requirements." These distribution requirements range from the carefully crafted course to the carefully crafted catalogue. Faced with the prospect of doing relativity theory, quantum mechanics, and the Big Bang in one semester, many a conscientious department exercises great pedagogical imagination in opening this extraordinary material to neophyte students—thus, the carefully crafted course. At the opposite extreme is the carefully crafted *catalogue:* enchanting catalogue prose on the breadth and depth of study, marvelously dividing the learned world into a limited number of areas and then sprinkling extant course offerings out upon the designated areas. Whatever the course content may be, it fits a catalogue area, and so it is "distribution"—thus, the course on Trafalgar and the meaning of life.

Whatever the diligence (or lack of same) from departments in crafting distribution courses, one should recognize how these courses fit into the average student's educational and life scenario. The most common comment of students to any and all requirements is that they are something to "get out of the way"—so that one can get on with what one *really* came to college for in the first place, the major. I have labeled this section "freshmen" because requirements generally fall upon their schedule like lead. Distribution requirements have replaced beanies: the academic equivalent of freshmen hazing. If one can survive the pain of required courses, then one is admitted into the true fraternity of the major. Underclass years create an underclass. It hardly seems an exhilarating entrance to higher studies to spend one's initial years "getting things out of the way." And it hardly seems an exhilarating outcome to think that students have got Calvin and the Buddha "out of the way"! (The most frequent comment from alumni when informed that I teach philosophy: "Oh, I took Phil 101 when I was a freshmen. I didn't understand a word of it!" Not my course, of course.)

If there is a final blow to be struck against general education, it would be at the placement office. Job applicants had better indicate what specialty they are really good at, and an applicant who boasts of his or her "liberal arts" proficiency is on the way to unemployment or graduate school (postponement of unemployment). A college president acquaintance, whose institution was the very epitome of liberal arts education, tells of extolling the virtue of breadth to a group of trustees. One of the trustees was the CEO of a small corporation. He listened attentively and appreciatively to the recital of the versatility of the liberal arts graduate, as contrasted to the "narrow specialists." Finally, the trustee spoke up: "How true. We need that sort of person in my corporation. But we only need one of them—and that's me." Something like well-roundedness may be immensely useful to senior managers, but few college grads are hired as CEOs.

In sum, one can look at the well-rounded instructional pattern and see superficiality and dilettantism—a drudge to faculty and students alike, a drug on the market. Why not abandon the very notion and vote for the departmental major straight off?

I have stacked the cards against breadth and distribution courses—this is a book of half-truths. Distribution requirements can open up areas of interest that become compelling for future life and study. Given the manifest uncertainty of freshmen about a major field and their own talents and capacities, sampling various fields is a rational choice. From the faculty side, it assures novel and unpopular fields an opportunity to display their wares to possible majors. Even the "hazing" factor may be useful as a means of building class solidarity. But for all that there are some direct and secondary benefits, the intellectual rationale for distribution courses is slim indeed. Brown University has virtually abandoned all requirements—even a traditional major. Letting students follow their enthusiasms may produce a more enthusiastic learning community than one where half the population is "getting things out of the way."

Distribution requirements are often defended as having some ultimate utilitarian value. One should know science in an age where scientific advance influences public policy. In a world of international business, it is important to know a foreign language. Yet these quite pragmatic aims seem flawed in both aspiration and execution. As a reading of world, national, or individual "needs to know," they have the sniff of the a priori and superficial. Yes, it is an international world with lots of science, but one could argue (on the basis of some dismal poll results) that American students do not know much about the United States Constitution, which could be even more practical than gluons and the French pluperfect. And if the aspiration seems sketchily defended, the execution is certainly minimal. Enough French to read the menu, not enough to compliment the chef. The superficiality of aim and result leads one to suspect that there is a subtext, a suppressed justification for distribution requirements—the "hidden" meaning of "well rounded." The "well rounded" graduate should be not "just a brain," but also a person able to deal practically with the "real world." "Well rounded" education may well express the longing that a university education should be practical and/or "moral," but as the previous chapter on moral tutelage suggested, it is not clear what moral message the university can or should convey. The moral claim to de-dogmatize the parochial student fits nicely with the well-rounded metaphor. But one wonders whether the end product is not as indifferent to moral depth as the smooth surface of the evoked sphere.

A quite different and more compelling moral demand on the contemporary quad, however, has been the call not for the smooth surface of "well-rounded distribution" but for the jagged *diversity* of the contemporary world. It is not so much learning to get along in French or Arabic, smoothing over the rough spots in cross-cultural conversation; it is appreciating— or revelling in—the depth and difference in diversity. Because "diversity" claims on the university are diverse, addressing populations and/or curriculum, it is necessary to clarify the issues involved.

Difference of Diversities

Education seems fatally determined to convert terms of relationship into absolutes, proper specific truths into absolute half-truths. The University of Rochester motto is *Meliora* (Better). Better what? would seem to be the next question, but university slogans seldom get to the next question. Rochester is not unique in espousing the dangling relative. Heavy educational philosophy seems repeatedly to fixate on similar notions as the key to educational rescue and reform. "Relevance" has had its day. Relevance to *what*? Life (here or in eternity), business, pleasure, peace, war, and so forth? Arguments about the classics or the core find it hard to proceed beyond proclamation to program. The most recent earnest watchword for education is "diversity." As with all the other educational emblems, it would seem to require a description of *what* diversity. An exasperated admissions director once suggested to me that he would increase diversity by admitting a lot of dumb kids! In the contemporary use, not only do I find "diversity" altogether too free-floating, but also, as it is discussed, it seems to be a serious misdescription of the real issues of diversity in American education. I want to address two very different "diversity" concerns: diversity of populations within the university-as-social-institution and diversity in the curriculum: "multiculturalism."

I had the privilege of being the chair of an accreditation team at Bryn Mawr College in the recent past. The most vexing issue on the campus by all reports was "diversity." Having read various self-studies and having spent several days on the campus, it struck me that the search for "diversity" was seriously misleading. For many years, Bryn Mawr had an enviable record of admitting foreign students. I have seldom seen a more "diverse" student body. Students were there in significant numbers from every continent, race, and religion. Buddhists could argue with *sabras* from Israel; Brazilians encountered mainland Chinese at the lunch counter. *The* underrepresented group at Bryn Mawr—as at most selective colleges—was American citizens of African descent. I am not certain that Bryn Mawr needed more worldwide diversity; it did need (and want) more American citizens of color.

While it may be politically astute to encapsulate the recruitment of African Americans under the "diversity" label, I believe it is dangerous to create vagueness when specificity is required. If "diversity" were only a polite label, it could be tolerated, but the word has led colleges and their administrators, faculty, and students down some peculiar pathways. Anyone who has participated in "diversity" discussions on any university campus knows that *the* issue involves African Americans. An administrator who points to the large cadre of Pacific rim and Middle Eastern graduate students as a proof of institutional diversity will be accused of frivolity on a serious issue. If there is a campus concern on that issue, it might be for *less* diversity—more genuine American PhD candidates, fewer Asian teaching assistants who supposedly cannot be understood by American freshmen.

The only major constituency included in the current "diversity" demands would be Hispanics—and at even further remove, Native Americans. If Hispanics are part of "the diverse," one needs to recognize immediately the difference in Hispanic diversity. Hispanics have certainly shared much of the economic and social deprivation of the African-American population. Most Hispanic students come from Caribbean and Central American cultures, which have been routinely ignored in the curriculum of American universities and colleges. Nevertheless, in a university curriculum, "Hispanicism" presents a less severe challenge.

Spanish is, after all, a major European language. Insofar as the university is a distinctly European invention—and it is—

Spain is a major participant. Hispanics can immediately retrieve a comprehensive and extant linguistic, political, and artistic heritage, either Peninsular or in the Western hemisphere, that fits at many points with the broad lines of the European assumptions of the university. One of the more pressing claims in diversity debates is that the curriculum is fatally Eurocentric. This may be so, but for Spanish-speaking students, applauding that argument seems self-defeating.

In comparison to Hispanics, *African* Americans present a formidable diversity. African languages are from a totally different linguistic root. Many of the African languages lack a long written history, and oral cultures are notoriously more difficult to retrieve. African linguistic and cultural roots are *radically* different from the European experience. In sum, Hispanics could easily pick up threads of their background culture in American universities; African Americans cannot. All the more reason, I would argue, for special attention to the African heritage because relative to the dominant European tradition, it really *is* diverse.

At the same time, however, while universities rightly may seek ideological diversity in Africa, the African American is probably more de facto American than African. Few African Americans speak an African language. Having been divorced from African roots by centuries of oppression, retention of that heritage is often subtle and indirect. A deliberate recovery of an African heritage is monumentally more difficult for African Americans than for Hispanics. Spain is a moderately small country, and in its period of empire, many of the assumptions of Peninsular Spain were exported intact to a New World. Africa is a whole continent, full of its own remarkable diversity of art, culture, and society. Recovering *African* culture for African Americans may share the foolish mistake of recovering "Indian" culture for Native Americans—assuming that Seminoles and Navajos are more or less the same.

For better or worse—and very much for the worse—the

dominant *experience* for African Americans has been American: specifically, *the American outcast.* Blacks have been defined in an American set of expectations *from which they are to be excluded.* The daily aspirations of African Americans are not so much diverse as denied. The civil rights struggle centered on black people obtaining what whites had all along: the vote, education, and the right to eat at any lunch counter, sleep in any hotel, and travel without segregation. One could argue that many of the current demands of blacks constitute a pure American wish list: a job, a decent home, safety in the streets, justice in the courts. Nothing very diverse there.

If one accepts this analysis, African Americans may seem to the universities and feel to themselves peculiarly alienated— more alienated than women, Hispanics, Catholics, or Jews. The university is a place of diversity of ideas, cultures, and styles. It should not have great problems adjusting to distant religions and strange customs. The alienation of African Americans at dominantly white institutions is something else: the university is an *American* institution attempting to *include* those defined as "the Americans *excluded.*" No wonder there are racial tensions on majority campuses.

My main objection to "diversity" as a slogan is that it masks the true plight of African Americans in the United States. There is more here than accepting those who are different—it is accepting those defined-as-different-in-order-to-be-excluded. In this regard, the charge of "racism" often raised in discussions of diversity has validity. Universities are accustomed to incorporating different "ideological" products: philosophies, religions, styles of art. Race is not an ideological product; it is a biological descriptor. (Note that the concept of "race" as denoting some special biological or psychic potential is highly dubious. "Race" is at best a superficial physical descriptor.) It is blacks as a *race* that are excluded in American experience. To the extent, then, that American educational institutions reflect consciously or unconsciously this historical sense of exclusion, they will appear to do so on *racial* grounds, and "racism" becomes an accurate perception.

From Diversity to Multiculturalism

Diversity in terms of the racial, ethnic, national, religious, and socioeconomic backgrounds of the students and staff seems an unimpeachable goal. It means opening this important social institution, the university, to the pluralisms of the society. What people-diversity leaves undecided is curricular-diversity. One could certainly favor *diverse* student bodies while advocating a *universal* curriculum.

If every student were a physicist, there would be one curriculum for many races. However, not all of university education is natural science. What about the humanistic curriculum? In earlier days, it was assumed that there was a common humanistic curriculum. It was certainly not as rigid as the chemistry course of study, but in some rough outline, the content was generally accepted as *the* cultural curriculum. Then it was noted that *the* cultural curriculum consisted of the thoughts of dead, white, European males; the diversity of the lively, multiracial, coeducational, ethnically diverse student body was not reflected in the designated cultural hitters. The standard, classical, common curriculum came under fire for its parochial narrowness, and the ideal of "multiculturalism" was proposed.

If a bad diagnostic on "diversity" in the student body prevails, one will run into equally misleading discussions of diversity/multiculturalism in the curriculum. There is a straightforward, unimpeachable argument for universities and colleges to treat seriously the radically different experience of the African continent—and the radically defeated (and, therefore, different) expectations of the African *American*. Both intellectual breadth and political commitment justify African and African-American studies. The argument begins to become wayward, however, when it centers on the curious issue of the university as

"Euro-centric." There is certainly justice to the charge, but as a structural "fault," I cannot see how it can be maintained.

The university certainly is "Euro-centric." It is a peculiarly European invention. I suspect it would be as difficult for the university to deny its historical culture as it would be for an African or an Asian to deny his or hers. The fact that universities have been as much Western institutions as *ashrams* have been Eastern institutions means that certain specific, distinct, and essential activities are associated with the "culture." Not the least of the cultural activities of the Euro-university has been the practice of natural science—the defining paradigm of the modern university. It may be an unappealing practice to some, but there it is. It would be as puzzling to imagine the university without physics as it would be a jazz band without a beat. If you want to play in either band, you have to follow the score. In the case of physics and the other sciences, I suppose that the score has to be seen as "European" *honoris causa.*

Physics is not the whole of life, but the modern university operates on "scientific" assumptions that have had a peculiarly powerful expression in something one would probably call "European." Having noted an honorific and historical European connection to the scientific thread of the modern university, one should hasten to make some important qualifications. First, "Europe" itself is a relatively recent invention. In the area of science, "Europe" has huge debts to pay to the Mediterranean basin, including northern Africa. Second, the meaning of "science" rests on a species of universalism that undercuts the accident of geographical origin. The scientific import-export trade between Europe and Asia is a fact of old history and new technology. If science was born and bred in Europe, it has proved eminently transferable to all regions of the planet.

If there is to be cultural diversity in the curriculum, the question is this: will it succumb to something like a European/university assumption, the assumption of "universal" reason?

That is the real issue for multiculturalism and its fundamental challenge to the research model.

Diversity Deconstructs the University

Years ago when I was an assistant dean at Princeton, I came to realize that one had to translate common sayings on campus into their real meanings. Because my position required me to see all the Princeton students unhappy enough to have flunked out or dropped out, I soon discovered an inner meaning of "diversity." It was a frequent complaint of my dropouts that Princeton lacked diversity. This was certainly true. There were, for instance, no women, and the number of African Americans was minuscule. Few blue-collar families were represented. However, this was not the real complaint. My dropouts were generally "sensitive souls," artistic folk displeased with the—as they saw it—unintellectual rowdiness of the average Princeton male. Their desire for "diversity" translated into "Why aren't there more students here like me?" As so often happens in the wonderland of academia, "diverse" meant "similar."

As with my diversity-seeking students who wanted someone similar to themselves, the banner of multiculturalism is often unfurled not so much for the sake of multiple multicultures, but to make sure that those of my group, race, religion, ethnicity, or sexual orientation are numerous, visible, and as represented in the curriculum as in the dorms. In other words, it is not clear that multiculturalists are interested in *broadening* their cultural horizons as much as they are in fortifying their particular sense of cultural similarity and solidarity. Multiculturalism does not necessarily deliver what the label suggests.

Mislabeling is probably a minor fault, since everyone knows how to read the code. And there seems to be no fault in wanting to study one's own racial history, religious beliefs, and ethnic origins at the depth and sophistication present in university studies. The fundamental challenge to university assumptions occurs if the multicultural crusade transforms cultures to be studied into cults to be protected. The "Euro-centric" scientific assumption of the university is then fundamentally rejected. There is no impersonal, transcendent, non-ethnic viewpoint from which one can observe cultures—certainly not mine! The demand for a deep "personalization" deconstructs the universal scientific assumption that is at the heart of the modern university revolution.

The issues involved in multiculturalism are a complex of intellectual, political, and moral concerns. It is important to understand the difference between an *intellectual* justification for the study of some particular ethnic, religious, or gender culture and the *moral* demands that resonate in the multicultural debates. I can illustrate the significant difference by examining a quite respectable form of "women's studies"—respectable within the ideology of the modern research university.

One of the charges against *the* cultural curriculum of yore has been that the venerated authors were all *males*—presumably because faculty were dominantly male. That is a serious fault needing amelioration. Women have been a minority among college faculties and remain so. One of the academic fields in which women not only have been represented but also have been leaders is anthropology (Margaret Mead, Ruth Benedict, Hortense Powdermaker). Why this congregation of women anthropologists? A plausible explanation is that Franz Boas, the founder of modern anthropology and the mentor of the above-mentioned distinguished women, realized early on that in the investigation of tribal societies, male anthropologists would often be rigidly excluded from the feminine culture. Not only did the men have male-only secret societies, but the women had their female secrets as well. If the women's culture was to be known, there would have to be women anthropologists in the field.

In this anthropology example, women have a unique capacity as observers. The role of sexual difference seems indispensable to the acquisition of knowledge; those "inside" a culture speak with special authority on that reality. The principle at work extends to any putative cultural group: Should Catholics expect Protestant scholars to be fully adequate reporters on the Roman experience? Whites on blacks? Women, blacks, or Muslims may be unique reporters on the character of class, clan, or cult. But under the intellectual assumptions of the "science" of anthropology, the purpose of the reporter is to report, to communicate as best one can to the outsider what the insider comes to know. The intellectual challenge in the diversity-multiculturalism argument comes when the need for special communicators between cultures seems to become an argument for *no* communication between cultures. The secrets of the Samoans are not revealed, but resealed. The culture remains a secret cult open only to those of special birth (or, for Christians, second birth in just the right baptismal font!).

Multiculturalists of the deconstructionist persuasion often sound as if they would be quite willing to accept the splendid isolation of cultures. There are many cultures, many sexual secrets, many racial truths that are incommunicable to the outsider. One may celebrate one's sex or race, but communicating to the others is impossible. "It is a matter of Faith," as they would have said in the old days. Those who do not have the Faith do not have a clue. Contemporary French philosopher Jacques Derrida (dean of deconstruction) talks about the "dance of innumerable choreographies"—which certainly suggests celebration over communication.

The anthropology example is chosen with malice aforethought. What, after all, is anthropology if it is not *multicultural* studies? In addition, it is a discipline in which women have been prominent investigators and in which it would appear that women as such are unique reporters on women's cultures. For all that, the intellectual assumptions of traditional anthropology conform to the overall assumptions of the university. From the standpoint of the modern multiculturalist critic, this misses the moral point. The cults, clans, and tribes displayed by the anthropologist are arrayed in a "natural history museum," just like the costumes and shamans of the tribes. Are these tribal displays moral challenges or simply curios of local custom?

Deconstructive multiculturalism will not settle for this "intellectualist/scientistic" assumption. By revelling in special cultures, the dance of innumerable cultural choreographies, deconstructive multiculturalism can undermine the universalist assumptions that have guided the modern university—and, to a certain extent, a great sweep of the European intellectual tradition. Multiculturalism is equally offensive if it moves beyond revelling to revelation: the notion that one must see the world according to cultic wisdom. Left at the level of an intellectual quarrel, multiculturalism may deserve the severe criticism and scorn that it has received from "traditional" academic circles. The "moral" issue involved in multiculturalism should not be ignored, however; multicultural moral claims point like Moses before the Promised Land. And like Moses, multiculturalism never seems to get to where it is destined to go. More of that when I return to the moral role of the university in the concluding chapters. I leave off with multicultural deconstruction as a direct antithesis to the "breadth" assumptions of the "well rounded" aspirations of the old cultural core.

If diversity and distribution create manifest disarray in the curriculum, a further disruption may be caused by a truly elevating notion: the importance of *teaching*. Teaching excellence is an individual accomplishment and one to be highly valued. Nevertheless, one might have an institution with wall-to-wall virtuosi of the classroom and yet fail at education. The continuing exhortation for better teaching in colleges and universities is itself a product of the research revolution. In the obvious case so often exploited in institutional polemics, the presence of this novel interest, research, is regarded as a serious distraction from the traditional role of teaching. No doubt there is some truth to this concern, but the deeper problem is the distraction that the research enterprise offers to a more fundamental notion: learning. American colleges and universities vie over the respective importance of teaching and research—they do not, however, advertise learning. There is a lesson in the choice of verbal weapons, and it is to this issue that we turn in the next chapter.

6 Teaching Is the Primary Task of Higher Education

Several years ago I was asked to present a paper at an academic conference on the subject "The University as a Place of Learning." It says something about academic conferences that anyone would think this was a discussable issue. It seemed like preparing a talk on "The Bachelor as an Unmarried Male." However, the more I thought about this bland topic, the more it occurred to me that in the United States, the rhetoric of higher education almost never promotes "learning" as the characteristic of the institution. Universities boast of "research," and colleges advertise "teaching"; no one that I know makes claims on *learning*. The avoidance of the term is more than accidental; it rests on suppositions that have significant ideological and practical consequences. In this chapter, I will discuss neglect of *learning* first in practical terms: how it blunts educational outcomes, how it prevents efficiency. In the second section, I will explore the philosophical implication of the university as a place of learning.

Teaching and Research versus Learning

Nothing is more often discussed—usually with high emotional valence—than the conflict in higher education between research and teaching. The discussion is painful and acute at research universities, which are eager—desperate!—to defend the adequacy of teaching, despite the advanced research and scholarship that mark the interests of the faculty. Smaller collegiate (teaching) institutions allude ominously to Brand X Research University, where graduate students do all the instruction because the researchers are off grabbing grants. It is nowhere proved beyond anecdote that graduate students are not inspiring instructors or that research professors are either better teachers or distracted absentees from the classroom—depending on which side of the polemic one fancies. My own experience suggests that the whole turmoil is beside the point. There is great teaching at research universities, there is lousy teaching at collegiate places, and vice versa. (And at the prestige *colleges,* faculty are as concerned to prove their research/scholarly credentials as their brethren at Brand X U.) The real issue for higher education is not teaching versus research; it is learning or, more grandiosely, education—a thoroughly neglected subject at most undergraduate and graduate institutions. (I make a significant exception for *professional* schools, of which more later on.)

I illustrate my point about what is missing from the research/teaching polemic with one of the most productive recent efforts to improve "teaching." Professor Uri Treisman of the Mathematics Department at UC Berkeley was deeply disturbed by the fact that the black students in his elementary calculus classes were performing so poorly. Failure in elementary calculus closed the door to all of the science and engineering curricula as well as a good proportion of the mathematically sophisticated social sciences. Treisman sought to understand the cause of underperformance. His first hypotheses were standard: poor high school background, low aptitude scores, lack of parental encouragement, concerns about money, and so on through a familiar litany of plausibilities. Treisman could make none of the supposed correlations. Black students with good high school backgrounds did as poorly as those with mediocre high school experiences. Wealth, parental pressure, and so on did not correlate any better.

Genuinely puzzled, Treisman wangled a small grant to investigate exactly what these underperforming students did each day that resulted in such negligible classroom results. He chose as a "control" a group of Chinese students who were doing excellent work. What was the difference? He discovered, among other things, that the Chinese worked together on problems in what they happily referred to as "work gangs." In contrast, the black students worked solo. (The Chinese were not cheating, just sharing insights and a sense of the subject.) On the basis of this research, Treisman reorganized his classes to promote cohort learning: students were required to work together. The improvement in results was striking.

The moral of this tale is that Uri Treisman was not a better *teacher* at the end of the process than before. Whatever vibrancy and ingenuity he could bring to explicating differential equations were presumably the same postcohorting as they were precohorting. Treisman had not improved his *teaching;* he had improved the *conditions of learning.* The distinction between *teaching* and *conditions of learning* as a means of improving education is profoundly important not only for the values that might be fostered by education, but also for the economics of the act.

I had the privilege, as a very young instructor, of assisting in a course supervised by E. Harris "Jinx" Harbison. Harbison, a legendary teacher at Princeton, taught a course on the Renaissance and Reformation ("Ren & Ref") that was a *must* on the student hit parade. When Harbison died at too early an age, the national teaching award was named in his honor. Each year a selection process designates the "teacher of the year" to receive the Harbison Prize. While I revere Harbison's memory and have nothing but admiration for the designees of the award, the whole process frames education in the "Noble Teacher" mode.

The Noble Teacher, through imagination, vivacity, dedication, or persistence, wrings enthusiasm and results from the masses before him or her. Indeed, it happens, and bravo for that! But the problem with the Noble Teacher concept is that it bypasses the conditions of learning. (Except, of course, that the unimaginative, torpid, distracted, and lazy instructor is a negative condition for learning. But as the Treisman example suggests, the teacher is not the *only* condition of learning—and may not be the crucial condition at all!)

By concentrating awards and debate on the individual teacher capable of a learned and bravura performance, the discussion of what is wrong with the college classroom bypasses the more important question of student learning. It is quite characteristic of Treisman's experience that he has recommended that colleges do away with teaching awards to individual faculty, redirecting funds and kudos to *departments*. A good teaching *department* is a very different entity than a brilliant individual teacher. A department may be excellent because of an unusual density of charismatics, but it is more likely that the awarded department is one in which the curriculum has been thoughtfully integrated and teaching assignments match the subject to be taught and the sophistication of those to be taught. Most important, the excellent teaching *department* is more likely to see itself as an integrated functioning unit than as a place where stars happen to reside.

The teaching versus research debate is yet another example of the half-truth that "the *faculty* is the university." Teaching and research are things that faculty do; learning is what students do. Of course, conscientious faculty consider student learning structures, but I submit that it is not usually a highly visible priority in educational planning. Students are more likely to be regarded as raw material, which the vivid performance of the instructor will energize. Students believe in the Noble Teacher model and expect to be stirred into action by vivacious teaching. There is nothing wicked in this pattern, but one could consider the wisdom of the ancient light bulb joke: "How many psychiatrists does it take to turn on a light bulb?" "None, it has to turn on itself!" Does emphasis on great teaching assume student passivity, when they really must turn on their own light?

The Virtuous B-School

Experimental proof of the claim for "conditions of learning" over "charismatic teaching" can be found in graduate professional schools. I was particularly taken with a discussion on teaching (a perennial topic) at a meeting of the AAU research universities. Many of the attending presidents admitted that their business schools displayed the best teaching at their respective establishments. This observation was usually uttered with an air of bewilderment. How could those mercenaries display better teaching than the concerned humanists, who constituted the core of the *real* university? When one attempted to unlock the B-School secret, it turned out that the secret was not the histrionics of the faculty; it was the conditions of learning created by the schools.

I take the University of Rochester's William E. Simon School as a case in point because it is one with which I am intimately acquainted and because the shaping of its educational structure seems to conform in general principles to that of the other successful B-Schools. During my time at Rochester, the Simon School embarked on a building campaign. Central to this effort was the determination to have very specialized classroom configurations. (The configurations were not original; they were copied to the millimeter from the Harvard Business School.) The classrooms featured tiered rows of desks with comfortable swivel seats, arranged in a semicircle with the instructor in the well. The architecture of a classroom is a non-trivial condition of learning.

Anyone from a Harbison winner to a harried assistant professor could be in the central well. Presumably, it will go better with the Harbison awardee—but it will go even better with this architecture, and it may rescue the bumbling beginner from disaster. The classroom architecture was intended to encourage significant *student interaction*. Student interaction is profoundly important for professional schools not only because students at such schools (particularly business schools) already have much knowledge and skill, which can be shared with others (their light bulbs are already lit), but also because, in most professions, communal work with colleagues is expected. (Doctors consult; lawyers team up; managers create task forces to address issues.) The tiered classroom permits eye contact with other students and becomes a facilitating condition of student-student conversation. Beyond this, the very shape of the space suggests a different sort of educational interaction than the "normal" classroom.

In contrast to the Simon School space, I taught an undergraduate class in ethics in a "normal" classroom. Students sat in rows; they could all see me—when awake—but would have to crane to see anyone else. Those in the back row saw the backs of heads, and few in the front would do a 180-degree turn to confront a back bencher. Since the subject was sexual ethics, the utter privatization of the students may have been a protective shield for the shy, but it did nothing for cross-student discussion.

A note on lighting: I have always admired a humanist colleague who, in directing the design of a seminar room to be used by undergraduates, insisted that the lighting be incandescent and provided via wall-wash units, rather than overhead fixtures. The rationale: incandescent light, in contrast to fluorescent light, is balanced to the red end of the spectrum and gives a pleasant warmth to skin tone. Warm light plus wall lights favors the flawed complexions of late adolescents. It is difficult to discourse on Goethe if you are worrying about your acne—which was not one of the sorrows of young Werther anyhow.

The architecture of classrooms is an obvious condition of learning—so obvious that it generally is neglected altogether in campus planning. However, if B-Schools urged only expensive architecture, they would not be singled out for "good teaching." The classroom was only the outward expression of the fundamental condition of learning that the Simon School judged to be productive: cohort learning. While it was important to have vibrant (Harbison-type) teachers in the well, a significant portion of the instructional program was based on the assumption of cohort learning groups. Classes were divided into two large cohorts and then further broken down into smaller units, who were expected to solve problems conjointly. The construction of the smaller cohorts was carefully controlled: there would be those with significant business experience and those with none; number-adverse types would pair off with accountants. Again, the assumption that the cohort replicated the professional life into which the students would graduate was itself a powerful learning device for the course offering.

It would be edifying to believe that the careful planning of the business school was the product of educational altruism. Far be it from business school faculty to admit to high motives. The initial concern was economic. The Simon School faculty was concerned with maintaining a high salary level. Of course, the individuals valued the cash, but as a school with high academic aspiration and achievement in a modest-sized, off-the-main-line city, it was judged to be important to sustain a high salary level to compete for faculty with Harvard or Wharton, where salaries were generous and consulting fees were a taxi ride away. Given a finite set of financial resources, the school leadership calculated the fewer faculty, the more for each. Faculty size was strictly limited to improve individual salaries.

One must satisfy the market of potential students. How to limit faculty size and satisfy the clients? If one accepts the simple axiom that faculty-student ratio is a marker of high-quality teaching, the Simon School would have to be down-graded because there were fewer faculty for many students. The answer to the seeming dilemma was to concentrate on student-student intimacy as a compensation for the lack of intimacy of the faculty-student ratio. It is possible to have genuine give-and-take discussion in a one-hundred-seat, specially constructed, tiered, semicircular room, and it is almost impossible with twenty students in a box with chairs in rows. Cohort learning creates an intimacy for and to the students that not only compensates for the smaller faculty number but also may be a more effective educational intimacy than formal faculty office hours.

Cohort learning determines curriculum. Large cohorted classes work only if there is a common core curriculum. Only when there is a significant mass of students reading the same material and solving the same problems can cohorting operate. If everyone is "doing her own thing," there is no point to co-horting with another. The educational potential of core cur-riculum and cohorting is enormous because it energizes the most underutilized educational capacity at the university: stu-dents. In the B-School case, this is obvious: because of their mix of talents and skills, the students were exceptionally effective in teaching one another. One did not have to depend on the single (happily highly paid) professor to do all the teaching.

Cohorting can have similar energizing effects with the un-skilled, namely, undergraduates. While at Rochester, I taught a course in and for a fraternity. All members of the class had to be members of the brotherhood. The subject was moral philoso-phy, and what I sought as a *condition of learning* was a situa-tion that maximized the possibility that the students would talk to one another *outside* the class. The normal class at any college of size will be a disparate collection of freshmen to seniors from various parts of the campus geography. The only time they assemble and discuss is in the three hours or so of class time. It is just impossible to figure out what is going on in Spin-oza in three hours—mostly dominated by the prof anyhow—

and, besides, next week it is Kant! My hope was that the fraternity brethren would have lots of time out of class to argue, grumble, and learn more from one another than they would from the Herr Professor.

Attention to conditions of learning, whether it is arranging the seats or cohorting the class, has much to commend it educationally, but it is the economic effect that should catch the attention of presidents and boards. (And faculty might note the lesson of the Simon School: attention to conditions of learning improves financial compensation.) Beardsley Ruml (of the withholding tax) many years ago wrote a perceptive pamphlet, "Memo to a College Trustee." Based on his own experience in that exalted role, Ruml concluded that the only thing worse than the educational confusion of the curriculum was its economic inefficiency. It made no sense and cost too much. Ruml argued for fewer course choices and larger classes: Econ 101 applied to the curriculum. The problem with such sensible cost containment is that it runs directly counter to the inherent faculty interest in a diffusion of specialties and the desire of students to shop variety in the course offerings. The unstoppable force meets the unmovable budget. The budget will prevail. But is the result educational disaster? Not necessarily.

Properly structured in a manner analogous to the business school example, less is more. The "philosophy" of the modern curriculum maximizes variety and choice at the expense of cohesion and concentration. Dabble before depth seems to be the watchword. But if there is to be economy *and* better education, it will be necessary for faculties to do as the B-School folks did: determine a core—or a set of cores. It is the very idea of a core for undergraduate education—*the* cultural curriculum, argh! —that seems virtually impossible to realize in the multisplintered edifice of the modern university.

It is not quite accurate to say that there are no cores in the modern university. Students in natural science and engineering are frequently cored solid. The accreditation requirements in electrical engineering, for instance, are so stringent that a student is likely to have no more than one elective in four years. (It was for this reason that the University of Rochester initiated its "Take Five" program: a free fifth year so that electrical engineering students could get an education along with accreditation.) The core problem in determining the core lies in the "cultural" curriculum: the humanities, history, social studies, languages, science for non-scientists. One cannot economize and/or improve education within a cultural "core" unless there is some cultural aim beyond dispersion. That aim seems to have gone absent. The vanishing of a cultural core is the philosophical issue involved in distinguishing teaching, research, and *learning*. No learning; no core.

The University as a Place of Learning

I have praised the professional school paradigm because of its attention to conditions of learning. That discussion of "learning" has been largely mechanical: cohorting, proper seating, incandescent lights, and all that. There is an ideological interpretation of the university as a place of learning that may help illuminate the puzzle of "cultural" education for undergraduates. The lack of attention to "conditions of learning" might be regarded as merely technical, easily corrected by imaginative architects and educational psychologists. Unfortunately, there are deeper ideological and cultural roots that have caused American colleges to avoid accepting distinction as "seats of learning." One can highlight the peculiarity of the American educational ethos by citing the counterexample of traditional British education at Oxford and Cambridge. University education at "Oxbridge" differs in both rhetoric and practice from the American system. If one can characterize American practice as teaching without much attention to conditions of learning, one might characterize Oxbridge as learning without much attention to conditions of teaching.

At Oxford, it is more than mere semantics that one "reads" for a degree. The university is a place of learning, and the student is regarded as a learner in a place of learning. There are learned dons, libraries full of learned treatises. One reads through this accumulation of learning and then certifies the attainment of learning in the honors examination. Students go to Oxbridge not to be taught, but to learn. To be sure, one does meet with a tutor on a regular basis, but his or her role is to direct the student into various plausible avenues of learning available. "Why don't you read the first section of the *Treatise* for next week and we will discuss it. Oh, Professor M is giving a lecture on a related issue. You might want to pop in to hear what he has to say!" The assumption of this colloquy is not that the student will rush off to be taught by Professor M, but that he or she will go about learning something during the week so that the conversation with the tutor will be productive. (Uri Treisman has opined that the key to curricular reform is making sure that the student comes to class prepared. Talk about radical suggestions!)

In the United States, one goes to college to be taught in a place of teaching. The method of grading and certification in this country underlines the importance of teaching. The teacher is the primary grader, and the grade is based more or less on how well the student has grasped what was taught by the instructor. This is a distinctly different mode than the Oxbridge climactic honors examination, when one must demonstrate that one is learned in the field, regardless of what teaching exercises have been undergone. At Princeton, there was a tradition of a senior general examination. Faculty continually complained that it was not really a general examination of the field; it was a reprise of the course work of the last two years. True enough, and the exam was abandoned.

It would be interesting to speculate on why teaching has such a different import in British and American higher education. I suspect that Puritan moral enthusiasm, religious pluralism, and the lack of an established gentry all conspired to create the special teaching impetus of American higher education. If students come from an established household to an established college sponsored by an established church, they may not need (or may judge that they do not need) to be molded from recalcitrant material into some semblance of culture. There may be an analogy between American agriculture and American collegiate culture. In both cases, the cultivators have assumed a virgin territory to be won by mighty effort from sheer wilderness.

The presence of an "establishment" creates an "external" rationale for the curriculum and makes "the university as a place of *learning*" an acceptable notion. The function of education is—at least—to inculcate the new generation in what has been established. Or, to put it another way, we have already *learned* something, so we should be certain that the next generation acquires what is already at hand. Cardinal Newman's famous *Idea of the University* is entirely based on the notion of the university as a place of learning. Although he shifted from the *local* establishment (the Anglican Church), Roman Catholicism presented him with an even older establishment. His religious commitments were also deeply embedded in the classical establishment of the great Greeks. Thus, Newman's university was exclusively a place where the established learning of humankind was to be passed along. He recognized the beginning of the "research" movement in advanced education, but advocated that research should be carried forward *outside* the university in separate institutes. Despite a presidential penchant for quoting Newman's eloquences, American higher education has followed the German research university model, of which Newman was only dimly aware—and of which he presumably would have disapproved. To the extent that a search and discovery mode comes to dominate the sense of the higher educational enterprise, learning as some accumulated historical wisdom vanishes from the scene. There cannot be any cultural core because culture was just discovered yesterday, along with structuralism, linguistic analysis, Noam Chomsky, or the Beatles.

It is the notion of some genuine, irreplaceable legacy of thought, a valued tradition about what the human race has already *learned,* that is at hazard after the research revolution in higher education. Considering all the things people definitely *knew* (the stock of genuine *learning*)—for example, the sun was at the center of the universe and the earth was flat—that turned out to be wildly wrong under the scrupulous gaze of science, one might well decide that an institution modeled on science should be wary indeed of accumulated learning. So it has been, and while much has been accomplished by this studied skepticism about any present state of learning, wariness about making a claim for *learning* virtually precludes any sensible view of morality and practical wisdom. Explaining why learning and morality are linked will be the subject of the concluding chapters.

The *core of learning* for higher education can well be regarded as the research university's central issue. Financial restriction pushes toward the *essentials;* moral critique demands some overriding ethical purpose. The inherent notion of the research revolution is highly resistant to either an economic or an ethical determination of core. At the research level, expansiveness into all the fascinating nooks of knowledge seems altogether justified. Restriction is condemned as "merely economical" without "educational" purpose. Surely, restriction may be demanded by economics; yet not every decision forced by economics is *solely* economic, despite the bitter complaints of aggrieved disciplines. On the ethical side, the problem is not the wonderful expansiveness of science; it is the complete disarray of cultural consensus. Scientific diffusion and cultural disarray at and on the core become acute problems when issues of institutional management arise. Thus, it is to the management of universities that the next chapter is devoted.

7 The Problem with Higher Education Is the Administration

Ask any faculty member what the major problem with his or her university is, and the answer will be "the administration." I happen to agree with that view, but for a reason opposite that of most faculty critics. The faculty member generally means that there is *too much* administration. My notion is that there is *too little*. Since this is a treatise on half-truths, I hope that these two half-truths add up to one whole truth.

The scope, size, and ambition of the institutionalization of research in the modern university necessitated a concomitant administrative burden. Legitimate (if inconclusive) arguments could be generated about the proper balance between fixing the roofs and funding the physicists. (I have never known a faculty that did not complain that the grass was mowed too frequently.) The administration might be accused of eroding educational funding, and thus affecting program on the sly, but it ought not dabble in direct educational planning—that is a faculty issue sole and secure. This uneasy, but happy, division between educational jurisdiction and janitorial services was fostered in the past century by the rise of the research university. The present (late 1990s) and future (as far into the twenty-first century as one can see) will not permit the amiable muddle of

faculty planning and administrative plunder—or vice versa—
that has marked the past one hundred years.

The Rise of Vice-Chancellors

I recently moderated a conference for the Salzburg Seminar on
the future of higher education in the twenty-first century. The
conference brought together senior administrators from thirty-
five countries around the world from Tajikistan to Chile. Without exception, the factors for educational planning in the
twenty-first century were the same in every country. Whether it
was a developed country such as Austria, a recently "liberated"
country such as Albania, or a third-world country such as Mau-
ritania, there was a brief scenario that prevailed. It can be set
forth in three propositions:

1. There will be an increase in the number of students attending universities and colleges.
2. There will be no proportionate increase in government funding for higher education.
3. Responsibility will be delegated to local senior management charged to make higher education efficient
   and economically viable.

The conclusion and forecast for the next century: more administration.

There Will Be an Increase in the Number of Students Attending Universities and Colleges

The factors underlying this predictive claim are varied. In the
underdeveloped world, college education is viewed as a personal hope for economic advancement. Governments respond
to this popular urge and belief—and then add the notion that in
a high-tech world, higher education will be the key to national
economic advancement. (That neither the personal nor the economic claim is by any means a sure-fire fact is of no importance
in determining personal or political choice.)

In the developed countries of Europe, the drive for greater college participation is often based on egalitarian urges. For societies historically defined by inherited class and privilege, college going is regarded as a means of democratizing the social structure. Austria is a case in point. The Austrian government, having passed legislation that eliminated the entrance examination for the *Gymnasium*—the traditional entrance program to the university—then decreed that anyone who successfully completed the *Gymnasium* program would automatically be admitted to one of the Austrian universities. The result has been an enormous increase in the university population—with a concomitant decrease in the postsecondary "technical" programs. A *university* degree in Austria is a social advantage not to be evaded.

The United States already has a very high proportion of high school graduates pursuing "postsecondary" education, and one might not expect a significant increase. But two factors suggest otherwise: a demographic upswing in the number of eighteen-year-olds after the "baby bust" of the 1980s and the continuing malaise of the American K–12 system. The combination of demographics and declining schools makes the projection plausible. Most of the demographic increase is in populations particularly ill served by the K–12 system. If these populations are to be educated at all for productive roles in society, the burden will shift to the efforts of the community colleges and remediation programs of senior institutions.

There Will Be No Proportionate Increase in Government Funding for Higher Education

In a book dedicated to half-truths, this assertion is 96 percent true. In a few of the "Asian tigers," government funds may be lavished on higher education, but almost anywhere else significant funding increases are manifestly impossible or monumentally implausible.

The only commentary on the matter of funding involves the role of government. In theory, not all universities are government funded. In the United States, many of our greatest universities are "private"; funds are derived from tuition, endowments, and fund raising rather than from government largesse. The independent funding of private colleges and universities is a more or less half-truth. For major research universities, the bulk of funding for research comes from a variety of federal agencies, for example, the National Science Foundation and the National Institutes of Health. At the other end of the education spectrum, I happen to be a trustee of a non-research institution that prides itself on dedicated teaching. The president noted to the board that given the low income level of the students and the access of that population to state and federal grants, loans, and work-study funds, about one-half of the income for this *private* university is ultimately derived from government.

American educators often point to the existence of "private" higher education as a special mark and strength of our system. True enough, but "private" higher education is not an American exclusive. It is important to delineate two significant "private" sectors elsewhere and in the United States. In South America, there are many de jure "private" colleges. These colleges happen to be wholly funded by government, although their legal status is "private." (One might argue that my American teaching institution is approaching that point. A "voucher" system for higher education in the United States would approximate the status of these South American institutions.)

In addition to these legally "private," economically "public" institutions, there exist in Asia and Latin America a growing number of "private enterprise" colleges. These institutions are established as for-profit corporations and are owned by their incorporators. In Korea, there are "family" chains of colleges established on the profit-making model. Westmar College in LeMars, Iowa, caused a sensation several years ago when it sold out to a Japanese "family" for-profit university and became Teikyo-Westmar.

In the United States, nomenclature distinguishes between

"private" colleges and "proprietary" colleges; the latter are profit-making enterprises in the same manner as Teikyo and its sisters proliferating throughout the world. In the United States, proprietary colleges, though they may appear to be strict free-market-education swashbucklers, are often even more dependent on government than the private non-profit institutions. Proprietary institutions are eligible for the full range of federal and state student assistance programs. In terms of the percentage of government funds received, proprietary colleges receive more in total than the aggregate of all the traditional private colleges and universities. Some of the proprietary institutions exist solely in response to federal and state grant and loan programs; tuition is set to the maximum government aid available, and students who are eligible for maximum government grants are aggressively sought. The problem of non-payment of federal loans is heavily concentrated in the proprietary sector. It would be unfair to allege fraud as the sole and principal cause. Proprietary institutions normally serve low-income populations and offer direct job-related skills, for example, hair dressing and TV repair. Given the meager resources of the students in the first place, the problem of securing a job no matter what, and the low wages offered for these skills, loan default is scarcely a surprise.

I have taken some time to sketch out the broad dependency of all of higher education on government funding, lest anyone would doubt the universal impact of restricted government spending for higher education. An expanding student population will occur in a situation of economic decline for higher education.

Responsibility Will Be Delegated to Local Senior Management Charged to Make Higher Education Efficient and Economically Viable

This is at least a 99⁴⁴⁄₁₀₀ percent pure whole truth—and the point of this chapter. Governor Christy Whitman recently abol-

ished the Department of Higher Education in New Jersey, argu-
ing that the presidents of the various state institutions could
manage very well on their own without second-guessing from
the Trenton bureaucracy. In Austria, the government has traditionally maintained very tight central control of the universities
down to the minutest detail. If you wished to raise the salary of
an associate professor at Linz by 200 schillings (not a lot), it required authorization from the ministry in Vienna. Faced with
the surge in students and the shortage in the treasury, the government has decided to delegate managerial responsibility to
the local institutions. We (government) cannot solve this mis-
match of educational aspirations and financial resources, so
let's pass the buck—not bucks or schillings, you understand.

The problem with delegating to local administration in the
European case is that there may be very little administration to
receive this mandate. The nominal "head" of a European university is the rector. Rectors, however, are—or have been—anything but *di*rectors. A common pattern saw the rector elected
for a two-year stint by the faculty "senate" and given the prime
responsibilities of presiding in ancient robes at ceremonial occasions, representing the university at state affairs, and greeting
distinguished foreign visitors. No heavy lifting. The actual
management of the university was elsewhere in the ministry.
Shifting management to the traditional rectorship is a journey
to the unknown. One change in Austria that recognizes the new
responsibility of the title has been to extend the rector's term to
four years, renewable if he or she is reelected by the faculty senate after the four-year term. In a time of economizing, it takes
heroic faith to believe that a rector up for reelection every four
years will serve a fifth year.

The result of devolving responsibility onto local managers as
a response to government economizing is most clearly seen in
Britain. Economizing under the Thatcher government seems to
have been driven by economic and/or educational ideology, but
the results are the same. In the British system, chancellors were

ceremonial, and what administration as might prove necessary was delegated to a vice-chancellor. The latter part of the twentieth century will be noted by the rise of the vice-chancellor. These former clerks have become managers by decree and default—even to the extent of having authority to dismiss tenured faculty.

The Austrian and British examples should be carefully considered by American administrators, faculties, and boards. Devolving management authority onto the formerly ornamental rectorships has its obvious problems: no managerial tradition and structure at the local level. But will the dual authority of American institutions (administration—finances; faculty—educational product) be able to meet the severe challenges presented not only by vanishing budgets, but also by emergent technologies? A senior officer at one of the major foundations recounted to me that her office was besieged with American university presidents who believed that their campuses needed fundamental restructuring, but they, the presidents, could not figure out how this reform was to be "politically" accomplished.

Consider a recent case in point on the problem of decision making: Yale University, projecting financial restriction, undertook a high-level review of the institution's needs. A select committee of faculty chaired by the provost made some rather modest suggestions for retraction, including a 10 percent decline in the size of the faculty over a ten-year period. Did faculty reduction commence? No, protest commenced, and the provost and the president resigned within four months—not the reduction projected. If one assumes that Yale's financial projections were correct—and all the macroeconomic signs point in that direction—this modest attempt at rational budget planning does not bode well for the critical decisions that seem all but inevitable for higher education in the next decades.

Economic stringency, *severe* economic stringency, will compel institutions to make critical decisions—many with harsh negative consequences for pet curricula and personal careers. I am told that in one of the ancient universities of Buda (or maybe Pest), there was an official called the *absolutorium:* it is a title to be envied by every rector, chancellor, and local president.

The rise of the vice-chancellor is a portent of the future. State institutions will be cut loose from state bureaucracies and the budget simultaneously, with the assumption that local management will suffice and prevail. Or the state will gradually—officially or unofficially—turn over higher education to "private enterprise," depending on private-sector management to offer economical education. California is a case of "privatization" in process without publicity. In California, as in many of the states, the flagship institutions actually derive less than 25 percent of their funds from state appropriations. The rest of the total budget comes from tuition, fees, room charges, board bills, research funds from the federal government, and fund raising. Paradoxically, UCLA may receive less government money as a percentage of its overall budget than many small private colleges, whose students bring government grants and loans. The proprietary colleges, which set their charges and recruit their students to maximize government grants, may be the real publicly funded sector of higher education. Former Chancellor Young at UCLA boldly stated that UCLA was not a "state university," maybe "state related" at best—and he was not so certain that he ought not go all the way and declare for "private university" status. (A reasonable prediction: United States "public" universities will become the inverse of the South American "private" universities—legally "public," economically "private." President James Duderstadt of the University of Michigan recently described Michigan as "a privately funded public university." The implications for university governance of such a claim should be significant. Why should a privately funded institution be governed by a state-appointed board?)

The trend toward "privatization" of higher education seems to me certain, though I would expect this conversion will be maximally disguised. "Privatization" stems from the defunding of education by the state, so that the local unit depends more and more on its own resources; bluntly stated, it is the management of the institution for a market. When the research universities were being formed, Thorstein Veblen referred to the entrepreneurial university presidents of the day as "Captains of Erudition"—comparing them with some disdain to the "Captains of Industry" such as John D. Rockefeller—whose "ill-gotten gains" were funding the new university enterprise. If funding and constructing the research universities created managerial "Captains of Erudition," the defunding and constriction may revive the title with a vengeance.

The Impending Crisis

While it is my view that the financial crisis in higher education worldwide will result in revolutionary changes to what are currently regarded as educational absolutes, I want to point out that the historical record does not necessarily support academic apocalypse. What it may illustrate, however, is how fundamental academic change may occur without clear decision or public notice.

Many years ago I participated in a collegiate group with the worst acronymic title ever concocted: ACNE (Associated Colleges of New England). This august group was created in the nineteenth century (before the invention of acne) and consisted of some dozen of the most prestigious of the Ivies and the "potted Ivies" (Williams, Middlebury, and such). Each year ACNE met at one of the institutional campuses. One year we met at Yale; it was the same year that Yale's president, Kingman Brewster, had been pictured on the cover of *Time* with this ominous caption: "The impending financial crisis of higher education." Financial crisis was the major topic of the day's discussion. The meeting began with an elegant lunch in the plushly carpeted Presidential Dining Room in Woolsey Hall. There were cocktails in the marble splendor of the Beinecke Rare Book Library, dinner at the palatial homes of deans and other high worthies. After a lunch of filet mignon on the following day, the group adjourned. Dartmouth President John Dickey, the senior president in office, officially thanked our Yale hosts, concluding with the remark, "Congratulations, Kingman—you are the only man that ever made poverty look attractive!"

I recount this tale from times past to suggest that economic crisis has been a permanent feature of higher education and also to suggest that no matter how bad the budget, colleges do persist—and even make it "look attractive." Muddling through is the key to eternal life. What happened to the Kingman-Brewster-financial-crisis? Ignorance and good luck helped: private universities were surprised to discover in the seventies and eighties that there was significant price elasticity for tuition; governments in this time period continued to have open coffers for the funding of flagship universities and the building of state and community college systems. By the 1990s, however, private colleges really had pushed tuition to the breaking point, while governments had soured on higher educational expenditures. The real lesson of the Kingman Brewster crisis, however, is not only that institutions can be lucky with history, but also that *economic* issues may well be "solved" invisibly by management—and these invisible solutions can radically change the educational mission of institutions.

Given the "philosophical" split between educational administration by faculty and "business" management by administration, saving the enterprise economically can be accomplished by administration. This was broadly done during the seventies and eighties. Economic cutbacks may, of course, do no more than shrink the status quo. At one time, Grinnell College in Iowa had a string quartet in residence. Impressed, I asked the president how that had worked out. He confessed that due to budget restrictions, they now had only a trio.

On the other hand, administrations facing the reality of a difficult student market may create new directions and emphases that truly change the institution, despite verbal allegiance to traditional educational ideals. The economic adjustments made by colleges in the eighties and nineties—after the Kingman

Brewster period—have led to *educational* changes that are as significant as they seem invisible to the general public. One of the major economic factors of these two decades in American higher education has been the decline in the traditional college-age population. The baby bust simply meant fewer paying customers. By rational rights, some colleges should have collapsed like department stores for lack of customers. Not so. While women were busy *not* having babies, they were busy entering the career world, and colleges created curricula to their tastes. The women in question were college graduates already and/or not at all interested in the liberal arts curriculum served up for the uncultured eighteen-year-old frosh. The average age of students in many traditional liberal arts colleges moved up into the late twenties, and the curriculum moved with them.

Compounding the economics of demography during the period were a number of significant cultural and general economic shifts that radically altered the curricula as a response to the customers' interests. Reaction to the hippy curricular choices in the protest years of the 1960s, plus recessionary times, plus soaring tuitions, led more students every year to seek "business" majors. David Breneman, former president of Kalamazoo College, undertook an investigation of liberal arts colleges. There were approximately 600 such in the United States, but Breneman's analysis suggested liberal arts graduates were a majority in less than 100. A variety of "vocational" majors have been introduced and have overtaken the ancient liberal studies. I was a commencement speaker at one such "liberal arts" institution and was fascinated to discover the horde of graduates receiving a bachelor in business degree. Even more striking, most of the other graduates received a bachelor of arts in business or a bachelor of science in business. Not many philosophy grads in the group. "Liberal arts colleges" have become "business schools" without changing the label.

What is important about this recent change is that it has largely been the work of the economics of universities, not educational planning. Insofar as administrators control the economics, they have been the ones to wither quartets to trios so that they could fund courses in cost accounting. Faculties have an interest in keeping the enterprise financially viable, so that they have by and large acquiesced to cutbacks and reallocations. In many cases, these changes have led to "death by a thousand reallocations" for the traditional mission of the college in question. Traditional liberal arts faculties (including those of the natural sciences) awake to discover that they have been relegated to rhetoric, part of the institutional advertising aura with as much connection to the ongoing life of the institution as the Gothic facade on the library.

Perhaps this subtle subterfuge in educational mission is all to the good. Clever administrators have managed to keep the school doors open right under the noses of the resident faculty. Nevertheless, despite my qualms about the transcendence of faculty above the nit and grit of institutional reality, turning colleges and universities into trade schools for the market would be an utter defeat of the faculty revolution of the last century—and not a good thing. But if universities and colleges are to have an inner educational meaning and not become alternative sites for commercial training programs, they will have to come to a much clearer sense of intellectual focus and social significance. If higher education is not to become *merely* market driven, it needs to have a clear sense of its own inherent capabilities and values. This will require real *educational* administration: neither the high clichés of the president nor the cobbled compromises of the curriculum committee.

Who—If Anyone—Is Minding the Store?

Several years ago an op-ed piece on presidential searches appeared in *The Chronicle of Higher Education*. (A critic refers to the publication as the academic equivalent of the old *Pravda*.) The author, a faculty member of a presidential search committee, recommended that colleges hire stage actors as presidents. The ultimate justification for this intriguing suggestion was that, as far as he could see from his perch on the search, what was wanted was someone who would *appear* to be a tough-minded educational leader and decision maker, but when it came down to it, the last thing that the faculty, student, and alumni constituencies wanted was someone who really had an educational philosophy (it might not be mine) and who would actually make decisions (they might not go my way). On the other hand, the president is called on to make a fine public appearance and speak eloquently about the liberal arts (to all those graduating majors in Bus. Admin.). Surely, a professionally trained actor could do much better than the average inorganic chemist promoted into high office. (In addition to the advantages for the institution and the president of signing on actors for the run of the academic year, it would also clarify the role of the presidential spouse. The president may be hired to appear philosophical and decisive; the spouse is expected only to appear.) After my first year as a president, I had presided at so many dedication and welcoming ceremonies that I decided that what was needed was not a president, but a Prince of Wales—a non-authoritative, but impressive, official greeter.

The president-as-actor suggestion is an amusing way of illustrating that in many ways, the direction of higher education is decided by no visible person or authoritative body. The institution "just growed." Boards steadfastly claim not to interfere with the academic prerogatives of the faculty; faculty only "recommend" action; the president is out making speeches. The university needs *more* administration? Maybe the university needs *some* administration!

It should not be presidents. Presidents are good fellows (non-sexist), but they cannot command the range of talents and interests embedded in the faculties. In the simpler days of Mark Hopkins, when all one needed was the Bible and a log, the president might well command the scene, but not on the Berkeley campus or its many sisters across the land. After the research revolution, "the faculty *is* the university"—at least by half and then some. If universities and colleges need more administration, the faculty in some form, part, or configuration must enter into administration. The next logical phase in university evolution should be faculty moving from *academic* management toward *institutional* management. This portent may strike faculty as a jolly good thing and time enough. But it is not so simple.

One of the proposed titles for this book was *Who Will Make Decisions in the University?* The title was rejected (boring), but the question is perhaps the central issue of the entire work. I have insisted that to examine the university is to examine an *institution,* not elegant rhetoric about the free mind, the joy of discovery, the search for self, or the love of alma mater. Institutions in turn are not simply geographic locations. The shopping mall is not an institution, though it may occasion a set of practices that give research material to sociologists. An institution has a set of internal governing structures, a set of "decision rights" distributed among various constituent parts. The temptation toward high rhetoric for high education elevates discussions of the university above the details of decision—the search for knowledge is eternal, so why worry about the decision of the day? But high ideals do not themselves create institutions. From the French Revolution to the experimental colleges of the American sixties, instantiating all conceivable ideals from love to justice inevitably degenerates into faction, reprisal, and chaos (which may also describe the university curriculum committee).

Why are decision rights such an important issue for the 1990s and beyond? Because for the past century one might argue that universities have not been making decisions and thus are out of the habit. "Decision" comes from the Latin *decidere,* which means "to cut off." During the grand expansion of higher education that has marked the century since the rise of the research university in America, one could argue that *cutting off* has been a minor activity compared to *adding on.* It is one thing to "decide" which of the delectables on the dessert tray should be appropriated; it is quite another to decide to diet and forbear desserts altogether. Of course, this is an exaggeration (score another half-truth) that will properly outrage several generations of exhausted administrators who have struggled with tenure decisions, visitation rights for women in dormitories, control of the athletic program, and a host of headaches. True enough, but most of those decisions have been peripheral to the core educational mission of the institution. Assuming that the president is *the* institutional decision maker (a presumptuous assumption), he or she has had only marginal influence on the direction of the *educational* process and product; faculty decide the educational program—at least their own division, at least their own department, at least their own course.

Decision rights are now central to higher education because of the current and projected restriction of financial support. Although all higher educational economists believe that the financial future will be stringent, optimists assume that it only means more frayed cuffs on the traditional professorial tweed. My own view is more gloomy not only about the severity of the economic cutbacks, but also about the prospect of more of the same with fraying edges. Not only does higher education need higher productivity, but also it needs to examine the nature of the product. One needs something more reformative than balancing the budget by fraying the least politically favored department. Higher education gets no more than a B– in its efforts to create effective structures of learning that address the needs of the nation.

I once asked Stringfellow Barr how he had managed the fundamental *educational* revolution at St. John's College in Annapolis back in the 1930s. (St. John's had been a standard "liberal arts college" but was radically transformed into its current shape as a "great books" college. Whether this was educational advance or retreat—I think advance—it was certainly radical, and remains so.) Barr explained, "When I became president the chairman of the Board said to me, 'Mr. Barr, this institution is financially bankrupt, we are going to close next year.

You can do anything you want!'" I don't wish bankruptcy on any college, but it may be necessary to approach the poorhouse in order create changes that will be not only economical but also educationally effective.

Management by Subjectives

If higher education is moving into decades and decades of decisions, it would be well to understand the institutional decision structure: who does manage the store? Several years ago two professors of management, Michael D. Cohen and James G. March, reviewed the management assumptions of universities. Utilizing the MBO (management by objectives) framework of analysis, they concluded that universities are not managed at all. Rather, they are a species of "organized anarchy." There are three salient characteristics of an organized anarchy: (1) uncertainty about ends, (2) low technology, and (3) fluid participation in governance. Universities fully qualify.

Uncertainty about Ends

Considering the varying competing functions assigned to universities, any institution might well be baffled by what it is really supposed to accomplish: advance science, improve the economy, bolster ethnic pride, improve morals, be Number One (in something)—and do it quickly and on the cheap! To avoid the confusion of specifics, universities turn to the universal transcendent: *Lux et Veritas* (Light and Truth). And at the end of the day, can one tote up how many units of light and truth have been produced? By placing its ends high enough, higher education can always aspire without achieving.

Low Technology

Despite some impressive scientific hardware, universities as teaching places are "low tech." It takes very little organization to clean a blackboard. A high-technology operation will be well organized, even if it is uncertain about goals, because it has to keep the machines in working order. The buildings and grounds department may make more decisions than the English department.

Fluid Participation in Governance

A social group uncertain about ends and managing a modest technical environment will eventually get some sort of organization if the same people sit in the same room long enough trying to decide a course of action. This is seldom the case in university governance, where faculty committees come and go, students graduate, and presidents serve even less than the biblical seven years.

Cohen and March conclude that in an organized anarchy, the role of the president is like that of a driver trying to control an automobile in a skid. If the driver/president manages to influence the direction of the skid in order to prevent a crash, he or she may well be applauded, but luck is probably more important. (Napoleon, in reviewing the credentials of his generals, used to ask, "Is he lucky?")

The current "anarchic" condition of management reflects the complex history of this institution. The old denominational college was clearly managed by the president solo, but it was a very small and simple institution. The research university, in contrast, is a highly complex organization both technically and educationally. The faculty sought, and received, academic freedom in order to escape the ideological restrictions of the denominational past. Faculty thus came to dominate the internal academic structure: setting curricula, appointing colleagues, setting admission standards for students and requirements for degrees—and even determining their own working conditions (teaching loads, sabbaticals, etc.). Presidents might tend the technology, but the academic system belonged to the faculty— and the faculty belonged first to their disciplines and only secondarily to the local establishment. If the mendicant medieval faculty were physically independent of the physically modest university, modern faculty can be ideologically independent of the physically dense modern university.

Faculty Are Managers—"The Law Is a Ass!"

A century of historical development has created a significant puzzle in the United States about just who does manage the university. In a landmark United States Supreme Court case decided in 1980, the faculty of Yeshiva University were forbidden to organize as a union, since in the Court's view faculty were not employees under the law but managers. (Had *NLRB v. Yeshiva University* been argued in the nineteenth century, faculty would have been employees at best—peons might have been more accurate.) The dilemma facing the contemporary university as it moves into the twenty-first century is that the shift in educational authority toward faculty remains within the old-style formal casing of presidential management. The heroic Professor Rabi, who had the courage to inform the General of the Army that "the faculty *is* the university," should have been encouraged by the *Yeshiva* decision of the Second Circuit, subsequently confirmed by the United States Supreme Court. The learned justices at both appellate levels appeared to confirm the importance of faculty.

This chapter is on "decision rights." The virtue of courts is that they exist for one overriding purpose: to make decisions. The necessity to decide is often delightfully distant within the leisurely debating culture of higher academic life. It is an essential characteristic of the life of *theory* that the argument shall go on until there is either knockdown proof or a tolerable consensus of current fashion. One of the endemic problems of the university-institution is cultural seepage from theoretical leisure (no decisions without demonstration) to practical demand (if I wait for proof, the bank will foreclose). The universal faculty comment on a disliked administrative decision is "The administration did not consult with the faculty." Usually, this is quite untrue. The problem is not lack of consultation; it is lack of agreement. Because faculty live in a world of proof, they assume that *their* arguments for some institutional arrangement are demonstrated truths. If, then, the administration does not agree with the faculty view, it cannot be that they were *wrong;* it was that the authority failed to listen, did not understand, failed to consult. For better and worse, the law when it tramples onto the academic precinct forces decisions in a body unacculturated to decision making.

The second virtue of legal intervention in academic life is that the resulting distinctions and decisions are generally wrong-headed. As already mentioned, in *Yeshiva* the Court had to decide between faculty as managers and faculty as employees as those terms are legally proscribed by the National Labor Relations Act (NLRA). Given the extant distinctions, *Yeshiva* is more right than not, but the distinctions are basic misfits. The fact that the law makes distinctions and generally gets it wrong can be of genuine assistance in understanding what is really going on inside the university. The *Yeshiva* case is instructive because of the paradox it presented about the de jure and de facto roles of faculty in the contemporary university.

The initiation of *Yeshiva* was simple enough. The faculty at the university wished to unionize—an action that seemed reasonably straightforward and one that had been successfully carried through at a number of colleges and universities. In this instance, however, the administration of Yeshiva refused to recognize the legitimacy of unionization. The administration's position prevailed in the Second Circuit and subsequently in the Supreme Court on the grounds that faculty are *not* employees under the definition of the NLRA.

What were the arguments in *Yeshiva?* The National Labor Relations Board argued that faculty are "professional employees," but in a telling riposte, the Second Circuit stated that a professional *employee* offers specialized, limited, technical expertise that may indeed be the basis of a management decision, but that the Yeshiva faculty were *"in fact substantially and pervasively operating the enterprise"* (emphasis added). Perhaps the most fundamental issue was whether the faculty acted on their own behalf or on behalf of the employer. The court noted that there seemed to be scarcely any actual instance that could be pointed to where the Yeshiva administration did not accept faculty recommendations. The conclusion drawn was that the interests of the administration (management) and the faculty were at least co-extensive, if not identical. The Court quoted a widely accepted AAUP policy statement to the effect that proper university governance lies in shared authority among faculty, administration, and board of trustees. "These three components have joint authority and responsibility for governing the institution . . . the essential and overriding idea is that the enterprise is joint. . . ." How does one apply the AAUP language when an AAUP bargaining unit is in negotiation with "management"? Does the faculty union bargain with itself as a joint manager?

You might think that faculty would be delighted to hear the highest court of the land proclaim that faculties are "substantially and pervasively operating the enterprise"—"the faculty *is* the university" after all. Faculty approbation for the Court was certainly not present with the Yeshiva faculty. Professor Paul Connolly, an associate professor of English at Yeshiva, quoted Mr. Bumble—"the law is a ass"—but went on to accept the Court's reasoning in a striking paradox:

> We, the Yeshiva faculty, have had to insist that we are non-managerial and non-supervisory in order to organize ourselves into a body that can assert its managerial and supervisory power. And it is the administration, paradoxically, that has insisted that the faculty *is* managerial and supervisory, in order to restrict faculty power. . . .

In short, if the Yeshiva faculty were declared *employees,* then they could really act as *managers.*

It is important to note two qualifications of *Yeshiva.* First, the ruling applied only to *private* colleges and universities. Second, a qualification was entered into the argument by an amicus brief from several private colleges to the effect that the argument against unionization applied only in "mature" institutions. Faculty unions are common in public universities because of special state legislative action. For many years, it was assumed in law that state employees as "public servants" could not unionize. That supposition has gradually faded from many states, and when state employees are granted specific permission to unionize, faculties at *public,* that is, state-supported, institutions are included in the new dispensation as "state employees."

The notion of "mature" university relies on an institution's historical record demonstrating faculty participation in major institutional decisions. Not all institutions are "mature." Presumably there are some institutions in which the trustees or a religious denomination basically determines all policies major and minor. The notion of "mature" may have some indeterminacy, but as a concept it certainly extends beyond the private college sphere. Many public institutions, certainly the great flagship state universities, operate as "mature" institutions with significant faculty determination of policy. If it were not for the specific quirk of "public employee" legislation, there would be no more reason to regard UCLA faculty as "employees" than their counterparts at Stanford. (A colleague of mine was appointed as the founding president of a public college to be created. With an eye to faculty unionization, he made certain that the covenants of the institution granted full managerial rights to the administration and clearly classified the faculty as employees according to the classic NLRA definition.) In sum, at most of the colleges and universities of the nation, faculty do not fit the category "employee," whatever the vagaries of local law and custom.

I think that one has to accept both sides of this paradox. The Court seems to me quite correct that under any reasonable reading of the NLRA, faculty could not be regarded as employees, but for all that, faculties do not regard themselves as managers of the enterprise, no matter how it may work out in law.

Faculty Cannot Be Managers

That faculty are managers (or employees) qualifies as one of this treatise's pure-gold half-truths. The significant expansion of faculty authority that marked the rise of the research universities came with at least one managerially disabling feature: academic tenure. When as president I was queried about why I (my office) had ultimate formal decision rights for the university, my reply was simple: "I can be fired." Presidents do not have tenure of any kind—most serve "at the pleasure of the board," not even on term contracts. What that means is that the president (and the senior administrative staff) is subject to dismissal for dismal decisions. In short, the president is ultimately accountable for decisions in a way that faculty (and students and alumni) are not. These various constituents may have lots of ideas, good and bad, about how the university should be managed, and it would be an idiot college president who simply ignored constituent opinion, but in the long run, the president decides and must live or retire summarily with the consequences.

Because the president and senior staff exist in a unique structure of accountability, it is difficult to give full allegiance (or understanding) to the AAUP statement quoted in *Yeshiva* to the effect that the governance of the university is essentially "joint" among the board, the administration, and the faculty. The statement seems more a muddy fact of the American historical landscape than a philosophical principle. The members of the triumvirate that the AAUP projects as joint governors of the university occupy very different positions in regard to decisions. When it comes to decisions, the board makes one, the president many, the faculty none (in theory). The board has one BIG decision to make: to hire *the* university decision maker (in theory), the president, and to fire same if they think he or she is making bad decisions. Finally, in the odd arrangement of collegiate governance, the faculty never really make decisions—even about graduating students. They only "recommend" action, which in turn is approved by the president and on some occasions the board as the proper legal entity.

As the comment about skidding presidents suggests, the distinction between "deciding" and "recommending" is a fig leaf of a fiction when it comes to actual effect within the university setting. When I was president at Bucknell, a faculty faction developed a considered theory of the president-as-conduit, a sort of decorative messenger from the "recommendations" of the faculty to the "decisions" of the board of trustees. They may be called "recommendations," but they can be ignored only with extreme prejudice. It was the efficacy of such "recommendations" that persuaded the Court that the Yeshiva faculty were "managers." The conduit theory of presidential authority is much overstated in fact, but as one approaches the notion that "the faculty *is* the university," one wonders just what real authority remains to the president's office. Was *Yeshiva* correct? Do faculty "in fact substantially and pervasively [operate] the enterprise"? It is to be doubted.

Faculty members are certainly not appointed to do any *university* management; they are appointed to advance physics in the field and in the minds of assorted youth. Dabbling in all the infrastructure from parking to parietal hours distracts from the meaning of the contract of appointment. To be sure, most universities have a three-part statement of faculty duties: teaching, research, and service—and the least of these is service. No one, as far as I know, has ever received a distinguished *faculty* award for "service above and beyond the call of duty." Too much *service* and you end up off the faculty, and damned as a dean. The prestige of the university is promoted by the great researchers and the charismatic teachers. Faculty may be quite expert in the management of their own disciplines: how to structure a curriculum, where to recruit faculty, but once off in the arena of asset allocation in the endowment portfolio, the average medieval historian is rather at a loss. Administrators should encourage them to stick to manuscripts.

However, for the twin reasons of economics and general educational policy, merely letting the thousand faculty flowers bloom—with occasional watering and trimming by the presidential gardener—is unlikely to be tolerable in the future. Unlike its denominational ancestor with its mission for the Church (whichever) One and Holy, the modern multidisciplinary university may lack a unified vision on anything except parking— even there the cry is "More!" To use the most objectionable business lingo: the faculty finally determine the nature of the product (the educational content) and the quality of the service (teaching). In the academic area, they "substantially and pervasively" manage the institution. What "product" will they decide is needed for God, for country, and for Yale? Given the modern set of professor-producers, what would it be reasonable to expect?

Talent, Time, Tenure, *and* Governance

In almost thirty years of attending earnest conferences on the problems of higher education, I became convinced that I was precisely the wrong person to attend—as were almost all the other attendees. We were almost wall-to-wall administrators, while the issues to be decided back on campus were largely faculty issues. The financial issues, which consume so much worry at national meetings, should have been addressed to faculty potentates. One could return from a dour conference on the financial crises of higher education, report that the sky was sagging, and yet be assured by the at-home constituents either (1) not here or (2) if here, a local issue to be solved by better management, better fund drives, better admissions, a new administration.

It would be a mistake to blame faculties for inattention to institutional issues; as argued repeatedly, that is not their mission, and there is no inherent reason why they should be concerned about anything except the advance of science, scholarship, and the service of teaching. Nevertheless, the *Yeshiva* Court was correct in observing that as managers of academic product and service, faculty substantially manage the institution. But the *institution* is not merely the pursuit of science; it is also the pursuit-of-science-for-clients. These "clients" may be individual students and their families, the nation, business, foundations, donors. Science may determine a splendid internal scenario of advance (the Super-Conducting Super-Collider) that is everything from unapproachable to unappealing to students and the Congress. Tragic that this should be so, but that is the price of institutionalizing the pure pursuit of knowledge. Science in the person of faculty (and presidents) is not passive in respect to client attitudes—even Congress can be persuaded. But in the long run, institutionalized science is not the same as the free, eternal, pure pursuit of truth.

There is no "cure" for institutionalization; what is needed is a healthy realization of the difference between the ideal of scientific pursuit and the reality of institutionalization. If faculty are to be academic managers and University H, Y, or P is the institutional product to be "sold," then there must be a much closer relationship between academic and institutional management.

The university is not the only institution that suffers from staffs that "substantially and pervasively [operate] the enterprise," yet are not managers. I take two examples from the University of Rochester experience: hospitals and symphony orchestras. The university had a notable medical school and the world-famous Eastman School of Music among its many attractions. Graduates of these two schools find themselves practicing their art within a specific kind of institution, the modern hospital or the symphony orchestra. Just how much did the average specialist in OB-GYN or oboe know about the economic and social realities of the institution within which much of his or her professional life would be spent? Too little. It may account for the facts that the American Medical Association has opposed every piece of national health care from Social Security to Medicare and that symphony orchestras exist in a chronic state of financial disaster. I give the medical school credit for making the economics of medical care a part of its curriculum and the Eastman School credit for emphasizing techniques of audience development with its students.

But if professional schools give some attention to the institutions of the profession, graduate schools in academic subjects give no attention to the subject at all. Yet one's recent PhD graduate and new assistant professor at Old Siwash, in the very first year, may well vote in faculty meetings on a range of institutional concerns from curriculum to benefit rates about which he or she has virtually no knowledge whatsoever. The first sentence in Professor Frederick Rudolph's synoptic history of American colleges and universities reads: "For some time the general reader and the professional historian have had greater access to the history of almost any skirmish in the Civil War than they have had to the history of education in the United States." This general ignorance of higher education, which has been only mildly alleviated in the thirty years since Rudolph published his study, is nowhere more prevalent than on the academic quad. University faculty are eager to recount the history and structure of everything from the Chinese opium trade to the World Bank, but they demonstrate virtually no interest in the history and structure of the very institution in which they live and have their academic being (thus, more professorial monographs on Shiloh than on Siwash).

Faculty Senates and How They Run

Despite the philosophical complexities of the issue and the general lack of knowledge (or interest) of faculty in institutional governance, the AAUP notion of "joint" governance has some warrant in reality. Much of the most important decision making concerns the appointment and promotion of faculty. ("The faculty *is* the university," *c'est ça?*) These decisions are deliberated with great care by the departmental faculty, the dean, sometimes a special committee on appointments, and the president's office. As long as one follows the slogan that "the faculty (specialists in departments) *is* the university," the decision process is careful and well structured. But as oft repeated, once one is forced to grasp the university overall and not in its discrete departments, decision structures are weak and underinformed.

Even in discrete departments, tenure decisions, though carefully considered, may fail on *institutional* grounds. Because individuals have differing strengths, one always has to strike some balance of virtues and defects. Thus, one may reasonably tenure a faculty member whose strength is with advanced students or a lecturer popular among freshmen who is less than cutting edge in scholarship. But unless the department-as-institution-for-teaching is part of the consideration, it would be more than possible to end up with a department in which all were excellent with advanced students, leaving the freshmen out in the cold. By and large, tenure decisions tend toward *individual* merit, without much consideration of departmental structure, and almost none for university structure.

The common means for assessing the voice of the faculty *as a whole* about the *whole* is the faculty senate or some similar formal body that purports to register overall faculty opinion. The problems faced by the faculty senate in managing the institution are significant. The principal problem is, as noted, lack of knowledge, interest, or time, "deficiencies" that are almost a necessary condition of faculty-hood. One might distinguish three areas of non-expertise: technical, personal, and educational. There is no reason at all to expect that faculty in general have much wisdom on recondite technical matters, such as intermediate bonds. In the personal area of wages and benefits, faculty have a compelling interest, but they often have great difficulty linking compensation with teaching, curriculum management, and the like. (The business school example cited previously illustrates very careful coordination between compensation and curriculum management.) Finally, only modest expertise can be expected, even in the area of overall educational planning. While there are numerous important philosophical examinations of the meaning of education and valuable empirical studies about the psychological effect on students of various patterns of college education, these are not at all likely to play a role in faculty curricular deliberation. Building a general course of study is mostly an exercise in earnestness, personal predilections, and anecdotes. There is very little "research" worthy of the research expectations of the university into the means and ends of the curriculum.

The fact that faculty as such are underinformed about institutional issues (by their own legitimate self-expectation or mere taste) means that many of the most distinguished faculty will be non-participants in the governance game. I recall the comment of a very distinguished philosopher at Princeton. He absolutely refused to participate in any of the "governing" committees of the university except the committee on faculty appointment and tenure. As he said, "the faculty *is* the university," and this was the only thing worth faculty effort in decision making. Every faculty will have numerous individuals who share this opinion, and they will not serve on the senate. If "the faculty *is* the university," it is a paradoxical outcome that the best faculty are so often not participants in the *institutional* reality that is the university: superb participants in their transcendent disciplines, absentees at the local franchise.

I have indicated that universities may well "muddle through" all the dire financial and philosophical problems that beset them. Despite Cohen and March's witty picture of organized anarchy, the fact is that all this sound and fury signifies something. Universities do come up with some sort of a financial and educational plan, which, like a Christmas pudding, is chockfull of goodies (and a few nuts). The downside is that the cooking is immensely time consuming and often ends in fudge (to change the culinary trope). My belief is that time is running out and that tomorrow's decisions will be hard edged. The century since the rise of the research university has been the "century of the faculty." I believe that the next century will have to be "the century of management." It will probably not be a return to the dominance of the president. The faculty revolution is permanent, but there will have to be significant changes to find a cohesion of faculty and management in the years ahead. The result, however, will have to be some change in the nature, structure, and status of faculties.

Faculty as Managers

The most important change that should accompany faculty assumption of a significant role in *institutional* management would be a change in the linkage between faculty and institution. If faculty are to administer—as I believe they should—then one needs to have a body of faculty with *institutional* competence (and probably special compensation in time or salary or both) who constitute an authoritative and accountable faculty voice. This group of faculty (council, senate, committee) would need authority in two directions: one toward the academic system, the educational product and process; the other toward the institutional realities of facilities and funds. This council would be the principal policy advisory body to the president, who (along with the board) should retain final decision rights. (Any council of any size—particularly of faculty—is likely to have serious differences of opinion about policy, so at some point a decision for this or that must be made.) The most controversial aspect of any such council would be its authority over *educational* policy broadly construed. While recognizing the proper authority of the various disciplines, the council would have to assay the educational program as a whole. Which departments fit the mission and/or the market? What should be added or subtracted? Is the pattern of instruction appropriate to the mission and/or open to the market?

If such decisions were to be made through the joint effort of such a faculty council and the president, the status of "ordinary" faculty would be subtly altered. Tenure would be subject to the direction of the institutional policy, not a vested employment right. If a decision were made to close a department, tenure could be abrogated. The institution may be able to cushion such actions by attempting to relocate the faculty affected or by offering a financial settlement, but in the long run, tenure could not be a barrier to institutional direction. "Ordinary" faculty would have to cede significant authority over the curriculum and patterns of instruction, becoming something more like "employees" following management's plans, while the council members would become something more like "managers" creating those plans.

Any such structure would address formal authority. That is the easy part. The imponderable problem is how any such council would be selected (election, appointment, seniority, departmentally diverse, ethnically diverse) and what principles one could expect the council members to bring to the table for institutional management. I save some specific suggestions for the concluding chapter. For now, however, I want to emphasize that an authoritative and accountable faculty concern about the shape of the whole is essential if the assumptions of the research revolution are to be maintained under conditions of economic adversity. Economic reality is placing universities more and more into the complexities and vagaries of "markets." Nimble, aggressive, and decisive management may be necessary to maintain viability in these markets. The ponderous consensus management of the past may be a luxury lost when assured funding dwindles. However, if universities become simply instruments of markets—vital as these may be—then faculty will have to become *just* employees. It is only because it is assumed that the studies of the university have some inherent reason to be supported that one countenances faculty tenure and dominance over the educational management. Market-driven education cannot tolerate either faculty luxury. The curriculum and the faculty will exist on an "as needed" basis.

Economic necessity has the capacity of wholly decentering the traditional collection of intellectual skills (and moral aspirations) that have been valued as "higher education." Higher education, the university institution, is moving—or being forced—in the direction of market dismemberment. If there is to be a check on radical marketeering, it must come from some better articulation from within the university of its inherent mission. After the research/faculty revolution, that articulation must come with significant faculty participation, but it cannot be with the casual, chaotic structures and assumptions of the contemporary institution.

Is there too much "market" in my analysis? In some ideal world, no doubt. Medieval mendicant scholars did not have to worry about markets—though they did do a brisk "business" in canon law; modern scholars ignore "market" at their peril. Too much market? All actual existent universities (not ideal academies) exist on a continuum between museums and markets. Museums preserve everything because of intrinsic value; markets hustle anything off the shelf that does not sell. Colleges and universities have to live somewhere on the museum-market continuum. Locating an institution on the continuum from market to museum really should be *managed,* not muddled through. Conclusion: universities need more administration—but in moving in that direction (by choice or circumstance), there will be a subtle, but significant, shift in institutional reality.

The focus of this analysis has been on *institution.* In this chapter, I have suggested that one of the traditional *institutional*

distinctions in American higher education—the difference between private and public higher education—is being eroded.
The private universities depend mightily on government, and
the real free-market profit-making institutions (proprietaries)
are more government dependent than any of the sectors. On the
other hand, state governments, by defunding public institutions, force them to act more and more like traditional private
universities (high tuition, major fund raising). One despairing
state university president told me that his budget had been so
eroded by the legislature that he no longer regarded his institution as a state university, or even a state-related institution; at
best, it was "state located"! In the next chapter, I turn directly to
some of the economic realities of public and private higher education—specifically, the issue of who does or should pay for
higher education and how various funding mechanisms affect
institutions. The trend toward "privatization" will be a continuing theme.

8 Low-Cost Public Education Benefits the Least Advantaged

The claim in the title of this chapter seems so obvious that it would appear beyond argument. Low cost helps low income. What could be more clear and direct? Paradoxically, the truth of the matter can be quite the reverse. "Can be"—it is not always so; but in some very significant cases, the statistical truth is that low-cost education helps the most advantaged. The root of the paradox is a high moral purpose called "financial aid" (government grants, college scholarships); the history of financial aid is a model of the slip between ideal and instituted reality. I take New York State as a case in point.

During the administration of Mario Cuomo, state policy was to keep tuition in the SUNY system of colleges as low as possible. (New York has two public systems: SUNY, State University of New York; and CUNY, City University of New York. CUNY is the descendent of the noble CCNY, City College of New York, which, on the point of city bankruptcy, was taken over by the state government.) Governor Cuomo stated on many occasions that his real hope was to offer state education with zero tuition. Given the governor's known advocacy for the less fortunate in society, the urge to charge no tuition was obviously intended to help the disadvantaged. The fiscal situation in

the state prevented the achievement of "free" public higher education, but during the Cuomo years, state tuition reached only
to $1,500 per year. Meanwhile, private college tuitions esca-
lated to anywhere from five to ten times higher. A modest private college might reach $9,000, while the high-prestige private
universities and colleges were $15,000 and up. The differential
in charges had a startling effect: the poor attended the private
(high-cost) institutions, and the rich attended the public (low-
cost) SUNY institutions. (CUNY is another story, of which
more below.) A state senator informed me that according to his
figures, the average family income was $40,000 for the private
colleges, $60,000 for the publics. That's right: the lower the tu-
ition, the richer the average student.

How did this bizarre inversion come about? The root cause is
the idealistic philosophy of financial aid in the private colleges.
"Financial aid," like so many terms of eternal verity in academia, is, in fact, less than fifty years old—and about to die an
early death from fiscal hemorrhage. Prior to World War II, colleges gave "scholarships." These were financial prizes or incen-
tives awarded to students on the basis of merit: the bright
science student, the brawny football player, or the student
whose "merit" was to be living in Monongahela, where the locals had established a scholarship for deserving residents. After
the war, private institutions, led by the elite universities and elegant colleges (the ones with money), decided that they should
democratize their student bodies and admit not just the wealthy
of Groton, but also the low-income whiz from Wahoo, Ne-
braska. Financial aid would be extended to make private higher
education affordable to those of modest income, and *not* on the
basis of some special merit or category. The amount of financial
aid was determined relative to the family resources. Low-
income families might receive full tuition and then some; those
in lesser need, lesser amounts.

Private college costs were moderate after the war, and tuition
was raised with reluctance. The differential between private

and public tuitions was in the range of four to one—and with room and board at the publics thrown in, the total cost differential was reduced even more. I recall agonizing for weeks during the 1960s over raising tuition $100 at Middlebury. When the decision was finally reached, the president breathed a sigh and said we would never do that again. Rampant inflation and a host of internal factors radically changed these ratios during the eighties and nineties to those prevailing in New York State. Financial aid remained.

How does high tuition + financial aid cause the inversion of rich and poor in college choice? Take the case of a substantially well-to-do lawyer with a $200,000 annual income. The family resources are such that they do not qualify for financial aid at High Price Private U. It is $15,000 out of pocket, plus room and board, books, T-shirts, and frat mugs, or about $22,000. But here is Public Ivy, charging $1,500, plus room, mugs, and the like, for a total of $8,500. Savings at Public Ivy: $13,500; over four years: $54,000! In contrast to well-to-do lawyer, take the $20,000/year laborer. His daughter applies to High Price and gets $18,500 in financial aid, making the total cost $5,500—less than what it costs the well-to-do lawyer for Public Ivy. From a financial point of view, the choice of High Price or Public Ivy has been more or less equalized for the modest-income student, while the cost remains enormous for the higher-income student. The lower-income student chooses on the basis of educational interests, the higher-income student on the basis of a bargain. If this pattern is repeated frequently enough, a trend will emerge that sends the higher-income families toward the low-price publics.

To be quite concrete: while I was at the University of Rochester, the neighboring small SUNY College, Geneseo, admitted a freshman class of 1000+—about the same size as the class at Rochester—but Geneseo had 14,000 applicants, twice as many as Rochester. Any admissions officer desirous of remaining in office sorts the admissions pool by "talent":

high school records, SAT scores, recommendations, whatever. However shaky the validity of the measures, sorting for strong secondary school credentials will inevitably produce a class that is dominantly white, wealthy, and suburban. It is a disgrace that this should be so, but the social fact is that black, low-income, urban schools do not produce profiles of students that compare with the records of students from the affluent suburbs. Even if the college admissions officer makes all sorts of affirmative action moves, and discounts doubtful records, it remains that the freshman profile will in all probability be dominantly white, wealthy, and suburban. As usual, the blacks go to the back of the bus. To a large extent, the private colleges in New York have been a haven for those pushed out of SUNY by the odd economics of the system. But given the cost to the private institutions in terms of excessive financial aid burdens, such a maldistribution of education funding cannot continue.

Public higher education for the well-to-do, private higher education for the poor is not a New York State phenomenon. In a recent study, the World Bank concluded that low-cost public education in third-world countries was largely utilized by the local urban elites, not by the disadvantaged (usually rural) poor. An official at the Ford Foundation to whom I related the Humpty-Dumpty world of private/public income distribution in New York assured me that on the basis of her extensive experience in Puerto Rico, the same pattern applied. The wealthier elites attended the public University of Puerto Rico, while Catholic colleges served the lower-income sector. Gareth Williams sums up the paradox of public education for the poor:

> The aggregate effect of subsidizing higher education by providing free facilities is often to transfer resources from relatively poorer families to richer families. Rate-of-return studies have shown that the effect of higher education subsidy has been to make investment in higher education more profitable privately than socially. The rest of society thus contributes to the advancement of some individuals, without an equivalent recom-

pense to the rest of society. The claim that a fully market-based
higher education system would be less equitable than other
models is not justified . . . a market-based system with subsidy
directed at students who need it is likely to be more equitable
than many currently in existence.

As so often in the United States, we have in public higher education another case of welfare for the middle class, in which resources are transferred from "relatively poorer families to
richer families."

The maintenance of low-cost, high-quality public education
is something that not only benefits a moderately well-off middle class, which is beyond the reach of private college financial
aid, but also is a boon to the moderately well-off members of
the state university faculty unions. Sharp price differentials that
deliver excellent suburban students in the classroom please the
professors, and the heavy demand for places creates clout in the
state capital for more funds. In New York, therefore, the faculty
unions have been among the most determined opponents of tuition increases in SUNY. In his first year in office as governor,
Mario Cuomo advocated significant increases in SUNY tuition
as a means of lessening the tax burden on the citizenry. The
unions bitterly objected, and a faculty union is a formidable political opponent. It has money, brains, and organization. The
capacity of the public-sector faculty unions to organize and to
contribute directly to a politician's campaign from PAC funds
is a reality wholly unmatched in the private sector of higher education. The combination of money on the political table and
the myth of serving the poor creates an almost unbeatable political position. Private colleges do not have faculty unions (see
Yeshiva), and as charitable entities, colleges are forbidden by
law to make political contributions—and their myth is that
they serve the wealthy elites. A true losing combination.

The very peculiar economic realities of low-cost public education and high-cost-*minus*-financial-aid private education are
about to implode. The principal cause for change has been the

altered financial status of the states. A host of factors—reduced tax revenues and rising welfare, medical, and police costs—has repeatedly restricted state university budgets almost everywhere in the United States. A sign of the times is that in the very recent past, the SUNY unions have reluctantly endorsed tuition increases. If the tax spigot is turned down or off, well, it is better to get the funds somewhere—even through tuition. The chancellor of one of the flagship California universities noted that 60 percent of his students came from families with incomes above $80,000. Considering that the state was cutting his budget by $25 million—and that the state contributed less that 25 percent of the total budget anyhow—maybe it was time to raise tuition.

A final highly important comment on the difference between private and public tuition: one of the most confused issues in the discussion of higher education has to do with the term "cost." When families think of the *cost* of higher education, they think of the *price*—specifically, the *tuition price*. (Interestingly, it is not the total price—tuition + room + board, etc.—that sticks in the mind or throat; it is the tuition.) In sharp contrast, when university administrators think of *cost,* they mean the *cost of providing the education*—paying faculty, sweeping the corridors. What is repeatedly lost in the public complaint about the high *cost* of higher education is the fact that the cost of faculty + janitors is virtually identical at public and private institutions of comparable scope and quality; the difference is *who pays* the cost to educate: taxpayers or students. In short, it costs the institution the same to educate your daughter whether it is Stanford or Berkeley, but at the latter, you get a heavy tax subsidy.

Who Benefits? Who Pays?

The philosophical justification for the relative financial obligation of state and individual in the area of higher education is murky at best. Flamboyant rhetoric and failing state revenues have not made the point of division any less murky. I have always been fond of a nineteenth-century legal case involving Middlebury College. It is a benchmark case, it involved tuition, and the college lost. The case is *Middlebury v. Chandler.* It seems that Chandler was a lad at the college who did not pay his tuition. The college sued, but lost. Why? Chandler was—as most students were at the time—a minor. The issue before the learned court was whether a minor could validly contract a debt for college instruction. Under the principles of English common law, a minor may contract a debt for "necessaries": food, clothing, shelter, and the like. Was college education a "necessary"? The judges decided it was not and, in a nice turn of nineteenth-century rhetoric, concluded that, while a "common school" education was a necessary, higher education was "an ornament of civilization and a benefaction of the law."

The state of the law and society has changed considerably since *Middlebury v. Chandler.* In order to make federal college loans legal, Congress lowered the age of majority so that a modern-day Chandler would have no out. Then, as this book has irksomely reiterated, higher education has changed radically from a moral indoctrination activity to a pursuit of science and technique. The learned justices of the Vermont Supreme Court might well have judged in 1844 that Chandler would have had sufficient moral tutelage in the common school (or church); higher education might ornament basic morality with manners and rhetoric, but the "necessary" purpose of education was already fulfilled. One cannot argue today that "common school" can provide the complex scientific and technical skills offered in the research university. The society of the nineteenth century was not yet into the active pursuit of technology that has marked the modern era and the university as a dedicated engine for discovery. It is relatively easy to argue the social and economic value of scientific higher education for a technical economy. But if higher education is moral in content and intent, one need not regard it as essential for the society. It would be disastrous in a democracy to make the assumption that college education is the necessary foundation of social morality, in the manner in which it is the necessary foundation for nuclear physics.

How much to charge for higher education and to whom remains an undecided and largely undiscussed topic. It is unlikely to receive any neat philosophical resolution because the modern university is so complex (as contrasted with its simple, moral forebears) and, more important, because economic factors and interest group politics (faculty unions, parents) are likely to overwhelm any conceptual clarities that might arise. The critical issue remains, however: Who is the beneficiary of higher education, the individual or the society? Are universities instruments of the public good—even if "private" in law and funding—or are they purveyors of services for the individual consumer, like plumbers and waste haulers? If *Chandler* tells us something about the court's view of higher education in the nineteenth century, the actions of the United States Justice Department during the late 1980s tell us something about the place of higher education today.

The Prestige Cartel

The origin of the notion of "financial aid" (as the offspring of "merit scholarships") was outlined above. When the concept and practice of financial aid were being formulated after World War II, the institutions leading the change agreed that they would base financial aid awards on family *need;* there would be no price bidding for students in the manner of price bidding for star athletes at some of the major sports schools. Students should choose colleges because they want the program, not because they get a bonus! Not only did that seem like a high-minded principle, but also it avoided the temptation of the wealthier institutions to outbid everyone for desirable students. In order to police this policy of high-mindedness and prudence, a largish group of the most prestigious colleges and universities agreed to share information about the financial need of mutual applicants and the nature of the aid offered. The colleges comprised what was called the "Overlap Group." It is no more.

During the Bush administration, the Department of Justice Anti-Trust Division decided that this financial aid arrangement was nothing more or less than "price fixing" and collusion. (As Senator William Proxmire observed at the time, after years of somnolence on anti-trust during the great merger mania of the 1980s, suddenly the Anti-Trust Division sprang to life and went after—Princeton!)

What is most interesting about this curious episode in federal vigilance is the relegation of higher education (at least private higher education) to the category of a for-profit business activity when it traditionally regarded itself (naively?) as a charitable non-profit activity in the public good. The colleges and universities in question (MIT honorably dissenting) agreed to disband the Overlap Group. Perhaps no great substantial harm occurred because of this tiff with the attorney general, but the principle established—or at least left hanging—was the legal and economic status of higher education as a private consumer good or a public benefit. I continue to believe that MIT was correct to resist the implication of the anti-trust charge. Some of the attorneys involved in the case pressed for a GODS (Grand Overall Defense Strategy), which was simply to argue that the framers of the Sherman Act never for a moment considered colleges as included under the legislation. With Standard Oil on their minds, why would they have been interested in Yale?

If there is a basis for the Justice Department's argument, it has to do with the elusive value of "prestige"—and the Overlap Group contained a high percentage of the high-prestige institutions. In the matter of university attractiveness to students and their dollars, *prestige* is the most important factor. Prestige is to college sales what location is to real estate. You may have the best program (a quality home), but with no prestige (the wrong location), you are in deep trouble. I have a simple marker for prestige: is your college one that is likely to be mentioned on a TV sitcom? If so, it has high prestige. We think that it tells us something about the character if she is identified as a Bryn Mawr grad. Visions of Katherine Hepburn swim into view. Unfortunately, there is no clear identification with Carleton, and Occidental sounds like foreign transplant.

I point out the importance of prestige because it is the one monopoly product that the Overlap Group might claim. Excellent, but non-prestige, universities compete on common ground with the lower-cost publics—many of which are excellent and mostly of lesser prestige than the Overlap brethren. Given the specific interest of anti-trust legislation, one might fancy that the Overlaps had "cornered the prestige market" and were prepared to "fix" prices for their elegant coterie of colleges. Outside the prestige club, however, it is hard to see how any private college could "corner" a market when a public institution across town is offering a relatively similar service at one-fourth the price.

The traditional American relationship between *private* universities and *public* purpose has a long and distinctive history. The trend line from the anti-trust action may suggest a very significant change in public and legal understanding of the two sectors. Private higher education in the United States was a colonial tradition, even though colonial Harvard, to take one example, was amply funded by the General Court of Massachusetts. After the establishment of the United States of America, private *religious* higher education appeared to be a constitutional necessity. The doctrine of separation of church and state suggested that, if religious denominations wished to sponsor colleges—and they were the main sponsors through almost the first century of the Republic—then they would not be supported by public funds. The history here is tangled. Many of the great state universities in their early years maintained a public Christian stance up to and including compulsory chapel. Whatever the history, recent Supreme Court rulings have effectively cleansed state institutions of the actuality and possibility of manifest religion. The distinction, then, between public and private higher education arises from history and constitutionality. The distinction would seem to remain as an important one, given the continuing interest in maintaining religious ties in higher education on the part of Catholics and various evangelicals. If one were to define public purpose by what is allowable before the great wall of separation (a judicial dictum, not constitutional language), higher education would be determinedly secular. While no one is about to decree only public higher education, the state obviously has the financial power to eliminate much of private higher education, including, of course, religiously based private higher education, by maintaining very low tuition rates at public institutions, refusing to offer state grants to students at private colleges, and so on.

If public and private rest on some important traditional and religious distinctions, there is a sense in which they have been regarded as one in purpose. New York University is the largest private institution in the country, and its slogan is "A private university in the public interest." The issue that remains after the Justice Department foray against the Overlap Group is whether these universities operate in the public interest or are essentially for-profit institutions that have cornered the prestige market. If Princeton is truly "in the nation's service" (the Nassau Hall motto), why should it not be subject to full governmental direction? Isn't an institution in the public service necessarily a public institution? If it insists on its "privacy," then it becomes a "for-profit" or "proprietary" institution operating for the benefit of its stakeholders (the well-paid faculty at the prestige colleges?).

All of these issues of private and public interest were hashed out in one of the most significant judicial rulings of all time: *Trustees of Dartmouth College v. Woodward* (1819). The legislature of New Hampshire, having chartered Dartmouth College, was displeased with its educational direction and sought to replace its board with members selected by the state. United States Supreme Court Justice John Marshall in his majority opinion established the principle that state charter did not imply state "ownership" or direction. The case is immensely important not only for private colleges and universities but also for all private corporations. General Motors must be incorporated as a business by the state, but for all that, it does not become a state enterprise like the Skoda Works under ye olde socialist regime. The *Dartmouth College* case is, in a sense, the charter of private business enterprise in the United States against any aggrandizement of the state.

The question that may face private universities in the future is whether their claim to be "in the public interest" is so vague and synoptic that it is more a matter of faith than demonstrable fact. If that is the case, the portent of the anti-trust suit may subtly come to pass: private colleges will become (or come to be treated as) for-profit institutions that directly benefit the individual stakeholders (students, faculty, alumni—via prestige), while their "public service" is no more than whatever contribution any prospering corporation may make to the general mix of the economy and social fabric. Washington and Jefferson College in Pennsylvania was recently denied status as a "charitable" institution because the trial judge decided there were not enough students on "scholarship"—despite a sizable financial aid budget. Although this ruling was reversed on appeal, the original judgment may be an omen for the future.

High Fees and Free Tuition

Although I have quoted above from a learned economist who claims that the individual benefit to students in life career outweighs the social benefit of higher education, I confess to being very doubtful about the methodologies for assessing and specifying these personal versus social benefits. The number of ad hoc assumptions necessary to measure the public benefit of higher education would do credit to pre-Copernican astronomy. The only thing that I am relatively certain about is that higher education is a considerable value to the individual in terms of greater earning power, more secure social position, access to leadership, and so on. Because of the manifest value to the individual, it seems appropriate to charge for that advantage. Free higher education in the public interest (or anything approximating the same) appears blind to the personal gain of the recipients. If one combines the sense of value to the individual with the apparent financial restriction of the state and federal governments—particularly in providing for real welfare benefits, such as Social Security, medical care, criminal justice, and the like—then the argument for reasonable charges at public universities seems sound and inevitable. The principle is often stated as "high tuition–high aid." One charges a significant tuition to the student *but* provides means-tested grants and loans for those unable to meet the sticker price. Whether high tuition–high aid conforms to some magnificent moral equation weighing public and private good, the trend line of state financing seems clearly to be in this direction—at least in the direction of higher tuition. The trend is worldwide. The Communist Chinese across the ocean from the Golden State have recently introduced tuition into the state universities. If the Communists charge fees, can capitalism be far behind?

A secondary advantage for capitalists in charging fees at state institutions is that this would create more competition within the American complex of institutions. Faculty unions at public institutions resist higher tuition because lower tuition "levels the playing field" with private higher education—particularly the modestly priced private institutions. Instead of competing with a tax-subsidized price, the state institutions would have to compete on quality and service. Tuition charges also would put a university education in play with other career choices in the society: entering the army, a business, or a technical training program. As mentioned earlier, Austria through a series of legal changes has opened up *university* education to a broad section of the relevant population. Higher education is free, of course, and a *university* education carries the most prestige and highest chance for advancement. Given the fact that this free good is now widely available, there has been a shift away from technical training schools, which is probably not desirable, even in the short run. One might argue that since the university education is of more value *to the individual,* there should be a differential cost for that advantage. Charging a fee would in some measure level the playing field for other life choices that may, in the long run, be more sensible for the society and the individual.

Having argued throughout this chapter for high tuition as a sensible state policy—one that would paradoxically benefit the poor if the New York experience is any guide—I want to make a modest exception. I return to my CUNY story. CUNY and its beloved ancestor, CCNY, have been institutions with a special mission and a special clientele. In the dreadful old days of rank discrimination and immigrant poverty, CCNY was a very blessing for the excluded in New York City. The Jewish immigrant population, with its passion for learning, could look to City, with its free tuition, as a passport out of the ghetto and the shirt factory. Today CUNY has a new population of ghettoized African Americans and some of the newest American immigrants. As long as the institution serves these populations, there is a very strong argument for free or very low tuition.

The arguments presented above about high tuition–high aid should make a lot of sense to state officials, and such a policy is likely to have no noticeable impact on the CUNY clientele. I recall the admissions director at Middlebury trying to persuade a low-income youngster from his own blue-collar township to apply to the college. "How much does it cost?" In those days,

"Three thousand dollars." "Man, that is the cost of a Chevrolet Camaro!" One could have argued with this potential student forever about financial aid or low-interest loans, and I doubt that it would have had any effect. It is one thing to talk price (and aid) with families where college going is an expected trajectory; it is very different in a society where there has been no higher education reality or expectation. It seems like a lot of money for something very distant and doubtful. Since bringing these populations into the mainstream is a profoundly important *public* good—and higher education is a grand boat for mainstreaming—I would argue to keep tuition as low as possible.

The argument is not intended for CUNY alone. There are other special colleges in special locations. Berea, for instance, serves the Appalachian poor, and you cannot go there unless you are from the region and financially limited. The community colleges of the United States have been an open door for populations traditionally shut out of higher education because of price and/or poor preparation. Perhaps the rational principle for tuition charges would be a scale from free for freshmen to a modest charge for a second year and escalating toward high tuition–high aid by senior year. As the student progresses, he or she not only acquires greater value in the job market, but also, within the college environment, can be "educated" into understanding the justification for tuition.

I do not intend to condemn the idea of public higher education. The notion of making education broadly accessible to the public is noble and democratic. The problem again is the slip between the ideal and the institutional reality. The institutional reality of financial aid has opened the private colleges to lower-income students—who now threaten to exhaust the budget; the institutional reality of faculty unionization in public institutions (more or less impossible in privates because of *Yeshiva*) has created political pressure for low tuition and high tax subsidy—which now threaten to exhaust the state treasury. If financially pressed "public" institutions trend toward "private" economic support, from tuition, fund raising, and so on (the University of Texas already has the largest endowment in the country), what will *public* education really mean?

The importance of higher education to the broadest public is an appropriate transition to the final "half-truth." If higher education is important to the public, just *how* important is it? Where does higher education rank with other goods, with other institutions, state, and church? How does higher education relate to the other goods and institutions of the community? Is it supportive, neutral, destructive? For various reasons, higher education has become increasingly important within the fabric of American society—world society as well. The final half-truth claims that the university is "axial," central and fundamental, to the world of the century ahead. Maybe not.

9 The University Is the Axial Institution of Modern Society

"Axial" seems to have entered the language in 1849 in a treatise on fish and has persisted as a high-tech word ever since. Despite its unprepossessing entrance into English, it was recently used in an enthusiastic article on the central ("axial," as in the axis of a wheel) role of higher education in the century to come. The new world will be an "information" age requiring high skills in advanced technology. High skills + high technology = high(er) education. *Q.E.D.* The argument has more than superficial truth, and it is vastly appealing not only to college presidents but also to people who peddle high technology. If the university is the axial, central, key, most important institution for the future, then surely it needs whatever financial support is required.

The argument for the axial university is so appealing and so effective in keeping the enterprise afloat that I would not wish to wholly refute the wisdom therein. Ignorance and stupidity have not been boons for the human race. To the extent that the university is a powerful engine for knowledge, it deserves major philosophical and financial support. Nevertheless, it is worth asking whether the university is more "axial" than the political and ethical institutions of a society. An even more crucial issue: does the "knowledge" available in the modern university offer a foundation for politics and ethics? The university may be an axis, but is it the one on the wheels that steer?

I recall attending a meeting of assembled academics back in the 1960s. It was during the tail end of the Vietnam War, when everyone—even the generals—seemed convinced that the war was at least a political blunder, if not a moral disaster. The speaker on the occasion, Julian Bond, pointed out to the gathered grey-suited deans and presidents that the war was not, after all, the creation of high school dropouts. Presidential cabinets have been dominated by "the best and brightest" from Dean Acheson (Yale) to John Foster Dulles (Princeton) to Henry Kissinger (Harvard). It would be nonsense to blame the war or the woe of welfare on the Ivy Leaguers who have made the highest-level decisions in the country, but Julian Bond's comment certainly suggests that sound policy and ethical discernment are not guaranteed by-products of elegant education. For all we know, high school dropouts might be even more obtuse in their decision making on complex moral issues, but the fact of the matter is that higher education has no necessary connection to political acumen or moral sense. If Ms. Doe graduates with a degree in chemistry, I have every right to expect her to know the periodic table; if Mr. Roe graduates in the "humanities" (even—especially?—moral philosophy), I have no reason per se to expect him to be an ethical person or a perspicuous moral judge.

Aspiration to axiality distorts the role of the modern university in the human community. To be foundational for society, an institution should have the inherent capability to assess, sort, prioritize, and commend the Good. For various reasons—modesty, academic freedom, priority of disinterested science—the research university in its sober moments will certainly withdraw from such high moral efficacy. (Columbia won its court case against Jacobsen. Despite the Greek inscriptions, the university does not produce *sophia*.) If the university maintains modesty of purpose, then its own intellectual efforts must themselves be assessed by the axial "moral" assumptions of humankind. In his famous American Scholar lecture at Harvard, Emerson stated the basic truth: "Character is more important than intellect." That was surely the truth at Emerson's Harvard; whether it would be so easily understood at modern Harvard has been a theme of this presentation. Intellect is not absolute when viewed in the light of moral needs and concerns. If there is a moral role for the university, it is far from foundational—and with the modern university, one can ask whether its fundamental intellectual strategy is capable of validating the moral life. Worse, if someone were to assume that the university encompasses all there is to the rational life, does it, in fact, undermine morality? That has been the complaint from the Court of Athens versus Socrates to Allan Bloom versus Cornell and Assorted Collegiate Co-Conspirators.

Ignorance Inherent and Inveterate

One of the popular ideologies for the university is borrowed from a notion about the character of the natural sciences. It is an ideology that, if adopted, wholly disables the university from practical life. That philosophy was summed up by a contemporary commentator, Professor Robert McCauley, in an article seeking to distance the world of the university from what was (to his mind) the unacceptable world of business:

> The process of seeking knowledge is not complete, and we have no idea what the final product will look like. Actually, I think that the view can be stated even more strongly. The process will never be complete because we cannot *ever* be certain what the final product will look like, even if we finally arrive at it. My claim, in short, is this: the process is all we've got and the process is all we ever have. What the university offers is not a measured portion of the truth for each customer, but an invitation to a way of life. . . . Learning how to ask questions is infinitely more important than learning to recite answers.

If ever there was a half-truth, this statement is it; I know, because it sounds like most of my convocation speeches. Intellectual freedom rings out in every phrase: who would shut down inquiry when there is no certainty? There are shades of Socrates and science in the claim. Socrates is the persistent questioner, who affirms only the wisdom of his own ignorance; science projects an everlasting critique of its own latest "results." The history of science is a chronicle of narrow-minded dogmatists opposing the revolutionary genius: Galileo, Darwin, or Freud. Einstein said that no series of positive facts could prove his theory; one negative could overthrow it. Truth yearns for a validated future; we are on an eternal voyage of discovery.

If you happen to inhabit a shaky academic field like my own (philosophy), questing and questioning may seem like the best one could hope for, but as a sensible view of natural science, the statement is at least half false. The folks doing cancer research really want to find out the *answers* to the origin and cure of that disease. Imagine your friendly physician telling you that he really is interested only in asking you questions, not in finding an answer to your problem. Dangerous as it may be to the spirit of creativity and free inquiry, the reality is that we do know some facts for sure. The earth revolves around the sun and not the other way round—and such like.

It is not at all uncommon for a Nobel laureate in his or her acceptance speech to proclaim the tentativeness of scientific theory. While it does credit to the modesty of great scientists to make such rhetorical flourishes, these speeches are a serious distortion of the actuality of science. Science is a long, complex endeavor, and, of course, one does not wish to shut it down. Further Funding for Physicists! But if premature dogmatism is a disaster for science, so is preemptive rhetorical skepticism. The great modern British philosopher John Austin made a significant point about the methodological skepticism of science and inquiry. He noted that the motor in one's automobile is *inherently* fallible, but not *inveterately* so. The difference is immensely important. To be sure, human knowledge is inherently subject to breakdown, but as with the auto, it is not inveterately the case that we make mistakes, or cannot get the car out of the garage.

In framing an ideology of the modern scientific-research university, one needs to be clear on the difference between inherent and inveterate fallibility. Unfortunately, there is a tendency to muddle the synoptic and the specific. In the day-to-day classroom, faculty and students act as if there are right answers to at least some questions. No one passes organic chemistry by copping a plea for the inherent fallibility of the human mind. Alas, while the faculty and students are busy pursuing and actually achieving specific knowledge, the president and Nobelists are out making synoptic statements about the intellectual life that read like the everlasting inquiry quote above.

All this skeptical posturing about present results might be regarded as relatively harmless, since no one pays the slightest attention to it in the research lab or at exam time, if it were not for the fact that universities occasionally try to decide what in general they are up to. Thinking about the whole university task invites synoptic thought. If such synoptic reflection focuses only on the idea of everlasting inquiry, the rhetoric may well emerge as inherent (or at least long-term) skepticism. Retreat to synopticism is neither surprising nor wholly inappropriate. The university is forever (I hope) because of the inherent fragility of our best achievements—even BMWs break down. From the forever standpoint, one can immediately defend academic freedom, eternal inquiry, and the endowment drive. The problem arises when the university begins to apply the synoptic rhetoric to its five-year plan. What is true enough in the long run is a half-truth (no better than a C–) for present policy.

The most immediate mess caused by confusing inherent fallibility with daily doubt can be seen in the wrangles of university curriculum committees. The wrangles can go on forever if one takes the forever horizon as the frame for argument. Any overall curricular suggestion can be undercut by the appeal to inherent fallibility. While Professor A on the curriculum committee is as unlikely as the hapless student who fails his organic chemistry exam to appeal to the general fallibility of the human mind, the rhetoric of long-term doubt and eternal inquiry, the notion that "we cannot *ever* be certain what the final product will look like, even if we finally arrive at it," sits like Banquo's ghost at the meeting of the curriculum committee, disrupting deliberation as surely as Macbeth's little party was upset by the ghostly apparition.

In sum, while the modern research university in its synoptic moments proclaims the *idea* of everlasting inquiry and the inherent fallibility of the human mind when it institutionalizes itself with required courses, examinations, and grades, it rather embarrassingly has to admit that there is some genuine knowledge already at hand. Not everything is to be discovered. The university may not be sure what things one ought to know in the great synoptic scheme of things, but one can be reasonably certain that, whatever one learns, it will contain chunks of genuine truth. Admitting to the sin of having something actually to be learned would be good for the intellectual soul of the university.

It should be obvious why synoptic skepticism will not do for university science, but even more so, it will not do as a prospectus for the moral and political life of a society. Everlasting inquiry may well be the *ultimate* condition of university study and the intellectual life, but it is a total disaster for morals and politics. The practical arts cannot wait for demonstration; they demand decision. Alexander does not solve the puzzle of the Gordian knot; he cuts it. While philosophers in some cozy quad may speculate skeptically on the subjectivity of morals and their utter relativity, law courts are assigning guilt, and reformers seek to reform our moral habits. A philosophical colleague, fed up with the reflex relativism of his students on moral matters, announced that he had graded the term papers by throwing them down the stairs and giving As to the ones that traveled farthest. The students complained bitterly that this was not just and fair. Case closed on utter moral skepticism.

To emphasize the difference between scientific demonstration and moral/political decision is not to affirm that decision is always right just because it is a decision. One can hope that moral decision makers adopt some healthy questioning about their own principles and motives. A certain tentativeness in proclaiming righteousness is to be commended. University historians and political analysts will gladly offer a myriad of examples of decisions that were perverse, wrongheaded, and wicked. What is not possible for the practical life, however, is the luxury of continued debate toward demonstrative truth. In morals and politics, one is forced toward a decision—often in a situation of irresolvable dilemma and tragic circumstance, but a decision nevertheless. Would that Sophie did not have to choose, but choose she must.

Everlasting inquiry is salutary for both science and morals insofar as it creates some healthy wariness about our best theories and our firmest moral dogmas, but in the moral realm, we must move to conclusion, even in uncertainty or contradiction. The intellectual strategy of ever-ongoing science is something the moral decision maker cannot finally accept. The pure scientist may have some pity on the practical man saddled with an impossible task; perhaps the learned savant will, in fact, remove himself as far as possible from the sordid world of politics in favor of the clarity of theory (a life strategy adopted by all too many German professors in the face of the manifest irrationality of the Nazi political program). The moral decision maker is not, however, quite as disabled as the pure scientist may believe. If the watchword for science is *discovery,* then for morality, there is nothing to discover—we have it in hand already.

An Ethical Einstein: Discovery and Recovery

The modern university model since the end of the nineteenth century has been the *research* university. For alliterative and accuracy reasons, I will here characterize it as replacing the *recitation* college. The educational and philosophical assumptions separating *research* and *recitation* are profound. The direction of research is *discovery;* the direction of recitation is *recovery.* It is significant that Professor McCauley's succinct and perceptive summation of one philosophy for the modern university concludes as follows: "Learning how to ask questions is infinitely more important than learning how to *recite* answers" (emphasis added). Surely, McCauley is correct—at least half correct—but there is more here than meets the rhetorical I.

The theme of this chapter is the capacity of the modern university to serve as the foundational institution for society. Ethical, political, and (I believe) religious institutions are essentially more important to human society. The intellectual endeavors of the university may be of great assistance to these "value" institutions, but the "science" of the modern university can neither serve to found these institutions nor—a modern temptation—to replace them. The university is a grand place, but it is not a vehicle of salvation.

The simplest indication of the failure of the research model in the realm of ethics, politics, and religion has to do with the different assumptions behind a curriculum of *discovery* and *recovery*. I am more than content to wait out the fate of the muon. Whether there are such, what they do, and why they are important may have to wait upon the abandoned Super-Collider. If the muon does not reveal itself in my lifetime, 'tis a pity, but let science forge on to its validated future. What I am not prepared to accept is that some ethical Einstein out there in the future will discover the real ethics, the perfect politics, the meaning of life. When Immanuel Kant published his *Critique of Practical Reason* (on the nature of morality), a correspondent wrote congratulating him on the *discovery* of the moral law. The old philosopher was horrified and hurried to reply that he had not *discovered* the moral law—what had humanity been up to all those years! Kant suggested that he may have provided a new *formulation* of the moral law, but that was all.

The modern research university and its presumed paradigm study, natural science, may quite properly direct themselves toward the future and toward discovery. All well and good, but to the extent that *discovery* becomes the sole watchword, the university incapacitates itself for the tasks of ethics, politics, and religion. We really do think that morality is somehow *already*—not in every jot and tittle—but somehow and substantially *already.* Science may come up with the most remarkable reversals and surprises, but no one expects that an ethical genius might just discover that justice has been a mistake. If one expands beyond lines of ethical conduct to religion or "the meaning of life," the establishment of a Nobel Prize for religious *discovery* is not to be expected. (As the philosopher John Smith once noted, when the angels appeared over the stable at Bethlehem, they did not say, "Behold, we bring you a topic for discussion!") Either I have some sense, however imperfect, of the good life and the meaning thereof *now,* or I should decide that there is no real ethics and life is just a mess. What is absurd is to believe that someday some successor of Kant will finally discover the moral law. *New York Times,* January 1, 2002: Philosophers in Pittsburgh Discover the Meaning of Life. Pope Resigns. Dalai Lama Refuses to Answer Telephone.

I am not making here any grand metaphysical claim to the effect that morality and meaning are somehow inherent in the mind, soul, or spirit. I only want to insist that morality and the meaning of life are not waiting to be invented like high-temperature super-conductivity. Whatever the metaphysics of moral faculties, the fact is that morality in some sense already exists—maybe gathered together bit by bit from the ruminations of prophets, sages, men of action, women of sense—but there it is. Whatever the metaphysics, morality is *already.* Socrates, who is repeatedly invoked as the prophet of everlasting inquiry by academic speech makers, is proof for my claim about morality. Socrates, like Kant, did not think that in his inquiries he would *discover* morality; his hope was to *recover* moral insight, getting his interlocutor through "reminiscence" to recognize what he already knew—but which had been clouded over by passion and immediate care. Socrates (or Plato) had a fancy metaphysics to go with this claim (eternal forms and reincarnation of souls). One need not buy the machinery to accept the essential notion that moral instruction is fundamentally recovery, not discovery.

This brings us to the problematic of any moral curriculum in the modern university. Given the dominance and proven power of the natural sciences in establishing the research paradigm, it is no wonder that professors in the humanities feel beleaguered and abandoned in the current curriculum. The humanities are concerned essentially with human values: ethical, political, aesthetic, religious—none of which awaits radical discovery. By rights, the humanities faculties should be engaged in recovery, or they betray the nature of their own subject matter. This is not to say that there are no ethical insights to be gained or that artistic creation has come to a stop. More of that below, but I do not want the reader to lay down the book in disgust (just yet) over the crusty conservatism of this claim. (Like all educational propositions, this, too, may be a half-truth.) But if the humanities essentially pursue recovery in an institution essentially dedicated to discovery, they are obviously in deep trouble. They *are* in deep trouble.

One can appreciate the dilemma of the humanities under the research-discovery paradigm by reconsidering the paradigm of the "classical" colleges, which were replaced by the research universities. As noted, the classical colleges were into *re*covery, not *dis*covery. Clearly, those old-time colleges believed that some things (ethics and religion) were *already*. The task of education was to recover the ethical tradition. Such an education is essentially *classical*—not necessarily in the sense of Greeks and Latins, but in allegiance to achieved wisdom, whether in the Bible or Plato, the Koran or Kant. The classical authors presented models worthy of imitation; they enshrine value. The modern university places invention before imitation, regarding imitation as mere rote and uncreative. But in the moral realm, it is better to imitate the bravery of Horatius at the bridge than to invent something better than courage.

The super-authoritative position of the Bible and the peda-gogical assumptions of the old-style college complemented each other. Morality may well be something that is already, but as Socrates' practice indicates, it may be a long road to recovery. Moral tutelage takes time; it involves many inconclusive argu-ments, wrong turns, an accretion of experience. The Bible seemed to short-circuit all that: there was the code; the only issue was getting the students to obey. Biblical pedagogy under this model was imitative indeed—and with some of the bad conno-tations of imitation. It was entirely possible to conform to the code, imitating the actions and manners prescribed, but in a merely external fashion. Schoolmasters in their exhaustion might well settle for such external order. One merely imitated morality; one merely recited the orotund phrases of the Latin or-ators, without internalizing ethical character or personal taste.

It is easy enough to see the limitation of the old-style peda-gogy, but it is worth noting that in learning ethical habits, the earlier stages are almost inevitably external and imitative. We are polite and say "Thank you" to the hostess because that is what our mannerly parents compelled us to do; only much later may we come to see the moral point of manners. We learn to "play fair" in children's games well before we grasp the power and scope of justice.

The modern university pedagogue looking at the practice of Classical College expresses proper dismay. That was not educa-tion, but indoctrination; that was not thought, but habit! The accusations—given the slipperiness of some of the terminol-ogy—are fairly put. But both Old-Style Bible College and New-Style Research U. fail in differing ways to address the issues of morality. How is that?

Religious Protest and Intellectual Critique

The view that morality is *already* can have two very different and opposing interpretations. It can mean that morality is something already revealed in some *historical past* or that morality is something *eternally present* to Reason and right conscience. The Christian college of an earlier period found morality in a revealed and exemplary past: the Bible and the Ancients. One can challenge the assumptions of the denominational college either because it picked the wrong past (or too narrow a past) or, more fundamentally, because the sense in which morality is *already* is a matter not just of historical revelation but also of rational insight. The difference between the two challenges is crucial to an understanding of a "moral" curriculum. Simply—oversimply—put, Old-Style Bible College has History without thought; New-Style Research U. has Thought without history. Neither has what is really needed: *tradition,* which is history + thought. My view is that morality exists inherently *in, through, by,* and *with* a tradition, and, thus, both the denominational college and the research university flunk Moral Pedagogy 101.

I have drawn the contrast between denomination and discipline, recovery and discovery, moral tutelage and intellectual search as sharply as possible. There is, however, an important perspective in which there is a commonplace between the denominational colleges and their research descendents. The commonality is "Original Sin." Jonathan Edwards, who died in office as president of Princeton, expressed a Protestant view that human nature was utterly corrupted by the sin of Adam. "Sinners in the hands of an angry God" was the best we could hope for. (Roman Catholicism tends to believe that human nature was wounded by primal sin but not *utterly* corrupted.) For Edwards, man is inherently sinful (Original Sin), saved only by God's infinite mercy and grace. For the modern academic researcher (in a synoptic philosophical mood), human intelligence is inherently fallible, saved only by the infinitely long march of science.

Radical Protestant emphasis on the aloneness of the soul before God undercuts the pretensions of established cultural and

ecclesiastical institutions. The Church as institution was replaced by the Bible as sole rule of faith. (In Catholicism, the
New Testament is the Church's creation; for Protestantism, the
Church is the New Testament's creation.) And since anyone
could read the Bible, it seems that anyone might interpret the
Church out of the text—thus, the divisiveness of Protestant sectarianism. Protestantism, in its reliance on the Bible as "sole
rule of faith," established that "authority" as an anti-authoritarian protest against the ponderous traditions of popes and
councils. The anti-authoritarian authority of the Bible passes
right on to the individual believer over and against any established "church." As the late Baptist leader Herbert Gezork
noted: "For Baptists there is the rule of the three 'F's'. One
Baptist is faith, two Baptists is fellowship, three Baptists is
fight!" Thus, Northern and Southern Baptists, General Baptists, Particular Baptists, and so on.

If Protestantism—as its name implies—arose as a protest
against the Church establishment of the day, the research university engaged in its own protest against the Protestant collegiate establishment of its day. The university protest was
undertaken in the name of science, reason, and universal truth
as against particular (biblical) revelation. The research university ideology (highly simplified) captured two anti-authoritarian strands: the eighteenth-century Enlightenment view of
reason over history and the nineteenth-century Romantic view
of heros over history. To the thinkers of the Enlightenment, reason was universal, accessible by pure thought alone. The human mind was either a blank slate on which the facts of the
common world were impressed *or* the transcendent, impersonal observer of natural science. Blank slates and transcendent
observers are necessarily sexless, racially neutral, religiously
agnostic, disengaged from king and party. The very disengage-
ment of Enlightenment rationality proved revolutionary; sheer
tradition and inertia may place the Bourbons on the throne of
France, but mere history must stand under the judgment of uni-

versal, rational sense. There are self-evident truths, natural laws discoverable by reason alone that govern the conduct of man and the state. Reason is inherently anti-establishment, anti-authority, anti-the-merely-historical—truly revolutionary.

The Romantic movement of the early nineteenth century added grace notes to the revolution against convention and tradition—revolution not by the iron law of reason, but with the towering passion of genius. History is transcended as genius (Beethoven) breaks the bonds of a sterile past. Enlightenment rationality and romantic genius play into the ideology of the new anti-authoritarian research ideology: the heroic quest of truth to be established only by transcendent reason. Heady stuff! The denominational college placed the Bible against this juggernaut of rationality, but it was no contest. Enlightenment rationality was categorically opposed to truth from *any* historical authority. The Bible may be the sole rule of faith, but Reason is the sole rule of science. And as if the categorical challenge was not enough, Darwinian science devastated the Bible at the beginning.

Consider, then, the possibilities for a moral and political curriculum within higher education as the new university merges *both* its denominational past *and* its research future. The Protestant heritage of private revelation and the Enlightenment's scientific demand for freedom of inquiry conspire to create a formidable barrier to any tradition-based curriculum. The natural science assumption of the modern university must find morality from pure reason, or else ethics is relegated to personal, subjective choice; Protestantism may assign morality to biblical teaching, but since individual conscience is supreme, there is the possibility of every man/woman—his/her Bible.

The common problem as one looks toward either the Enlightenment ideal or the Protestant faith is the role, if any, of tradition. Protestantism judged that it could do without the Roman Church tradition, going directly to biblical Revelation for spiritual direction. The Enlightenment believed that access to Pure Reason would be sufficient to establish proper government and true morality. Either Reason or Revelation could conform to the basic thesis that "morality is already"—but not "already *in any established tradition*." Jefferson is a child of the Enlightenment when he proclaims the moral truth that all men are created equal and endowed by their Creator with the rights to life, liberty, and the pursuit of happiness. That truth, he says, is self-evident—self-evident to any person of reason.

All the Knowledge Already There

Nothing has been more controversial in the recent past than the content of the "core" liberal arts curriculum. Is there really some "tradition" that is valuable to convey, or is the traditional core merely the propaganda of dead, white, European males? The traditional core is denounced as a fundamental ethical and political distortion. Claimants to the curriculum clamor and clash for acreage in academic turf. Moral denunciation mixed with the synoptic skepticism of ongoing inquiry can easily subvert any selection of classic texts. *If* there is to be a moral and political curriculum—and that is a significant "if"—neither the denominational roots nor the research graft is likely to be fruitful. Insofar as the two "traditions" are in their differing ways anti-tradition, they would defeat any moral *tradition* from having a validity *as tradition*. The denominations did, of course, admit the Bible—not as part of a tradition but as a direct revelation to the believer. These two transcendent judgments upon tradition, upon history, pose a serious challenge (or threat) to the moral, political, and religious *institutions* that are historically embedded or historically encrusted. Jefferson, as true Enlightenment thinker, believed that there should be periodic political revolutions so that the dead hand of encroaching history should not thwart the rational will. Calvinism declares *ecclesia semper reformanda* (the church always reforming). As to "Protestant" politics: one might hope for a perfect polity, as in

John Calvin's Geneva or the Puritans' "City on the Hill," or adopt Martin Luther's "conservative" stance, which, in effect, left the German princes to their own bloody business during the Peasants Revolt.

This chapter is concerned with the relationship of the university and its "skills" to the moral and political institutions of society. The university might, of course, restrict itself to pure science, regarding all value claims (ethical, political, aesthetic, religious) as quite irrational and unscientific. The Enlightenment was right in proclaiming the transcendence of Reason, but wrong in believing that Reason played out in the messy world of morals. In such a case, the university would hardly claim to be an axial institution for society; from the standpoint of "science," political organization could be regarded as a form of public neurosis. Certainly, this is the claim made by Freudian science about religion, and the mania of modern nationalism or social tribalism could easily be taken under a similar ban. On the other hand, if politics is not assigned to irrationality, one could believe in a purely "rational politics": a form of social organization that could be derived from pure reason with the same clarity and assurance as a geometric proof. This was the ideal of the French revolutionists. The problem with the politics of pure reason is that it does not seem to work either practically or theoretically—which leads back to the conclusion in many minds that politics, ethics, and religion are finally irrational expressions of passion, pleasure, or preference.

The purpose of this chapter has been to raise issues regarding the contemporary university's relationship to the moral and political life of society. In particular, I have been concerned to see whether the studies of the contemporary university could be "axial," fundamental for society overall. I believe that there is a fundamental fault line in any such claim. Since the moral and political institutions are the real foundations of society—and since institutions are necessarily historical—a well-functioning (moral and political) society depends on *tradition*. But there is a very deep anti-traditional strain at work in the university. (If our contemporary society is in trouble, it is because it has lost a sense for tradition—indeed, for America, there is always the worry whether it ever had or wanted a tradition. It was the *New World*, after all.)

I have deliberately highlighted incapacities and some negative outcomes. It is, of course, not true that the modern university has become the mere engine of Enlightenment Reason, the detached scientist unconcerned with history and tradition (though it is worth noting that history majors have declined by 50 percent in the recent past). I have already noted the "moral hangover" of the modern university, and it is obvious that materials from various moral traditions are all over the course offerings in the catalogue. It is not the content of the catalogue that is at issue; it is the spirit of the enterprise that is subject to question. Having pieces of a tradition is not the same as understanding and exercising the modes of thought that define a living tradition. The denominational college, after all, had a piece of history, a piece of a tradition, but it failed to deal with it as a *tradition*. If, as suggested, the modern university is founded on philosophies that are deeply anti-authority and suspicious of any tradition just because it is traditional, then whatever the moral and political *content* of the curriculum, it exists in alien territory, lost in a Slough of Despond. That does seem to express the mood of humanities faculties. In the next chapter, I want to return to these themes—particularly to explain and justify the role of tradition as both social necessity and possible university study. If successful in that effort, we may locate a few directional signs out of the Slough.

10 Synthetic Morality

These concluding chapters offer "synthetic solutions" to at least half of the problems masked by
the half-truths delineated in the text. They are synthetic in
as many dimensions of the term as I can conjure. First of all,
they are not *the real thing*. Paper solutions to the complex
economic, ideological, and political problems that beset the
modern educational establishment will miss the whole cloth.
It can be ironed nicely, but it unravels in the wash. Second,
as a cautious Hegelian (oxymoron), I am fascinated by synthetic resolutions to dilemmas. One basic framework of this
entire presentation has set forth two radically contrasting
models of higher education: the denominational collegiate
model of the early nineteenth century and the research university model of the twentieth. The former espoused clear
"moral" aims, the latter dominant "intellectual" goals. To the
Bible colleges, "moral truth" was already and needed to be *re-
covered;* to the research universities, "scientific truth" was yet
to be *discovered*. Moral recovery created a pedagogy of *recitation,* intellectual discovery a pedagogy of *interrogation*. Bible
College had all the answers; Research U. has nothing but questions.

A Hegelian synthesist is tempted to sublimate the opposition of moral college and scientific university, inexpensive ethics and exorbitant science, in a grand educational *Erhebung* (German word that somehow manages to mean cancels, preserves, and raises to a higher level—all at the same time!). One would like to cancel the negatives in the two models, preserve their decided virtues, and raise the whole establishment to a new and less expensive synthesis of the two.

Because this chapter is concerned with moral issues within higher education, the solutions are "synthetic" in two further meanings. Moral wisdom, if it exists at all, is a synthesis out of a tradition of moral deeds, decrees, and deliberations. One does not "clear the slate" and then deduce a pure morality outside historical experience. Finally, if there is to be any form of moral "instruction" in the college years, it will have to be a sort of "substitute" for the real thing, a synthetic education in morality, as opposed to the actuality of moral training and the ethical reflections raised by life experience. Plato referred to such learning as "the Garden of Adonis"—the classical equivalent to a greenhouse for plants. One can indeed raise plants in a hothouse, but the real test is out in the field. Moral discussion on the quad is necessarily a hothouse product. That is not all bad: it is helpful to have this artificial nurturance of morality, but the real test is outside the classroom. Finally, to persist in horticultural metaphor: the university ought not to imply that moral plants are rationally inedible.

The Persistence of Ethics

The passage from collegiate old-style to university new-style could well be regarded as a transmutation so radical and so profound that only the name has been preserved to protect the innocent. Both are "higher education," but they are as different as old Church from new Physics. Perhaps that should be the final conclusion, but as detailed in the text, the new research university, with its clear scientific prospectus, was somehow

grafted onto the old denominational model both organization-
ally and ideologically. The new research universities, with their
authoritative faculties, did not jettison the (ad)ministering
president or wholly overthrow the moral rhetoric characteristic of the office and the institution. One could conclude that the
graft really did not take and that the successor scientific institution will eventually discard its moralistic past.

I am disinclined to accept such a prospective slice across the
educational knot. I am not certain that it could be done, given
the extended moralistic history of American higher education
and the curious persistence of moral claims unto the present
day. The American social experience tends to project moral
concern onto college life. If the universities really wanted to jettison moral urges as they happily jettisoned *in loco parentis* and
single-sex dorms, I doubt that the public would accept such
purist academies. Thus, the continual complaint from various
publics about liberal faculty/conservative institutions that fail
to support family rights/spousal rights for homosexuals. Nobel
scientists may consider all this public moral interest in collegiate affairs distracting to the search for laser fusion, but it is
just not likely to disappear from the American scene.

More fundamental than the externalities of American history is the fact that the modern research university cannot escape certain inner moral structures and cues both positive and
negative. As discussed, the research university's mission "to
discover truth" carries with it certain "moral" implications
centered on cooperative search. Fraud misleads the search; plagiarism moves us not an inch forward. The *cooperative* search
implies dispassionate participation free from mere idiosyn-
crasy and personal demands. The private enthusiasms of drugs
or dreams fail to contribute to a common search—my id is *idio*-
syncratic. Personal passion (the older view of sex) must be
guarded against in the stern restrictions of scientific inquiry.
The inner morality of research is a demanding asceticism,
which attracts noble minds as surely as the monastic ideals of

the first faculties in medieval Europe. ("Ascetic" was Max Weber's precise term for the spirit of the modern academy.)

This "ascetic" research mentality has been the dominant philosophy of modern higher education. It is a philosophy that is inherent in the very notions of research, discovery, and scientific truth as they were set forth in the divorce from the older sectarian collegiate tradition. Unhappily, one can conclude about this new and noble idea of a university that it is a nice place to visit, but you wouldn't want to live there. This is precisely what the advocates of diversity, multiculturalists, and fraternities have concluded. One may study and do research *impersonally*, but no one *lives* that way. The internal asceticism of the modern academy becomes a *morality to reject*. Being "neutral" is being neutered, and that is morally objectionable.

The university may bluster back and insist that it is just into science, and warm personal morality will have to look out for itself somewhere outside the collegiate cloister. Moral mission really is an undesirable denominational hangover, a painful headache for a scientific establishment. Such "modesty" of purpose for the scientific task is not likely to prevail. Whether it wishes to be "axial" or not, the university is more and more seen as a trustworthy source of guidance on everything from medicine to morals. Given the enormous authority of science, the general public and university students may legitimately ask the university in its "scientific" cast of mind to proclaim on the nature and content of the moral life. What will alma mater say—what can she say?

Multiculturalism to the Rescue?

Jefferson founded the University of Virginia, but his is the founding spirit of the modern university overall: the deep faith in transcendent reason. Can this spirit of reason be the foundation for morality? Can science found a moral course of study for the university? There are deep philosophical reasons to be suspicious of the Enlightenment program for morality—and thus the place of moral learning in the Enlightenment's child: the research university. What interests me here is not the philosophical intricacies—though I will indulge in some—but the present challenge to the Enlightenment ideal presented by the heated multicultural debates currently raging inside the academy walls.

I have already touched on multiculturalism in the discussion of the "intellectual" curriculum, and I suggested there that there was more to say if one opened the issue of the moral implications of university education. Diversity and multiculturalism do not challenge the university simply on the *intellectual* justice of including the formerly excluded. Standard material in anthropology, sociology, and alien histories already makes intellectual multicultural claims on the curriculum. What these standard subjects do *not* do (at least overtly) is to commend or condemn the culture under review. Margaret Mead obviously liked the sexual freedom she thought she saw in Samoa, but as anthropologist, it was her business to describe, not proscribe. Intellectual diversity would be enough of a challenge; multiculturalism goes further in challenging the basic assumption of university "rationality."

Multiculturalism challenges the Enlightenment's "scientific" ideal, the detached "rational" observer, without historical position (and thus without historical prejudice), without sex or race or religion or ethnicity (and thus without all *those* prejudices). Multiculturalism rejects the fundamental mind-set of the Enlightenment—and thus of its great creature, the (merely?) scientific university. There is no transcendent intellect, no "view from nowhere-in-particular," no universal scientific point of observation. Like it or not—and the university definitely does *not*—things are always seen as male, female, black, white, and so on through an extended litany of ethnicity.

It is obvious why multiculturalism is such a deep problem for the modern university. It seems to destroy the possibility of dispassionate, universal communication, which is essential to the scientific assumption. Speaking as a multiculturalist, if you are the wrong sort, you cannot possibly understand my point of view. I am the unimpeachable source of "truth"—understanding that there are as many "truths" as there are ethnics available. I do not have to listen to your sort, since you could not possibly understand "where I'm coming from." You (wrong sort) are not free to talk about my subject matter, and if you try to do so, I will insist that you stop uttering such distorting "falsehoods." Thus, multiculturalism is seen as a threat to open inquiry, to academic freedom. An open dialogue toward Truth is nonsense, since there is nothing that we and "you guys" can dialogue about. We don't speak the same language!

Multiculturalism seems like old dogmatism in deconstructionist disguise. It is a fundamental rejection of science and universal truth. Like old dogmatism, it sees no point in academic freedom because it rejects the universalist learning assumption, the transcendent mind, on which inquiry is based. I should be free to expound my own sex's or sect's truth, but that "truth" is a personal, intuitive possession that is unchallengeable.

As a broad-scale frontal attack on the modern university overall, I think that multiculturalism is dead wrong. Much of the intellectual work of the university and much that it has achieved demand a kind of personal *ascesis*, a transcendence of sex, race, and ethnicity. At the level of fundamental scientific theory, there is no feminine or masculine astrophysics. Feminist critiques of the course of natural science have tended to concentrate on biology and the choice of *problems* in that science. In problem choice, gender bias clearly has been important. In medical research, white and male diseases have occupied the dominant interest of mostly white and male medical researchers. But once one picks a masculine or feminine, black or white scientific *problem*, the scientific solution will be genderless and raceless.

However, if multiculturalism is bizarre in astronomy, it is not so in the area of the lost moral curriculum. It starts in the right place. If morality is *already,* there are, as noted, two interpretations of that view: that morality is derived from some past *and* that it is already and is always present in pure reason, unadulterated by historical facts like male, female, black, and white. Multiculturalism opts for the historical. Denominationalism also opted for morality-from-the-past in the revelation of the Bible and the example of the Greeks. This choice is fatally patriarchal for feminists, but it is at least historically rooted. The whole trend of modern thought since the Enlightenment has been to reject the merely historical, bringing the Bible, the Greeks, and any other cultural claimant under the judgment of Reason. The Enlightenment position created the scientific cast of mind so much admired by the eighteenth-century philosophers—and so marvelously exploited in the great science of that age and subsequent times. But there is a serious question whether Pure Reason in the sense indicated could possibly be grounds for morality, politics, or religion.

Morality and the Veil of Ignorance

The argument against morality-from-reason is long and complex. In the context of this treatment, I only wish to throw ice water on the plausibility of transcendent reason as the grounds of morality. An elegant and profoundly valuable treatment of morality-from-reason is contained in John Rawls's *Theory of Justice.* Rawls creates a useful fiction (which I here adopt without in any way doing "justice" to the subtlety of his presentation). Imagine yourself setting up a just state. How would you wish it to be structured? He is concerned that you set up a system that is fair. If, for instance, you are a white European male, you might well decide to arrange things such that your sort gets most of the cash and kudos in the society. To prevent such special pleading, Rawls requires you to set up the state from behind a "veil of ignorance." What sort of polity would you wish if you did not know whether you were born male or female, black or white, rich or poor, Hindu or Muslim? The "veil of ignorance" is the equivalent to "transcendent reason" in that one is asked to drop away just those determinants that the multiculturalists wish to bring into play.

The overriding problem with this intriguing strategy is that, if we were really ignorant of these specific determinants, if we saw the world from the standpoint of eternal reason, we would probably make no sense at all out of moral and political life. Moral life is inherently a matter of these poor and those rich, the sexes, the passions and beliefs of very specific, actual folk. How exactly would a sexless intelligence understand the nature of that interesting desire and the physiological characteristics through which it is expressed? Having an Enlightenment mind forming morality would be like having an angel decide on the proper behavior of humans. If angels are not available, consider the proverbial Martian who, as is well known, reproduces by cell division like the amoeba. No sexes at all. What would the Martian make of human sexual goings-on? (In fairness to Rawls, he believes that one preserves enough humanoid data behind the veil to be constitutive. I side with his critics, however, in believing that he cannot have his veil and see through it at the same time.)

To sense the defects of a morality-from-reason and the plausibility of a morality-from-history, I recount an encounter I had in a course I taught on philosophy of art. At the beginning of the course, I asked all the students to indicate with which of the arts they were familiar: painting, ballet, music, and so on. One student said that he had no acquaintance with any of the arts. Why, then, was he taking this course? To get the general *theory* of art so that when he actually started to look at paintings and listen to music, he could discriminate the good stuff from the trash. The student was a true Enlightenment savant. If one knows the theory of art, then one can apply the theory to the actual instances. But this is not how it works. No prior "theory" of art, such as my earnest student hoped for, could direct the artist's work or inform the critic. The notion of art and the standards of value are derived only from knowing actual historical artifacts.

To an Enlightenment thinker, if morality is not *already* in transcendent reason, then where does it come from? One straight answer for the scientific, universal mind has been this: from nowhere! If morality is not grounded in reason, it has no ground to stand on; it is a subjective attitude, passion, belief of individuals and groups without any universal warrant. Multiculturalism rejects this starting point in universal reason—that is why it is anathema to so much of the modern university tradition. The multiculturalist insists that value is grounded in the highly specific historical experience of quite specific peoples in specific circumstances. Morality is not spied above history in the insights of reason; morality is a product in and of specific histories.

Multiculturalists and rational scientists may actually agree on the fact that morality is buried in specific histories. To the scientist of universal mind, so much the worse for morality. It is one of those subjective facts of human behavior, no more to be given universal value than the odd behavior of some remote tribe should be taken as standard for the race. The multiculturalist may in turn be more than willing to accept this "subjectivizing" of morality. There is *my* culture and mores, which certainly are not *yours* (thank [my] god!).

The multiculturalist need not, however, accept the Enlightenment assessment of his or her cultural claim, namely, that any such cultural claim is "subjective," a "private" experience for women or blacks, a unique value that cannot be communicated to those outside the group. Such a claim would indeed remove multiculturalism from *university* consideration—as many would wish. Cultures are cults, enthusiasms of true believers that, whatever their psychic value, are not part of any common dialogue. What is lacking in the argument (or agreement) between the rationalist and the multiculturalist is the notion of reason in history or, more concretely, the notion of *traditions* of value. Culture and morality are not isolating revelations; they create traditions, which in their turn subject particular revelations and enthusiasms to discipline, order, and, one may say, "rationality," albeit not transcendent, a priori reason.

Multiculturalism is a demand on the modern university for "moral" content. Critics of multiculturalism in the university are properly worried about a fundamental deterioration of the research university ideal. And they are dead right about the fundamental challenge. Should one then pay attention to the multiculturalist? Can one preserve the importance of open inquiry and academic freedom and at the same time make moral claim on the curriculum?

How to Be Moral and Not Lose Your Mind

In the days of the denominations and their colleges, higher education was perceived as morally subordinate. "For God, for country, and for Yale," as we have reiterated. The subordination of intellect to Christian character abstractly fulfilled Emerson's injunction—but there are those who would question that morality and, worse yet, denominational dogma appeared to seriously hamper the free inquiry of the intellect. The struggle of the research ideal was to liberate the inquiring mind from ecclesiastical as well as other social restraints. That battle has largely been won. Concomitant to the history of "scientific liberation" for the university, and perhaps because of the academy's ultimate victory over denominational dogma, the moral institutions of American society seem to have diminished notably. Certainly, this is true of the Protestant establishment, which promoted the denominational era of colleges. The churches seemed so wrongheaded in the battle against Darwin and real science that they lost much social credibility—particularly with the intellectual cadre that occupied the now liberated universities.

It may have been dangerous to win that battle with the churches; now the victor is expected to fulfill the role of the vanquished. But as we have insisted, the university appears decidedly ill equipped to fulfill this new moral task. My contention is that denomination, discovery, and diversity—from sectarianism through science to multiculturalism—all suffer from rejection of *tradition* as the unique locus of rational morality and value.

Although the claim is abstract and simplified, I believe it is correct to note that both the Protestant "tradition" of the sectarian colleges and the rational "tradition" of our research universities have serious problems with the very idea of tradition. The anti-authoritarianism of both the religious and the rational critiques requires whatever is historical to stand before the bar of better judgment. Protestants placed the Church tradition at the bar of the Bible and found it wanting; rationalists put the biblical tradition to the bar of science and found it wanting. Both Bible and Reason transcend the merely historical in God's word or Jefferson's self-evident truths. When it comes to transcending, science commands the heights these days.

Failure to deal with the power and character of traditions disables the older sectarian institution and the newer research institution from engaging the inner process of the moral life. Morality must be deduced from on High: the High of the Bible or the Heights of Reason. But morality is not deduced; it is developed out of dialogue with history in an ongoing tradition. All this talk about "tradition" may seem a mark of deep conservatism, as in the famous definition of a conservative as "someone who never wants to do *anything* for the first time." While morality is indeed "conservative" (it is *already*), it is only because of a "conservative" assumption that one can expect moral "progress." I hope to prove that claim.

I have already suggested that "art" is a creature of "tradition." Where is reason *in* art? Consider music. Music begins as a revelation in the sense that someone just does it; no prior theory—it just happens. There may have been whistlings and tootings before the Original Tune appeared; for music to happen means not just that some ancient flutist warbles in the woods, but also that listeners decide this kind of event is something valuable to be continued. To value X is to foster X. There is now a Tune to be carefully passed along. Before first flutist dies, there should be a successor, a new flutist to play Original Tune. Thus, first flutist teaches someone else to play the Original Tune. But the very act of pedagogy underlines the separation of the artist from the Tune. Second flutist is strictly second fiddle—or second flutist invents Variations on Original Tune. What to make of this Variation? Is it part of a Tune "Tradition" or something altogether different? Not only has Original Tune become an object of value, but also it has covertly established a "rule" for Music. It is decided that Variations on Original Tune has an organic relationship to the Tune Tradition. And so it goes with third flutist, and so on to Stravinsky.

The important aspects of the music tradition—and of any genuine tradition—are *origin* and the *act of passing it on.* The origin is *historical,* rooted in a highly particular set of circumstances. Imagine a "veil of ignorance" from behind which one would try to construct the "ideal symphony"; the notion is bizarre. A Beethoven symphony is a particular construction out of the historical existence of violins, woodwinds, and the like in the course of European music. From behind the veil, however, one might get a concatenation of gamelan and oud, whistles and claps—anything. Music is just some contingent historical development of instruments, patterns, and sounds. There is no "pure theory of music"; there is just the development from an original sense of value, with each "new" step being fitted into the tradition so that one can declare "That is music!"—even though one had never heard such a crash and crescendo before. The essential role of tradition in music explains why musical pedagogy follows in part the pattern of old-style denominational education. One imitates and recites from the tradition.

The past tradition is a fixed repository of value to be conserved and passed on, *and* novelty and variation can be assessed only as they grow out of the past as a "rule" for the art. Without a sense of Mozart and Mahler, the modern composer would be composing behind a veil of ignorance—we would not have any sense of "progress" because every product would be an Original Tune.

A proof of the centrality of tradition for music would be the work of "anti-musicians," such as John Cage. In his infamous composition *4'33"*, a pianist carefully sits down at the piano, adjusts the bench, inspects the keys, and then closes the lid and sits there silently for four minutes and thirty-three seconds—arising, one assumes, to applause for the "performance." Is Cage's work "music"? Only if one places it against the tradition of piano playing. Anti-music—if one can so characterize Cage's ingenious efforts—like *new* music, exists only in relationship to an actual body of work so far accomplished.

In the course of the development of the musical tradition, in terms of both learning to recite the tradition and expanding the tradition, there are various levels of reflection. At first, there may be simple imitation of the tunes at hand, but as one realizes that each new artist may vary from the standard (well or ill), one reflects on techniques of teaching and learning. It is no longer "I play this, you do the same"; one begins to be very self-conscious about how the bow is held, the reed cut, the sonata developed. Each of these self-conscious reflections inherently suggests different ways of proceeding. "Choice" is introduced into musical composition and performance. Finally, one develops a "practical wisdom" for music, an ordered set of reflective comments about the underlying forms of music. If this is called a "sonata," then it is not just Sonata K.545; it has a general character that could be instantiated in a novel sonata. (Not, mind you, instantiated in the manner that any frog is an instance of the species. This sonata is not at all the same as K.545, but it is a wonderful *sonata*.)

Some of these novelties are judged to be productive; others are clearly retrogressive. How do we know which is which? By trying to fit the practice alongside the actual achievements already before us. The "genius" who invents a new musical form or style of playing must convince us that it is as enriching as something extant. To switch arts: Cezanne said that his aim was to "redo Poussin in nature." Artists do not learn from nature (despite the popularity of the claim); artists learn from other artists and then carry the tradition (Poussin) forward in a new way. Music—as a tradition of revealed value historically positioned—develops through the fact of tradition, from passing the value down, from the reflective judgments that are the "reasons" in the tradition. A powerful and extensively developed tradition, like music, creates its own inner "reason," its own shared language of critique and appraisal.

Contrary to the Enlightenment notion, tradition is reasonable—or, more accurately, a tradition that works reflectively creates standards of discourse and reasons for assessment. These standards and reasons become apparent only if someone is "initiated" into the tradition. That is why my student's desire to have a theory of art so that he could judge the arts whenever he got around to paying any attention to them was bizarre. Only one who listens to music, who listens carefully and has some of the sense of original revelation, will ever arrive at the "reasons" for that tradition.

The music example is, I believe, a sufficient case of what I mean by the irreplaceability of history and tradition. I want to emphasize that the musical scenario is *essentially historical* in contrast to the scientific "tradition." Science also has a history of achievement—thus, the half-truth of the notion of never knowing the final answers. The critical difference is that science is genuinely *progressive,* such that the truths of Newton are subsumed into the broader theories of relativity. Newtonian mechanics are fine at the small scale, wrong at the cosmic level. Art, however, does not subsume its history. Poussin remains

Poussin and irreplaceable even after Cezanne redoes him in nature. Science continually incorporates its past into a present (timeless) structure of theory; art preserves its past as the touchstone of its present and future. Science discards its past by incorporation; art keeps its past—and it is in this sense that art, morality, and values are "already."

If a tone-deaf person cannot understand the fuss about music, a morally deaf person will not have any understanding of the "rationale" of morality. First, one is musically/morally initiated; then one comes to understand how and why it works. Thus, Aristotle's rather sour injunction that it is no use giving lectures on moral philosophy to the youth, since they have not had the requisite experience to understand what you are talking about. The virtues, moral habits, are the originary givens of morality. The tune is the thing done; the moral action is the thing done. We learn moral habits by inculcation and imitation, as the musician learns to play the piece. Then we want to see if the thing done is a matter of chance or choice. If there is a *habit*, the musician can repeat the tune; the actor can be brave again. Moral philosophy is not the ground of moral habit; it is the other way around. One who does not have moral habits is as deaf to moral philosophy as the musically illiterate is to Bach. The "missing" moral curriculum of higher education has to assume that the student has some historically grounded moral habits and opinions, as I had to assume that my student had some acquaintance with the arts. Practical wisdom is a reflection back on these habits. It assumes initially that there is value in the habits attained—as the beginning musical pedagogue assumes that the value is somehow in the extant body of works. As one reflects back on the body of morals (and music), one derives a sense of underlying forms, which in turn can be used to refine a sense of value: one starts with liking Strauss (Johann) and ends with liking Strauss (Richard).

Reflection, then, suggests new ways of proceeding within the values of the tradition. If there is to be a moral curriculum, then it will be nothing more than a reflective exercise *within* a history, a tradition—which is a lot. The Enlightenment wants a reflection *above* history in Pure Reason; the Biblicist freezes history and thus denies reflection—Bach did it once and for all! If morality is *essentially historical,* it raises serious questions about the modern university's pedagogy of "deparochializing" students in the interest of moral enlightenment. If morality exists in some Enlightenment heaven above all local parishes, the strategy is well placed. But if morality is always historical—in some sense always from some "parish"—the thoroughly deparochialized pupil will also be thoroughly demoralized. Of course, old-line denominationalists see just that threat in the modern university and send their offspring to Bob Jones University.

Tradition = The Open Mind

I believe that, properly understood, "tradition," education in and through a tradition, is not only essentially historical but also *essentially open-minded.* Both the Biblicist and the Enlightenment savant, on the other hand, are committed to ways of thinking that are *essentially closed-minded.* That is easily seen in the case of the biblical fundamentalist, but it is equally true in the rationalist case. Science, as the paradigm of rationalism, is open as a *strategy,* not as an essential characteristic. Despite all the discussion about the "tentativeness" of scientific inquiry, about the everlasting questing extolled by Professor McCauley, the fact is that in science, certain historical positions are definitively closed, refuted, abandoned once and for all. No one will revive phlogiston or Galen's physiology. Ideally, at the end of an infinitely long inquiry, science will reach surety and as firm a closure on Truth as any Biblicist.

Why is tradition *essentially open-minded?* "Tradition" means "giving over," handing on from one generation to the next, and it is there that any cultic, closed-minded interpretation collapses. It collapses through the very process that is the subject of this book: education. Take any cultural claimant: class, cult, clan, church, or culture. Each generation must *acquire* the dogmas and values of the "cult" into which it is born. If one is born into a special cult, that group must communicate *its* truths and values. This is the process we call education—or, more accurately, it is a process that needs finally to "collapse" into education. Unfortunately for the ideal of a cultic isolation, passing on (educating for) the cultic way of life undercuts its own dogmatic aspirations. It is not that one must abandon the beliefs of the special group; it is that beliefs into which one has been *educated* cannot be held in the "absolute" manner, which is the cultic temptation.

The best illustration of the inner failure of the dogmatic and isolating ideal is Socrates' scandalous suggestion of the noble lie in *The Republic*. Socrates is in the process of imagining an "ideal" state. If the state is to function well, different classes of citizens will have to display particular virtues and traits of character. The military (guardians) will have to believe that displaying courage in defense of the state is eminently worthwhile. Indeed, they must gladly die for this belief. Socrates lays out an elaborate program of training and education to inculcate courage in the guardians. They are not allowed to read "sacred scripture," which shows the gods acting in a cowardly fashion. What sort of example would that be for future warriors! It is important that warriors be true believers in their social role.

Having most carefully "educated" the various classes of citizens into their social roles, Socrates said that it is now necessary to convince members of each class that they were *born* into that role as "gold, silver, and brass" offspring. Being born to a "silver" role (the courageous soldier) establishes the necessity to act in the unequivocal manner to which the "cultic" society aspires. If the guardians were to realize that they had only *learned* these roles from others, they could well begin to wonder why they have these roles and not others, why these teachers and not others. Freedom of thought arises in the detachment between self and any role that we come to realize has been socially inculcated. If social education is the only way that special cults can be created, the very idea of cultural identity is threatened. Once education is self-consciously recognized, either the fact and devices of education must be shown to be an ultimate support of morality or any and all societies will dissolve in sheer skepticism about any proposed cult or belief.

(This is the next step in *The Republic:* at the beginning of the next book, Socrates' interlocutors become very interested in the community of wives already sketched out. They wonder how this sexual revolution will work. This raises the *real* problem of intergenerational continuity—no more lies about gold and silver babies—and is a new starting point for the dialogue, leading directly to the need for the reflective wisdom of the philosopher king. With the internalizing of philosophy, the love of wisdom, one learns that proper education can defend ethics by something more than dogmatic declaration or genetic fallacies. Practical wisdom is a possible subject matter. One need not accept Plato's specific curriculum for practical wisdom, but the basic issue is extraordinarily important: *does higher education inherently undermine/reinforce ethical value?* The Athenian court decided that Socratic "higher education" corrupted the youth of the city. *The Republic* is Plato's defense of higher education as the ultimate ground of value.)

Plato accepts an initial grounding of morality in social reality: philosophy does not overthrow that social training; it educates it. Socrates starts his inquisitions from "where the interlocutor is at," in his social role, at the gym, or in the market. The alternative "rational" strategy of the Enlightenment attempts to transcend the social (historical) inculcation of morality by grounding morality in Pure Reason. As the most profound philosopher of the Enlightenment, this was Kant's great purpose. But if *pure* reason is historically neutral, the morality will be that of angels, not of men and women. It is not clear that angels need a morality! Socrates' strategy is an ascending strategy from historical reality to critique and a "rational" ground for morals. Kant's is a descending strategy from rational insight somehow back down to actual history. I am not sure that the Sage of Königsberg ever makes it back.

The noble lie argument is roundly condemned as Socratic high-handedness, but it is interesting to note the persistence of arguments from natural determination in modern multicultural debates. One is not born gold or silver, but we are urged to believe that sexual orientation or gender wisdom is genetically determined. While that claim may have some validity, it is interesting that "education" into the special group remains a central issue. Feminists are urged to *discover* and *proclaim* their true female self, even though this "self" is supposedly given by nature. Whatever the "natural" base of the discovery of sexual ideology, it seems clearly to be subject to "education" in a manner that discovering biological sex difference is not. One discovers a separation of present self and sexual identity that makes the sex role "learned" at some level of function. Homosexuals are urged to discover and proclaim their true sexual character, not their biological reality.

Unhappily for dogmatists (denominational or multicultural), the demand to "raise consciousness," to join the true culture of women/blacks/homosexuals, inherently breaks the absolute character of the cult. What I have to *learn* is given not by nature but by teachers, by education. What I learn, I could unlearn. (For most oppressed groups, *unlearning* false stereotypes is critical to progress.) Once I believe that my values are what I have learned, I am placed in a situation of openness to those very values that I did not have when I thought that they just came with the natural territory as gold, silver, brass, female, male, and so on. I may now *choose* silver or female values, but to choose is to exercise freedom from the values so chosen.

One of my great, but terrifying, philosophical mentors, Richard McKeon (the professorial villain of Robert Persig's

Zen and the Art of Motorcycle Maintenance), argued for *education* in the following fashion:

> We have tended in our analysis of communication to reduce the minds of men to opinions and to neglect active attitude and ability by concentrating on what is passively received. Communication is education, and education should train men to judge all communication. . . .

Insofar as any cult or society must communicate/educate in order to make (its) truth known and effective, it unwittingly begins to create the "active attitude and ability" that is at the essence of "being educated." Being educated cannot be "passively having opinions." Education is a habit of mind relative to opinions, even one's own. The philosopher king has "opinions," but his or her habit of mind relative to the "opinions" has been established through the self-conscious awareness of what education can or cannot accomplish.

There are certain reflective "truths" that arise from appreciating the difference between having an opinion and having an *educated* opinion. One of the things that education cannot accomplish is bypassing communication; there is no *education* by pill, program, or golden, brass, black, white, male, female nature. Education as active ability establishes its own set of necessary "moral" values. I have already outlined the definitive moral assumptions of an educational community guided by a research ideal: no fraud or plagiarism, bring your mind to work, and do not confuse sex and science. Education in a *cultural* (moral, political, religious) way of life also requires necessary "moral" values beyond the specific moral content of the cult.

If scientific knowledge proceeds by assembling evidence and drawing conclusions, knowledge from a tradition assembles the extant tradition and draws its "moral" from the collection. The advantage of the scientific process is that it can and does manage to close issues definitively on the basis of evidence. The earth *is* round. Drawing "conclusions" from tradition has the disadvantage of depending on the historical "state of the art." One could come to certain general ideas about musical form after Beethoven, but along comes jazz—where does that fit?

Saint Thomas Aquinas—properly interpreted—is an example of a thinker-in-a-tradition. As a Christian, he is stuck with an odd assortment of Fathers of the Church who, as Abelard had shown in his scandalous *Sic et Non* (yes and no), disagreed on almost everything. Just to make it more difficult, Aquinas knew something of both the Jewish and the Muslim theological traditions, and they had to be assessed. On top of that, along comes Aristotle with a powerful "scientific" set of claims that hardly seem synchronous with the prevailing Platonic-Augustinianism. Aquinas sees his task as synthesizing the traditions, summing them, *Summa*ing them in an elaborate network of questions and answers. What Aquinas did *not* know about was the Buddha and modern biology—and lots of other things. As a thinker-in-a-tradition, he would necessarily be open to effective and powerful additions and challenges to the items in his own stock of science, theology, and moral insight. Just as the musical tradition cannot close down, so morality-as-tradition cannot close down. Again, it is important to emphasize that the open character of tradition does not mean that everything is up in the air—the transcendental air of the Enlightenment. One develops from the values-given-so-far until or unless one's tradition collapses from inherent contradiction or is overwhelmed by some countertradition or emergent reality.

If the university has some moral, cultural role, it is not to be realized by returning to a single dogma, presenting a jumble sale of ethical views, or delighting in the dance of diversity; it is to move students toward an (educated) attitude of mind toward all values—even and especially their most cherished values. Dogma, distribution, and diversity are all dead ends, half-truths, if they do not synthesize the givens of traditions of value using the rule that traditions are depositories of value *and* essentially open-ended to history.

Education as Moral Tradition

If there is to be any place for genuine moral education in the university curriculum, it will have to come from a curriculum of, for, in, about tradition. Denominational recitation and imitation freeze tradition; rationalist science finds no use for it. In neither set of assumptions could morality develop its inner rationale, any "reasons" for moral belief and conduct. If, as I believe, morality, like music, is essentially a tradition of performing that develops its own reflective reason, I would be more than prepared to defend religiously based, or ethically based, institutions of higher learning. A Catholic university genuinely exploring the meaning of its tradition—and morality as tradition—is not an aberration from higher education unless one is utterly committed to Enlightenment rationality, in which case both tradition and morality fail to register as worthy of discussion. Similar comments could obviously be made about a college dedicated to women's issues, ecological concerns, or social action—again, provided that it is genuinely *working* a tradition, not simply expostulating on the latest fashionable cause.

While recognizing the legitimacy of certain powerful moral traditions as principles for the curriculum, it is equally important to emphasize the *fundamental tradition:* the tradition *of* traditioning, that is, the tradition of education. Any sectarian or "sextarian" college legitimates itself not just by right of birth, but also by development out of its origins into an educating tradition of inner judgment and rationale. The "sectarian" tradition needs to reflect on the general fact of tradition-as-value-carrier. Traditional knowledge, wisdom, is essentially open to history; therefore, a value position that closes itself to history dies from inner contradiction, since it denies its own status and fundamental "method." Tradition is necessarily open to the potential challenge of alien traditions. The essential demand and "limitation" of working in a tradition lie in the realization that these (traditional) values are not from nature, but from education and history, and thus must always be open to education and history.

I have suggested that higher education is necessarily enmeshed in moral issues. Clearly, that was the case for the denominational colleges of yesteryear; clearly, that is the desire of multiculturalists, who seek to affirm their own ethnic values. It is also the case for the "scientific" ideal of the university if it implicitly denies "rationality" to morality, thus creating basic skepticism about moral value. Insofar as the university cannot help instantiating some moral stance—even if it is a demoralizing stance—it must understand itself within a tradition of education. One of the hoped-for lessons from this book is to reemphasize the history (and traditions) of higher education. The modern university, following its own roots in a priori rationality, often acts as if its current structural and pedagogic assumptions are absolute axioms, when they are, in fact, the results of social, cultural, and economic circumstance. By contrasting the denominational college with its research descendent, one may come to sense that there may be quite different cultural assumptions guiding education. The modern university, if it justifies itself by its own inner logic of science, may assume that it has utterly surpassed all the previous models in the manner that Copernicus surpasses Ptolemy. But the proper model for the university *tradition* would be to note that Stravinsky did not finally eliminate Bach from the musical canon. Reflecting on its own traditions, higher education might become less "dogmatic" about its own presumed moral "neutrality," if not downright dismissal of moral education.

A Pedagogy of Practical Wisdom

It is relatively easy, as stated earlier, to understand how one might add a thoughtful tradition to denominational beginnings. Denominationalists and diversity advocates start from the right place: historical origin. Bringing historical origin into the *university* setting is legitimated whenever reflection, review, and revision form articulate standards within a tradition of reflection. Christian revelation, the black experience, and female consciousness are not simple data, given whole and entire and infallible—despite the claims of dogmatists in each and every party. If one holds an *educated* belief, there is an assumption that the belief has an inner rationale and that this inner rationale can be communicated not only to those inside the tradition, but also, in some fashion, to those outside the tradition—no matter how lame and imperfect that communication may be. The alien in this case is at least theoretically in the same position as the neophyte in one's own tradition. Both need to be "initiated" into the tradition. Consider trying to initiate someone into an appreciation of classical music. There is some mystery in the process, but it is done. It is a combination of presentation *and* the use of the reflective and critical language that has developed about presentation. The reason that one must regard the alien like one's own neophyte is the general truth about education. Christian or Muslim, Whig or Tory, one is not *born* such; education is the fundamental vehicle of whatever tradition is at hand. Refusal to attempt communication to the alien denies the basis of one's own ongoing initiation, indoctrination, and elucidation.

Beyond deep appreciation of alien traditions, however, there is the profound, delicate, and extraordinarily complex assessment of the place of any moral tradition in "the world." If I accept or reject this or that tradition—or my own tradition—how does "the world" change? Alfred North Whitehead said that religion is "world loyalty." Insofar as morality creates a meaning for my life and actions, is it loyal to the world—or is the world loyal to it? The world-as-science is not loyal to any moral tradition, having transcended that concern into the angelic status of the mere observer. But if I am not a detached observer, but a participant actor, where and how do my actions fit the world I can shape and comprehend? It is not beyond belief that from such profound and searching questions, one may reject certain moral and religious traditions as the ultimate, no matter what their multiple insights and excellences. Practical wisdom, then, is the task of tradition and the assessing of traditions in the light of the reality revealed by traditions—including the world of science.

The continuing theme of this presentation has been the institutionalization of high ideals in higher education, in the universities and colleges we have at hand. Having praised practical wisdom, is it not an ideal so lofty and so deep that the Columbia officials were surely correct to oppose Jacobsen? Can one *institutionalize* practical wisdom?

To the extent that the dominant ideology of the university in either its rationalistic or its multicultural mode suggests that morality is *merely* a historical given, a subjective attitude, mere opinion (not educated opinion), it blocks the road to practical wisdom. Multicultural morality may be a dance, but it is not a deliberation. The multiculturalist, however, is more vulnerable to critique and correction, since, as I have attempted to show, no culture could exist beyond the primal scream without a tradition that perforce develops an inner rationale, a practical wisdom of the cult. Further, the very building of the cultic tradition necessarily acquires modalities of thought and appraisal that are characteristic of all traditions, are characteristic of tradition-as-education. One can move back down the structure from the general nature of tradition to the inner rationale of specific traditions, toward the initiatory experiences that are *culti*vated by the specific group. Obviously, this is a complex and extensive endeavor requiring patience and imagination, along with a keen critical sense that measures traditions against one another and the world within which they purport to "work." No wonder it is not one of those "rights and privileges" conferred at university degree ceremonies. Jacobsen was mistaken.

Is Practical Wisdom Practical?

The question to ask is not whether the university curriculum *arrives* at practical wisdom but whether it is even on the trail. As stated, an Enlightenment university *ideology* could defeat all practical wisdom, and that ideology may be expressed in the pedagogy of the place. The preferred pedagogy in the area of morality is what I have called *deparochialization*. By questioning and challenging the set beliefs of the student (assuming that by luck he or she has some), one is presumed to have pushed youth onto the Pathway of Prudence. Perhaps. Perhaps it "wakens him or her from dogmatic slumber," and that is a positive change. But if, having awakened our youth, all that follows is a dance of innumerable choreographies, a jumble sale of "choice," the last state may be even worse than the first. From dogmatism to diffusion in one set of distribution courses. Is there, then, some pedagogy for practical wisdom?

Practical wisdom is much more difficult to acquire than quantum theory, not because it is so esoteric but because it is so everyday. The very removal of quantum experiments from the everyday lends them a clarity and precision that is difficult to acquire in regard to value concepts, which occupy almost every waking hour. We pay as little self-conscious attention to our moral views as to our breathing—both of which are continuously at play. Because we are immersed in moral habits, ideas, and beliefs, we lack perspective on them. The at-hand character of value makes it particularly susceptible to evaporation (destruction) by a prevailing scientific turn. Quantum theory reveals the *reality behind the appearances;* it is a standard turn of science to show us something going on underneath the surface (atoms, genes) that explains some surface appearance. One may come to believe that this is the *key* strategy for intellectual investigation: find the reality behind the appearance. On the whole, this is a destructive approach to values, which are, in a sense, just what they are and not something deeper. If I "explain" moral conduct as sexual sublimation or genetic urge, I evaporate it as moral.

If looking for the reality behind morality-at-hand is a methodological mistake, a common pedagogical mistake is to look at situations that are "out of hand" as models of moral thought and action. There is a certain fascination about "lifeboat" morality—after the crash, is it moral for survivors to eat the bodies of the victims? Posing these outré situations presumably sharpens the wit for dealing with the ordinary case. I am suspicious. My first suspicion is that we work from the known to the novel in seeking solutions, not the other way round. Without some grounding in the big musical Bs, I would have no idea what to say about Karlheinz Stockhausen—not to mention John Cage. If we have a deep understanding about why we thank Grandma for preparing Thanksgiving dinner, we may come to understand why we should or should not eat our fellow passengers (deceased). My second objection is that lifeboat situations often pose genuine moral dilemmas, tragic situations in which any course you take is a bad one. If students come to take lifeboat cases as typifying moral decision problems, they may (1) be blind to the morality of the everyday moment or (2) decide that moral deliberation always ends in a hopeless, tragic dilemma where no clear right or wrong can be discerned. In a genuine dilemma, chance, luck, and impulse may be as good a guide to action as practical wisdom.

Charles Sanders Peirce, the most profound of American philosophers, said that he had learned philosophy by reading Kant's *Critique of Pure Reason* every day for four hours, for ten years. Just the thing! I assume, however, that, if reading Kant for ten years is my "synthetic solution" to practical wisdom in the curriculum, it is neither wise nor practical. Yet Peirce was onto something. The problem for the curriculum of practical wisdom is finally not discovery, distribution, and diversity; it is *density*. Peirce achieved density through the reiterative, ruminative reading of one of the most dense and structured treatises on the character of the human mind. In the long run, I think—and Peirce thought—that Kant did not quite get it right. But that was no matter, since he who finds it possible to disagree with Kant (after ten years) has moved ahead three places on the road to wisdom.

Can one create "conditions of density" in the undergraduate course of study? I suggest various ways, any and all of which exist ad hoc, here and there, from time to time in the American collegiate experience: concentration, cohorting, continuity, connection, commitment, conversation—I have run out of Cs.

Concentration

This may be no more than "catching the critter's attention." The scientific and technical curriculum necessarily occupies the student's attention because it is so different, esoteric, abstract, and difficult. She knows that she does not know the Krebs cycle, so she must pay attention and muster effort. The humanistic curriculum seems to be familiar territory that one "knows" already. The difference between calculus and ethics is like the difference between maneuvering in the Moscow subway system and moving about one's own household. The practical effect of this difference in managing the academic terrain is that the student will pay the least attention to what he believes he knows best. Calculus captures attention and time.

Given my own argument that morality is, in some sense, "already," one might make the mistake of thinking that it does not bear much time and attention. Yet nothing is quite as strange as the familiar. A professor colleague had the ingenious spiritual exercise of looking at something utterly familiar—like the face of one's spouse—as if it were for the first time. Then, since moral traditions are merely, magnificently the best we can cull from history, they are everywhere open to the enrichment and challenge of history. Nothing may be more important than that the student develop a deeply sensitive eye to the household of his or her own values. This is particularly the case given the discovery and deparochialization ethos of the modern university culture. Dazzled by all the reversals of common sense displayed in great science— the sun does *not* move in the heavens!—the student may be tempted to regard the common household of values as superficial and boring. Sadism is the true self! Or masochism? Or . . . ?

One of the strategies of a moral curriculum is to concentrate attention on the household of values at hand. One mechanical means of accomplishing concentration is to isolate a time for this meditation on the mundane and the moral. Colleges can offer terms devoted essentially to a single course (the Colorado College curriculum: a string of course sausages, not a stack of course pancakes; the short, single-course "winter term").

Cohorting

Beyond concentrating the time, it is beneficial to *cohort* the learning experience. Having to discuss values with others is like inviting a stranger to your house: she sees things that you have forgotten to notice and queries you about that ghastly wallpaper! Cohorting in turn requires some common curriculum. The common program may be a cohorted course, as in my fraternity course, or an extensive program, such as the Columbia University General Studies program, which occupies much of the initial two years at the college.

Continuity

The Columbia program adds a further C. (Jacobsen was half right—but he had the wrong university.) If moving to an *educated* morality is important—and I believe it is—this is a particularly difficult task not because it involves discovery of startlingly new revelations, but because it involves re-viewing the ordinary—as Jan Vermeer raises the mundane Dutch household to sublime art. One needs a continuity: a continuous, concentrated sifting and resifting to create insight and assurance. Extending the cohorted course over two years creates a continuous process.

Connection

If practical wisdom relates traditions to "the world," *courses* in ethics are essentially perverse. Insofar as ethical argument is located solely in the classroom, it will have only a literary relation to the "real" world. Nowhere is it easier to be a sheer ethical skeptic than in Phil. 101. It may even get you an A+ as a thoroughly deparochialized outcome. I was heartened, however, to read of an elementary ethics course at Boston College in which part of the assignment was working in a place of practical decision: law court, social service agency, government office. Ethical skepticism may rate well on the term paper, but it does not rate at all when dealing with divorce claimants or welfare policy. It is not accidental that Socrates chose the marketplace as the locus for ethical inquiry. Cohorting my fraternity friends and teaching *in* the fraternity placed talk in a place where ethical decisions and disasters often occur.

Commitment

I have already registered a demurrer on the Noble Teacher concept, but the time has come to pay tribute to the Noble Teacher. There are times, blessedly, in a student's course of study when he or she experiences a Noble Teacher: an individual obviously committed to a deep tradition of value. The committed teacher may well compensate for all the other Cs in my list. Jinx Harbison, after whom the teaching award was named, was just such a Noble Teacher, a deeply committed humanistic scholar who believed that "Ren & Ref" was not just a chance to view the oddities of the species, but also a pivotal time in history when the very meaning of human existence was at issue. I would not wish any of the complaints about the *university* as *ideology* to suggest that there are not hundreds and hundreds of Jinx Harbisons out there in the classrooms of the nation. There are, but they are not necessarily "displayed" in a manner commensurate with their message—which leads to my last C.

Conversation

One of the great paintings of the world is Georges Seurat's *La Grande Jatte* in the Art Institute of Chicago. For years, it hung in a small gallery room, where it properly dominated the space. Lately, it has been rehung indifferently in a long corridor in a row of paintings large and small. The latter display is a disaster. As one of my friends remarked, "It takes genius to take one of the world's great paintings and make it look cheap." The lesson for the academic curriculum should be obvious: how does one display the great moral traditions in a manner that does not cheapen their impact? If the university is only a "scientific" space, the austere palace of Pure Reason, displaying the peculiar historical artifacts of ethics and culture will seem only a curiosity in a cabinet, one of the exhibits in the "Unnatural History Museum" of human behavior.

One might analogize the modern university pattern of value studies to a great museum, full of magnificent works displayed in a higgledy-piggledy fashion. The contrast would be a museum with exactly the same works arranged in an order of dialogue. Both museums would contain greatness, but the latter would be constructed for the purpose of education. In the "educational" museum, landscape paintings would be displayed to enable the viewer to understand how they develop over time; the use of color, size, and spatial shapes would be instructively ordered to sense traditions of form, color, and line. The arrangement would place the works in "conversation." Lacking some sense of ordered conversation, one will fail to grasp rationality within the history of art.

The splendor of the Noble Teacher can therefore be dissipated or enhanced by the pedagogical space or, more prosaically, by the structure of *conversation* within a particular college or university. The "conversation" may be in the form of a coherent curriculum or in the conversational ambience of the particular place. Here let me pay tribute to the University of Chicago, which, in and out of season, has maintained a tradition of conversation that, in my experience, is distinctive and seldom found in other institutions. Given the diffusive specializations of the disciplines, it is no wonder that most institutions seem to operate as collections of soloists. The essential dialogue of values is defeated or deferred when faculty-faculty, faculty-faculty-student, student-student conversation is not present and vivid. In the heyday of learning from tradition, the Middle Ages, one of the major pedagogical practices was the public debates between scholars. Now one writes a scathing article to be published in Holland and read by two other specialists in Canberra.

None of my Cs alone or in combination will be the equivalent of Peirce's ten years holed up with Immanuel Kant. Undergraduate (or graduate) education can hardly contain the full "course" in practical wisdom. That is indeed the life task. The trick of any curriculum of practical wisdom is to create *belief in practical wisdom*. The choice is between diffusion and density. My negative judgment is that the research agenda moves naturally toward diffusion in the moral curriculum, to the naive deparochialization ideology of the present day. If the university takes up the task of practical wisdom, it will have to be by creating ethical conversation in coherent, concentrated, cohorted, connected, continuous learning patterns. By so doing, the university will present to students the fundamental conditions for the pursuit of practical wisdom.

In addition to its ethical value, the moral curriculum of the older denominational colleges was, as it happens, economically efficient. A compact student body of common believers, instructed in a common faith by a small faculty that taught almost everything in the curriculum, is essentially inexpensive. Mark Hopkins + the Bible + a log = the ultimate institutional downsizing. I turn from morals to managing the money.

11 Ultimate Synthesis: Money, Mission, and Management

At one point during budget debate in the faculty senate at Bucknell, a member of the faculty asked whether it would be helpful in my discussion with the board if the faculty voted to approve the larger of two salary recommendations. I suggested that at the least, it would not be informative. As Eugene Debs noted years ago, when it comes to salary negotiations, you only need one word, "More!" "More" may be the demand, but "Less" will be the answer in the financial crises that face higher education in the coming decades. Having mulled over the moral crisis of higher education, I turn to the easier task of managing the money crisis.

Money Talks: Economics and Eloquence

My "solution" to the moral issue is "density"—and I am certain that readers (if any) may well consider the solution *dense* indeed—philosophically convoluted and maybe just plain thickheaded. So be it, but before abandoning density for research distribution or multicultural dancing, I would point out that "density" can also address the economics and the (nonmoral) efficacy of higher education.

A concentrated, cohesive, cohorted curriculum is essentially an economical curriculum, since it reduces redundancy. A prescribed four-year curriculum may be a philosophical headache, but it is a fiscal relief. In theory, the "great books" curriculum of St. John's College in Annapolis approaches 100 percent efficiency in the factors of production, since all faculty teach in all parts of a common curriculum taken by all students—no pockets of esoteric and expensive specialties.

In economic terms, a fully prescribed curriculum constitutes a form of "command economy." In the real economic world, command economies are generally a disaster because no commissar can command sufficient knowledge of consumer needs and production supplies to make an efficient match. Free markets are by no means 100 percent efficient because suppliers make the wrong suppositions about sales—but the advantage of free markets is that the unlucky firms fail and go out of business. In command economies, one continues to send tractors to Novosibirsk whether they are needed or not.

The sharpest contrast to the "command-economy curriculum" can be found at Brown University, which approximates a "free-market curriculum." Students have virtually no requirements, even for a major. Students pick and choose courses with no constraint. Such a free-market curriculum would also be 100 percent efficient in the long run—except that there is no academic equivalent to bankruptcy. Departments or individuals not chosen by the student consumers do not necessarily go out of business; they continue in their previous tenured state. Because of tenure, a complete free-market curriculum is probably the most inefficient of all possibilities. The determinedly specialized skills of faculty exacerbate tenure; unlike in business firms, faculty do not get transferred from production to sales, that is, physics to classics. If Brown is *not* an economic disaster, it is because it controls its customers, if not its curriculum. The admissions office makes certain there are enough chemistry consumers in the freshmen class to match the faculty forces on the ground. One must be a "highly selective" university to choose your customers ahead of time. Most institutions have to control customer choice after the customers arrive.

Distribution courses and majors are a means of managing a free-market curriculum so that there is some flow toward areas and individuals less likely to be "purchased" by the consumer. While there is philosophical justification for distribution requirements, much of the motivation for maintaining the pattern is economic: making sure that each department has a directed shot at the student's time. Given the fact of tenure, some form of command-economy (core, distribution, customer selection) curriculum would seem to be essential. The contrast exists in community colleges, where prevailing philosophy—and tenure—is reduced to a minimum because of fundamental customer orientation.

The command economy of a cohesive curriculum may appear to share the faults of the real command economy, but not really. After all, there are 3,000+ American universities and colleges, and no one need advocate a single national curriculum. On the contrary, it would be a great benefit educationally and socially to have a true variety of cohesive curricula offered by competing colleges. As it is now, most institutions try to be all things to all customers: intellectual department stores. Running intellectual department stores offering every variety of good for all possible tastes is not only educational rummage but also an inherently expensive approach. Diversity should be *between* institutions, not necessarily *within* them.

It is highly unlikely—and undesirable—for most research universities to adopt anything like the four-year core (though it is worth noting that Hutchins's Chicago approximated this pattern while retaining a forefront position at the graduate and research level of study). However, even some lesser core or set of cores offers economic solace. For example, one of the perennial problems of productivity in higher education is what to do about courses with small enrollments. If it is judged that a small-enrollment course is not financially viable (or educationally essential), the problem remains of deploying the faculty member productively. Canceling small classes without reassigning the faculty decreases productivity. The presence of a core offers an opportunity for reassignment on the assumption that specialists should be able to teach in the broader areas of their discipline. (Perhaps even *outside* the discipline! There was a legendary—perhaps fictional—faculty member at Princeton who, on being reassigned from his special niche to a broad humanities core, gleefully told his students that he had never read any of the books assigned and had no intention of doing so. Their responsibility was to persuade him every week that he ought to have read the assignment!)

More important than juggling faculty is the fact that a coherent curriculum energizes the most underutilized university factor of production: students. Only in a concentrated, cohesive, cohorted curriculum (even if only a portion of the overall plan of study) can students educate one another. Whether it is Treisman's calculus students or my fraternity brethren struggling with Heidegger, the concentrated back and forth of student conversation is a powerful instrument for creating discriminating judgment.

The proper cohesive curriculum is particularly effective in addressing the most vocal complaint about contemporary graduates: they cannot read, write, or speak the common tongue, that is, English. Various studies that have been made about teaching writing indicate that the only sure method to improve writing is—surprise!—practice. Students need to write continually, have their work corrected, then rewrite, have their work recorrected, and so on. It is, I hesitate to say it, the "classical" curriculum's pedagogy of repetitive practice. (As noted, performance pedagogy in music is definitely about practice. Little girl with violin lost in New York: "How do you get to Carnegie Hall?" "Practice, practice, practice!" In the business world today, you get the same answer if you want to be Andrew Carnegie.) If students cannot read, write, or be eloquent, one contributing cause is the scattering of their studies and personal interactions, which works against repetitive practice. The value of the cohesive curriculum is that the authors "talk" to one another so that a nuance and density of language can be developed. And if the authors talk to one another, so can the students, thus developing articulateness around articulate exemplars. (I am assuming here a core in "ordinary English," not ordinary Engineeringese. Students are already significantly cored in the sciences; it is the disarray of the "ordinary language" curriculum that creates the perceived problems of reading, writing, and speaking.)

A Bucknell geologist friend took a field trip to Arizona with a group of undergraduates. The group drove across country in a van. My professor friend was concerned about how conversation could be sustained during that time. What would he have as a subject for conversation with these young people? It turned out that not only did he have difficulty finding a common topic, but also the students had equal difficulties—except for rock music. On that subject, they were eloquent and discriminating. (Unfortunately for my colleague, he was only interested in igneous rock.) The anecdote is telling. In an area of common experience and obviously much common talk, a language of nuanced appraisal had been developed. If contemporary grads cannot *talk,* it is no wonder. Aside from the Rolling Stones, they have little common subject matter on which to practice the art.

One can start, then, from economic efficiency, ethical interest, or eloquence and end up with a similar result: a concentrated, cohesive, cohorted curriculum. Obviously, a fully prescribed and cohesive curriculum will not do for every undergraduate. St. John's has always had to make adjustments for premeds, and it is not the route for an aspiring laser scientist. Admitting all that, the vast majority of students passing through American higher education do not directly pursue a career in the subject of their particular major, and if reports from outside the ivy walls are correct, what the majority of graduates lack is general literacy—and any knowledge of history and culture before the Beatles. This perceived lack is bad for business and the voting booth; a broadly coherent four-year general education could address those defects and would by no means disadvantage many graduates.

Disciplinary Diffusion and Distance Learning

The high cost of higher education (to the student or the taxpayer) *and* the perception that graduates cannot even handle basic English would strongly suggest that these instruments of learning (colleges and universities) could well be replaced with more efficient and effective mechanisms.

I noted early on that almost all of the modern curriculum developed *outside* the university institution. To the extent that the research university ideal is "scientific," it is sobering to consider that science led a highly productive existence outside and often in opposition to the universities for centuries. In contemporary South America, the physical sciences have often avoided connection with the universities, finding the bureaucratic and careerist culture of the institutions quite unsupportive. The conglomeration of various studies from physics to musicology in the complex institution of the modern research university is not something inherent in the various arts and skills. The rise of the mega-university probably proceeds as much from vast social and economic changes in families and factories as from the needs of the intellectual disciplines. I can only guess at the social forces that moved so much scientific and cultural firepower into the university. From the standpoint of the nineteenth century, such a concentration would have seemed bizarre. That those frail, feeble, dogmatic little institutions, attracting only a trace element of the population, would become the academic juggernauts of the present day would not have been believed.

If, then, the varied arts and skills that comprise our current universities have enjoyed life outside the academy in the past, and if the actual formation of the modern research institutions is as much a factor of social, cultural, and economic forces as the inherent need of the disciplines for deans and registrars and fraternities and the NCAA, one can certainly ask whether equally important changes in external factors at the end of the twentieth century may not presage the demise of the university-institution as now constructed. I would point to three potent factors for change: economic, technical, and cultural. Any of the three, and all in combination, may change higher education as profoundly as the research revolution of the previous century.

Economic Change

Adjuncts and beyond: money isn't everything when it comes to understanding the university. It is theoretically possible that a drastic reduction of funds for higher education will revive the monastic orders. New Age faculty will opt for poverty and chastity in order to pursue chemistry. The reader is entitled to have doubts. Assuming that the professionalization of faculty away from monastic and ministerial vocation is with us for the duration, the economic consequences of professionalization will have to be worked out within significant economic constraint. The principal effect of limited funds may further distance faculty professionals from specific institutions, which, after all, will be even less able to reward them financially than in the past. Since the *ideological* connection between faculty and institutions has already been undercut by allegiance to *discipline*, economic circumstance may sever this tie altogether.

Deinstitutionalization of faculty is not wholly conjecture; the trend is already clearly visible. One of the noted and much deplored phenomena of the present day is the rise of "adjunct" faculty. In the terms of *Yeshiva*, adjunct faculty are definitely *employees*. Adjuncts are non-tenure-track appointees, often working part time on ad hoc assignments to specific courses. Adjuncts are economical; they are only hired as needed, and as part-timers, they do not normally have access to costly fringe benefits. Adjuncts have been used by university management and acquiesced to by regular faculty as an economic expedient, but the practice is viewed as educationally undesirable. If "the faculty *is* the university," temporary faculty create temporary universities. Adjuncts therefore are not enfranchised to set academic policy; that is the prerogative of the tenure-track faculty. Like one's anesthetist, adjuncts are specialists who do a specific job and then disappear from ongoing life.

The rise of adjuncts may be seen largely as an objectionable management ploy to balance the budget, but regular faculty on their part may well respond to the new economics of education by quite a different mechanism. A clear example of a possible strategy would be the "franchising" movement in Great Britain. Suppose the University of Aberswych decides that it cannot afford to teach a specific discipline, so it franchises that area to the University of Bosthlewaite, whose faculty are more than happy to receive a portent of steady employment. The next step is obvious: the faculty at Bosthlewaite form a private consortium of physicists or paleontologists and franchise services in various locations throughout the United Kingdom. And if they are a private consortium selling services on a franchise basis, what exactly is the point of tenure at U.B.? Instead of a specific university having to load itself up with a permanent staff of faculty who may in time become redundant or dull, the university can contract with the Einstein Consortium to supply physicists. Physics and food services will be "outsourced." The economic advantages to the institutions seem obvious, and the economic advantages to the physicists could be equally favorable. By careful selection of the members of the consortium, the company can utilize staff with maximum productivity such that even with lower unit costs to the university for physics service, the income received by the consortium will be spread over a smaller employee base, thus maximizing individual salaries.

Adjuncts, franchising, shared appointments, and attenuated tenure all seem feasible, if not fully upon us, and all erode the assumption of an early chapter of this book: "the faculty *is* the university." A fully adjuncted or franchised university would be the creation of "management," with an eye on the market for services (students, business training, governmental research).

Technical Change

Beam it up! Someone will certainly object to the adjunct/franchising scenario on the grounds of sheer logistics. We are so used to the classroom instructor in a stuffy room with a piece of chalk at hand that it is difficult to realize that interactive television may allow the Einstein Consortium to deliver the product from a permanent central location. (That this is already done by large multinational corporations in their in-house training programs should be impressive to academic planners—though it probably is not.) The student may not be at any institutional setting at all, but safely at home preparing for final exams from the Open University. The economic advantage to the student over institutional learning is too obvious to mention. In short, economics has had a history of forcing technological change—at least where cheap replacement technology becomes available. The current higher education "technology" (physical locations called universities and colleges) is very expensive, an expanded apprentice system left over from the Middle Ages and the time before telephones. A technology that delivers the "same" education without the costs of dormitories, permanent staff, and campus security may prove economically irresistible.

If adjuncts and franchising loosen the connection between faculties and institutions, technology may, of course, eliminate faculty altogether. Some of the California state colleges have already agreed to give full academic credit for a precalculus course completely taught—including examinations—by computer. I have seen the product, and it is very "user friendly," even to the extent of adjusting the homework problems to the level of achievement displayed in the course of the lessons. The program has enticing and instructive graphics, and, of course, the great virtue of computer instruction is that the "instructor" will never lose patience and will give you just as much time as you need—or can stand. For any instruction that involves problem solving and drill, it is not clear that Mlle. C. D. Rom will not prove an attractive teacher. There goes half the French Department!

I am pessimistic enough to believe that the computer will not wholly eliminate people—even academic people—but the nature, role, and status of those who attend at those vibrant screens may be not at all like current university faculties and staffs. Even more realistic than college-by-computer is college-by-coaching. While it is true enough that one can learn a lot at a distance, experience over time does not suggest that it works all that well. One did not need television to create "distance learning"; the invention of books would have been sufficient. One can read almost anything that a computer can screen, but there have been few real autodidacts in the history of the species. Learning is often just hard work, boring drudgery, and repeated practice, for which a live, enthusiastic mentor may be a highly effective antidote. But these "mentors" do not by any means have to be rocket scientists; they are rather like athletic coaches, who, through a mix of regimen and rhetoric, carry athletes through the boring drudgery and repeated practice required to achieve athletic skill. All language departments and some mathematics departments have such a "coach" (most usually female), who is far from being an advanced scholar, but who has just the right mix of personality, basic knowledge, and pedagogical acumen to carry the student forward. Of course, as the complexity increases, the coach needs ever-increasing levels of knowledge, but one can proceed a considerable distance at the undergraduate level before a "research" level of skill is clearly productive of increased learning.

Cultural Change

Information can come from nowhere in particular. Economics may create the technology to replace located institutions, but it will require cultural acquiescence to accomplish collegiate demise. The modern university is a product of the research revolution, and that change in learning culture, the *meaning* of higher education, may offer a final push toward deinstitutionalization. It would be ironic if the revolution that created the mega-university also planted the seeds of the dissolution of learning into banks of PCs serviced by franchise faculties. (For a Hegelian, the failure of success is always assured.) Yet the seeds of that dissolution are inherent in the ideology of the scientific idea. Insofar as education is seen as acquiring certain bodies of knowledge—particularly knowledge that exists under the impersonal and abstract eye of the scientific observer—the reason for creating an at-hand physical college is diminished. The *moral* mission of the older denominational college had an essential tie to an at-hand institutional setting. To the extent that the aim of the older college was moral tutelage, that is something that cannot be accomplished very well by television—if for no other reason than the easy passivity of the viewer. If I do not like moral instruction on the tube, I switch stations. The older college was prepared to act *in loco parentis,* and while there may be learning at a distance, there is no parenting at a distance. If physics is the whole of life, it is difficult to see what "the Princeton experience" adds to quantum mechanics.

The university institution began in an era when faculty (vowed monks) were as inexpensive as one could imagine. Monks gave way to ministers, who earned their mite. The monks and ministers are gone—even modern Jesuits earn salaries—to be replaced by "professionals," who are appropriately expensive. Comes the present and future financial crunch, and expensive faculty professionalization is bound to be assaulted by adjuncts, franchising, detenuring, distance learning, and so on down the hill. If economics and technology make these assaults plausible, the social perception of the "meaning of higher education" may be the final blow to located-institutions-with-tenured-faculty. The wonderful universality of scientific knowledge may universalize the particular place (Prestige U.) right out of existence. While *information* is not the same as *knowledge,* the contemporary clamor of an information age, with information superhighways delivering data on every home screen, might well suggest that education is acquiring lots of information—for which a PC is less expensive than four years at UC.

If one is pondering the possible passing of universities and colleges because of some internal intellectual incoherence, it is well to recognize that the rationale for their specific existence may have absolutely nothing to do with research, teaching, learning, the arts, the sciences, and all that. Parents will continue to send students to the named institution, Prestige U., for the prestige. In a complex and supposedly "classless" society, one needs every assistance in standing out from the crowd on the road to success. Enrollment at Prestige U. is a definite plus— not *education,* just enrollment. A Japanese example is instructive. In Japan, there is ferocious competition to enroll in a prestige university like Tokyo University. On the other hand, it is generally acknowledged that, once the students are admitted, they do very little during the course of their "education." Of course, not every institution can sell prestige like Princeton or Tokyo, but a careful examination of college and university brochures will indicate that what is often being sold is the sizzle, not the scientific steak. (Sizzle = prestige, swell city, peaceful rurality, new swimming pool, etc.)

The complete deinstitutionalizing of rational research intellectuality is probably a chimera for inherently "intellectual" reasons as well. At the very highest reaches of any study or practice, there is a nuance of behavior and insight that is going to be conveyed only by immediate personal contact. Musicians pursue master classes to gain insight into the very highest levels of performance; scientists benefit from the immediate contact with research leaders, who overflow with productive ideas for lines of inquiry. So, in the long run, and at the highest level, nothing beats being there in person with the maestro or the Nobelist. The great research universities have one real distinction and advantage for the intellectually adventurous and advanced: they have no top, so that one may proceed from practicing pronunciation on a PC to writing a French novel under the tutelage of a resident artist. Properly realized in the specific university culture (and it often is not), the presence of cutting-edge, advanced research and breakthrough scholarship gives an excitement to the specific institution that may even compensate for a high prestige factor. A faculty member once opined to me, however, that at his institution, the undergraduate curriculum was what "seeped down" from the graduate program. An undergraduate curriculum of research seepage has little to commend it. The challenge for the research university—and for the research-oriented faculty at collegiate institutions—is to construct undergraduate programs that have a more vital connection to all that research. Trickle-down education is no better than trickle-down economics.

It is altogether plausible that the future of much of higher education will be supplanted by some combination of economic, technological, and cultural shifts. One could imagine the simultaneous opening in twenty major cities of Microsoft Colleges, with programmed instruction, interactive video instruction, and friendly at-hand coaches and technicians. While I think that the price for higher learning (information?) can undermine the rationale for located, named institutions of higher learning with departments, tenured faculty, and musty libraries, it probably will not happen. There will be significant inroads, and perhaps some subtle shifts, which may finally emerge as radical change, but it is altogether likely that the landscape will continue to be dotted with the Harvards, Slippery Rocks, and St. Swithinses. Just *what* they will be teaching, and *why*, is the mystery. Harvard was "Harvard" when the curriculum consisted of Demosthenes and Paley's *A View of Evidences of the Christian Religion;* it would still be "Harvard" if it taught Derrida, deconstruction, and Shirley MacLaine's theology. The issue is this: will we drift from Demosthenes to Derrida or decide on new directions under some plausible educational principles? And *who* will decide?

The University *Is* the University

A large overall concern of this book has been the management of universities, an issue made acute by the financial constriction at hand and forecasted for higher education. Financial crisis forces some sort of management, but whether it is educationally wise, driven by inner mission or external market, will be crucial to the future of the historical institutions we call colleges and universities. Some simple economics might well suggest that these institutional frameworks are on the road to obsolescence. One can easily construct a technological scenario that makes the university *library* obsolescent; why not the university overall? Powerful political, economic, and social interests may keep the library and university in business—no one has yet solved the economics of copyright when anything can be obtained on-line. Closing down your local college puts a lot of people out of work, and prestige is not instantly constructed. But if the rationale is only politics, the local economy, or prestige perception, the university institution is ultimately vulnerable to those notoriously variable conditions.

It is entirely possible, in my judgment, that any one of the above factors will be sufficient to dissolve the universities with as much finality as Henry VIII dissolved the monasteries. What I would not like to see is the universities conspiring in this dissolution—but it is just such an unwitting acquiescence in evaporating universities that the modern culture of academia makes possible. To repeat a much-repeated repetition of this argument: the modern university as a *research faculty* university is neutral to institutional existence. This is an ideological claim; it obviously does not apply to all—or perhaps any—actual individual professors, associates, assistants, and so on. Faculty, like other members of the human race, become attached to familiar surroundings; they have to be *somewhere,* and on the whole, these cozy cloisters are nicer than most alternate locales. The problem is that faculty, like students, may be attached to a specific place for reasons quite irrelevant to the inner rationale of their professional expertise. Prestige is as important to professors as to parents of prospective students!

The initial "half-truth" in this book has been its governing motif: "the faculty *is* the university." If the *faculty* is wholly defined as the research revolution and Enlightenment rationality would have it, then the resulting institution is inherently unmanageable. Or, less pessimistically, the university is only a "nominal" institution, a loose conglomeration—hardly even a confederation—of trades and skills. There may be extrinsic reasons why a particular configuration exists at a particular time—for example, these skills are needed by external markets—but there is little inner rationale. It may seem better and cheaper to pass French teaching off to Berlitz and physics to the Bell Labs. For the reasons mentioned above, I do not expect the universities and colleges of the land to be dissolved into industrial training and TV instruction. Rather like shopping malls, they may continue to exist, peddling all sorts of wares whilst discarding what non-sellers they can. Sheer inertia and nostalgia will probably keep physics and philosophy in the catalogue. Higher education will muddle through.

Muddling through may be the "answer," but it seems a sorry state for a collection of folks who claim such high rational ground. Surely, one would like to believe that there is some inner philosophy that guides the destiny of higher education. To discern such a "philosophy," however, one would have to begin by denying my lead "half-truth." Instead of "the faculty *is* the university," one would have to assert that "the university *is* the university." (Since the latter is a tautology, it is obviously a whole truth!)

The problem with whole-truth tautologies is that they are true but empty. What is being asserted? Simply that the institution should have a specific *mission* and that the mission overrides appointment, tenure, departmental program, and all the associated extracurricular paraphernalia. Don't all universities and colleges have missions? They do have mission *statements,* but as a long-time reader of these statements, my sense is that they seldom say anything specific enough to offer policy direction (Cohen and March's point that the goals are so lofty that no one can be sure they are ever accomplished). The mission is "excellence": appointing "leading" faculty, recruiting "talented" students, educating them for "productive" lives of "leadership" in the nation and local community, and so on. The key terms commend without content: what sort of "excellence"? Are "leading" faculty established scholars, avant-gardists, feminists? Is leadership of the nation exercised in the halls of Congress or on the CIO picket line? Few of the latter are grads of Prestige U. The mission statement will eliminate the dull and disastrous, but one hardly needs a pompous statement to do that. MIT and FIT (Fashion Institute of Technology) have *content* missions that direct the customer's choice. If one has a fuzzy mission for "excellence," there may be no way to differentiate Siwash from Hogwash.

There are, despite these negative comments, what Burton Clark labels "distinctive" colleges—but they are few. Swarthmore, Haverford, Reed, Antioch—most women's colleges, historically black colleges—are examples of institutions with a "saga." The saga is the expression of a mission-with-content. As Clark notes, faculty and students who attend a distinctive college are absorbed into the saga; the institutional saga uses them, rather than their using the institution for some extrinsic end. The saga of the distinctive colleges is "moral" in the largest sense: it creates a specific character. The character may be "the intellectual" (Swarthmore), but the "(Swarthmore) intellectual" is not merely a talented brain; he or she is someone who believes that intellectuals should play a leading social role.

Institutional mission and saga are not always easy to define, and they will (should) vary considerably among institutions. Roughly speaking, however, the saga flows from a special historical placement for that specific institution. An illustrative anecdote: Bryn Mawr, a tiny college compared to almost any, graduates approximately 5 percent of all the women physics graduates in the entire nation. Bryn Mawr's mission has been women's education at the very highest level. What saga leads to the results in physics? Because Bryn Mawr has cross-registration with Haverford and Swarthmore, which are coeducational, there are men in most of the Bryn Mawr classes. But not in Introduction to Experimental Physics; that is a course for women only. Why? Introduction to Experimental Physics is actually Introduction to Gadgets; students have to construct, wire, and solder. It turned out that, when the men were in the class, the male saga of Mr. Fixit took over and intimidated the female students. (Even Bryn Mawr women can be intimidated!) Women are, of course, every bit as good—if not better—at wiring and soldering, except that it was not part of the "normal" female saga. Once the women were introduced into the soldering saga, they continued brightly on to produce the surprising statistic.

If mission-with-content creates saga, the saga may be expressed in either content or form—or probably both. The Bryn Mawr Intro to Gadgets involved form and dealt with the *conditions of learning*—a topic discussed at length earlier. The physics faculty were not more charismatic teachers for expelling the males, but they were acutely sensitive to a condition of learning for women students. A saga of "form" may be neutral to content. What was being taught was just physics as physics; this was not physics for poets or female physics; it was the same stuff taught at Cal Tech.

On the other hand, one may develop a saga of *content*. "Specialty" curricula, such as engineering, music, art, and design, all have dedicated missions that may generate a proper saga of content—though content alone may not develop a *learning* saga. Content alone did not develop Bryn Mawr's physics learning saga *for women*. The example of two art museums— one arranged to teach a lesson, the other as a random collection—suggests the difference. Both museums have the same *content*, but the pathway through the content of one is not supportive of learning. The ideal situation is one where specific mission is translated into a crafted saga of content and form related to the potential student. Science may exist in the transcendent; students are historical particulars. The more a university crafts its physics to the student, the more it creates a special saga—and justifies its institutional existence.

Clark's "distinctive" institutions are all relatively small colleges; can a large university also have a saga? Probably not *one* saga, but it could well have several clearly defined pathways in content and/or form through the institution. A clearly defined school or schools of social science or a natural-science-and-engineering saga at a larger institution would be educationally efficacious and create economies of cooperative instruction that seldom exist across departmental divisions. I know one engineering department that finally gave up on the same institution's mathematics department as a reliable tool for developing the skills of engineers. Engineering and math were not in the same saga.

My higher educational ideal for the future would be a proliferation of "distinctive," mission-driven institutions. One does not, of course, need three thousand different missions; a women's college in Oakland, California, may be similar to one in Northampton, Massachusetts. But within some general geographic distribution, professed mission would create rational choice for students and parents. Sharpening the mission of the institution directs resources economically. Failure to focus on a truly directive mission opens the institution to the diffusion and dissipation of both the disciplines within and the market without. Mission defines the institution and can create a distinctive market niche. Mission is a powerful barrier to the sheer power of the undifferentiated market; belief in a distinctive mission can energize an institution to find its constituency. Mission may, of course, fail; many women's colleges have found that despite a proven record of success and cogent arguments for the special power of a single-sex institution, they cannot prevail against the unisex revolution. There is no reasonable choice but to change mission (admit the men) or close the memorial gates. There is no metaphysical law that decrees that every college must continue "as long as grass grows and water runs."

The modern research universities and their collegiate cousins "just growed," and now that they are faced with economic restriction, they can either focus on a directive and content-rich mission or succumb to whatever market thinks it can use their services. Market dismemberment is aided and abetted by the level of arbitrariness involved in collecting the disciplines at hand. To the extent that the varied fields are either inherently unrelated or distant from institutional mission, they are each and every one expendable to the budget. (While it is true that physics needs mathematics, it is not true that it needs math at hand and at the research level. For undergrads, enthusiastic calculus tutors could be more valuable than a Fels Prize superstar. And if one is into high-level math-physics collaboration, you are more likely to have the Fels Prize winner in your Internet chat group than across the quadrangle. And so on with variations across all the "linked" disciplines.)

The research university rests on the ascendency of disciplinary faculty as the definers of higher education. Academic tenure is not just a guarantor of free expression and an economic benefit; it also signals ownership rights over the curriculum. But if the market calls the curricular tune, the rationale for tenure is eliminated, since the consumer now owns decision rights over what is to be taught. Mission as an internal principle for management buffers the market, but mission cannot be a mere tabulation of academic disciplines on the ground. If institutions are to be mission driven, *internally* governed, this will not be the equivalent of the current interpretation of "the faculty *is* the university." The university (mission) *is* the university; the saga *is* the principle, and faculty are subject to the saga. The faculty may help to shape, refine, and modify the saga and mission, but to do so calls for a perspective that transcends a mere additive vision of the parts. This view of the whole, the shaping of a saga, is not something for which the PhD degree is an obvious preparation.

Managing to Mission: The Necessity of History

Institutions with a mission will not be run by Franciscan missionaries, so there will be a face toward the market, but mission-directed management involves testing and adjusting mission and explaining and justifying mission to influence the market, not letting the market directly dictate mission. The research university revolution established a strong *internal* principle for managing higher education: the curriculum and course of study are decided by discipline-oriented specialist faculty. Faculty *internal* direction was seen as counter to the *external* influence of the traditional denomination or the political and economic views of powerful trustees or interest groups. Academic freedom and internal direction formed an essential linkage. Giving away internal integrity would be a sorry next step in the history of higher education.

If the research revolution is right in asserting the need for academic integrity and internal "management," it is only half right in interpreting that internal management as the cumulative outcome of various more or less unconnected disciplines—particularly if the disciplines are all cast in the model of natural science. Science has its *scientific* mission, discovery of truth, but that mission is as indifferent to the university's *institutional* mission as balancing the food service budget. *Institutions* are necessarily historical, tied to some set of particular social, political, and personal needs—precisely what science transcends (for good reason and with good results). The historical roots of institutions are the source of *institutional* mission. Failure to both support free science and balance the budget will destroy the university, but for all that, providing science labs or three meals a day is not the rationale for the existence of a specific institution.

Institutions are rooted in history, and missions are connected to specific histories; the dehistoricizing tendency of the natural sciences is, in its subtle fashion, one factor in deinstitutionalization. If, then, institutions are to be guided by *mission,* they need to seek for institutional ground elsewhere than the fact that "science is done here"! I suggest that this is true even if one were to confine the course of study to the natural sciences. The Bryn Mawr example is appropriate: it is a college for *women.* The institution was founded at a time when women were excluded from the most advanced studies. Bryn Mawr's founding aspiration was to provide for women an education every bit as sophisticated as that then available at the Johns Hopkins University, the premier American research university. My contemporary tale about the Bryn Mawr physics program indicates that the historical mission to women remains as its basic institutional saga. Physics may be transcendental; women are historical realities. So even if the whole curriculum at Bryn Mawr were natural sciences, the institutional mission would be grounded in the historical needs of a special population. Similar remarks could obviously be made for historically black colleges, Native American institutions, religiously sponsored colleges, and so on.

Because universities are *teaching* institutions, they become historically engaged with the historical reality of the students attendant. This may be strikingly obvious in a women's college or a black institution; it should be no less a concern in every collegiate institution. Not the least of the historical factors is the age of the students; if science does not speak to the male or female, Asian or African mind, it also does not speak particularly to the adolescent mind. Nevitt Sanford's voluminous study of the academy and its relationship to adolescent development,

The American College, received scant attention from the profession. I would suggest that it is because the academic mind has a hard time de-transcending toward the historical particulars in the front row. (Sanford claimed it was because the book was too heavy for college presidents to carry onto airplanes.) At the bare minimum, therefore, universities establish missions based on teaching responsibility—or, as I would prefer, based on establishing the conditions of learning that are productive for the actual men or women or minorities or geniuses on the quad.

Students may be the historical tug that converts pure physics into physics instruction for women, but the content of the curriculum remains undetermined. There may be similar problems teaching cost accounting to women and ballet to men. Why do colleges teach physics and not fly fishing (not an uncomplicated skill)? What is the difference between the manual dexterity of the fly caster and the flutist (at Eastman, Oberlin, Peabody, etc.)? In Mozart's day, musicians were regarded as below valets in the employment hierarchy. Frankly, that is not a question I propose to answer. I only suggest that it cannot be answered *for university institutions* on the basis of the inherent value of knowledge; I fear that God and country will be back in the act if one is to address that properly. Finally, the justification for the traditional "liberal arts" studies at colleges and universities rests on deep moral and political foundations. Because the modern university is both wary and weak on moral argument, it is also poor at articulating the basic values that justify its own choice of studies. Lacking much depth on its own *value* choices (the curriculum), the university almost inevitably reverts to external economics or internal politics to guide decisions.

The Faculty *Is* the University! *Which* Faculty?

The initial and guiding half-truth of this book was the claim that "the faculty *is* the university." The claim is a *half*-truth if the faculty we have in mind are simply the creatures of the learned disciplines. Since I believe that it is vital that faculty define the institution as a guarantee for academic integrity, it will be necessary to redefine—or refine—faculty understanding so that it is *institutional* faculty who constitute the *institution.*

One of the oddities of arts and science faculties, the core faculties, of colleges and universities is the monolithic assumption about faculty roles and tasks. All faculty are somehow the "same": all follow the same time track to tenure; all have equal voice (more or less) in institutional decisions. (It is typical of the AAUP that in its recent statement about downsizing at St. Bonaventure University, it criticized the fact that, although restriction had been thoroughly vetted with select faculty committees, not *all* faculty were consulted about the proposed changes.)

I was particularly struck with the "oddity" of a single track for all faculty when I became president at Rochester and contrasted the faculty structure at the school of medicine with that in the school of arts and science. Medicine had three distinct faculty tracks, labeled (imaginatively) A, B, and C. A-track faculty were *clinical* faculty who saw patients and acted as practitioner tutors to students; B-track faculty combined practice with research, often clinical research; C-track faculty taught classes and did more fundamental research (sometimes practice as well). A-track faculty never received tenure, B-track faculty received it only at the full professor level, and C-track faculty followed the standard seven-year evaluation pattern of the arts and science faculty and received tenure as associate professors. It seemed to me that the medical school designation of differential faculty tracks was most appropriate to the differing and necessary tasks within medical education.

Some analogous refinement of types of faculty appointment in the core areas of the university would be beneficial and could be structured to create a class of *institutional* faculty about whom one could say, "*This* faculty *is* the university." Traditionally, universities state that the tasks of the faculty are teaching, research, and service. These functions could be clearly designated by differing faculty tracks along with appropriate definitions of rights and rewards. Some of the larger and wealthier institutions designate certain faculty as "research professors." These individuals may do some teaching, but it is usually in highly specialized areas to a few student apprentices. "Teaching professors," however, are seldom so designated—probably because one assumes that everyone teaches. Nevertheless, reality would suggest that, as there are research professors who do some occasional teaching, there are great teaching professors who do occasional research. (Like the B-track medical faculty, it may be more "clinical" than cutting edge.) Then, of course, there are the model faculty who supposedly are brilliant at scholarship and on the lecture platform: great researchers and teachers.

What does not exist at all, to my knowledge, are "service professors"—that is a nice extra, not a necessity. Yet, in theory at least, it is those faculty members with a sense of "service" who have appropriated the saga of the institution; they are serving not only their discipline in the abstract, but also the discipline-to-these-students, the discipline-in-the-reality-(financial/ethical/social)-of-this-institution. (Not every faculty member who appears to serve—e.g., on policy committees, in the senate—is someone who serves the *institutional* saga. On the contrary, he or she may "serve" only to advocate a special disciplinary interest or a personal gripe. A true "service professor" would demonstrate a keen awareness of and allegiance to the large historical mission of the institution as it impacts his or her own academic specialty, and vice versa.)

I would then add one more letter to the faculty tracks: A (research), B (teaching), C (teaching and research), D (research and/or teaching + service). The University of Chicago has had for some time the title "distinguished service professor," and one could borrow the title, if not the description. "Distinguished service professors" would hold tenure appointments because of distinguished research and/or teaching and would have demonstrated over time a special comprehension of and concern for the mission of the institution: the historical reality of Bryn Mawr or Berkeley or Bloomsburg. Appointment to this rank would carry special salary and privileges in setting policy for the university.

Differentiation of faculty would allow a more differentiated salary scale overall, which would be another boost for the budget and could avoid the unhappy resort to adjuncts. Differential tracks would, of course, raise the specter of "second-class citizens." It was part of the genius of the Rochester medical tracks that, *if* there were second-class citizens—and I am not sure that there were—they were the A-track faculty! I believe that one could construct an even more elaborated set of tracks than here suggested without stigmatizing anyone if one accepted the obvious truth that there are lots of different and essential tasks in higher education. It is not generally accepted.

I end, then, where I began: "the faculty *is* the university"— but the faculty that is the institution is a faculty engaged in "distinguished service" to *institutional* mission, not just distinguished service to *disciplinary* mission. Creation of such a cadre of faculty suggests not only different promotion policies but also different patterns of "faculty formation," beginning in the graduate schools, where PhD students aiming toward teaching careers would be expected to study the historical and philosophical roots of the institutions of higher learning in which they would be pursuing their intellectual interests. Colleges and universities, in turn, should take seriously the acculturation of faculty into the special mission and saga of the institution. Faculty who demonstrate a special interest in the "service" side of their role, those who pursue the D track, would be given the opportunity to attend programs such as those run by the Harvard Institute for Education Management to gain a deeper insight into the structures of academic institutions. The individual university would have specific ways of nurturing these faculty toward a complex and well-grounded view of the specific institutional mission in the context of the social, economic, educational, and political realities that impinge on institutional decision making.

Mission-guided "distinguished service faculty" would have authority over areas now regarded as sacrosanct to the individual disciplines. Because the service faculty would enter into the institutional *mission*—guarding, shaping, refining, and maybe even changing it—they would have final authority over appointment and tenure, curriculum, disposition of departmental resources, and teaching.

Do I expect mission, management, money, and morals to synthesize into the ideal university? I am not that much of a Hegelian! The political cost of changing entrenched interests is staggering; I cannot imagine any extant faculty rushing to create the rank of distinguished service professor with all *those* rights and privileges! But if the structure is fantasy, the practical need is not. Those institutions in which faculty and administration truly conjoin to maintain an articulate mission will be the success stories—if not just the survivors—in the years ahead. Whether the "conjunction" is formalized or simply part of the local collegiate culture, the alternative is simply more *non-faculty* management: a necessary increase in the action of presidents, boards of trustees, or state authorities in the determination of institutional policy. If the twentieth century has been the century of *faculty*, the twenty-first will be the century of *administration*. The issue that faces higher education is whether current faculty expectations and education will allow them to join in with administration or cause them to fight a generally losing battle against the social and economic forces that have created the need for decisive institutional direction.

In the terms of my initial disclaimer, the visible outcome for higher education is likely to be muddle. This is particularly probable because of the ability of higher education to live so comfortably with undigested hyperbole. Realities change; the rhetoric remains. But even in the midst of muddle, it may be useful to know what forces constitute the confusion. And, finally, while muddle may define the short term, some of the economic, technical, and cultural factors cited will, I believe, prove so compelling that we may well look back on the end of the twentieth century as a period of academic revolution truly as profound as the research revolution of the century past. Then we will ask, "How did *that* happen?" And we are not likely to think then that the *that* that happened was educational advance.

References, Acknowledgments, and Afterthoughts

This is not a book of and for footnotes. I prefer that the reader move on through the text unhampered by apparatus. Many of the examples stem from my own experience as faculty member, administrator, accreditor, and so on; I have tried to use personal anecdotes to illustrate broader characterizations of university life. It is appropriate, however, to indicate some source material. The general history of higher education, contrasting the nineteenth-century denominational college with the twentieth-century research institute, is a commonplace of historians. Frederick Rudolph's volume was my introduction to this history and remains an eminently readable and succinct account: Frederick Rudolph, *The American College and University* (New York: Knopf, 1962). Laurence Veysey, *The Emergence of the American University* (Chicago: University of Chicago Press, 1965), is the standard chronicle of the research revolution in higher education. Charles Wegener, *Liberal Education and the Modern University* (Chicago: University of Chicago Press, 1978), is unique in its attention to the basic philosophical and institutional assumptions that guided some of the great founding presidents of the new universities. George Marsden, *The Soul of the American University: From Protestant Establishment to Established Nonbelief* (New York: Oxford, 1994), announces in its title the extraordinary conversion (reversion, perversion) of the "soul" of higher education. Finally, Philip Gleason, *Contending with Modernity* (New York: Oxford, 1995), is a meticulous and revealing account of the persistent, largely losing battle of Catholic higher education against the inroads of the new university mentality.

The book takes its epigraph from an essay by Burton Clark in a volume he edited, *Perspectives on Higher Education: Eight Disciplinary and Comparative Views* (Berkeley and Los Angeles: University of California Press, 1984). I find Clark's collection particularly valuable because of the international character of the essays—several by non–United States authors—and because of the clarity that emerges from structural analysis around such areas as politics, economics, status, and the influence of science in and out of the institution. Several of the key quotations and opinions in the book come from this volume.

Full-Face Preface

The comment about the positive role of administration in the American university context is contained in Henry Rosovsky's charming *The University: An Owner's Manual* (New York: Norton, 1990). I applaud the humor in the title, but I am not sure that there are any "owners." That is a major theme of my presentation.

I hardly think it necessary to "bibliographisize" all the various critiques of the university made within the recent past. The weightiest physically and philosophically remains Allan Bloom, *The Closing of the American Mind* (New York: Simon and Schuster, 1987). Bloom's book was a best-seller, but I have a hard time believing that it had as many readers as it had buyers. The first and last chapters are richly invective, but the vast middle part struck me as a lugubrious downward path toward Nietzsche. Bloom was a great admirer of Plato; thus, it seems most peculiar that he should think that modern philosophers (or faculty) invented moral relativism. I thought the ancient sophists and their pupils—Socrates' frequent antagonists and interlocutors—had first claim on "man the measure of all things."

Chapter One: Anyone for Higher Education?

For anyone more interested in God than higher education: George Dennis O'Brien, *God and the New Haven Railway: And Why Neither One Is Doing Very Well* (Boston: Beacon Press, 1986). (The book didn't do so well either.) Although my work is critical of "faculty," it is on wholly different grounds than those alleged in Charles Sykes's muckraker, *ProfScam: Professors and the Demise of Higher Education* (Washington, D.C.: Regnery Gateway, 1988). If modern faculty have vices, they are the vices of their virtues. For Sykes, it is vice all the way down.

The quotation regarding the development of science outside and even opposed to the university is from an essay by Harold Perkin on the historical development of universities (in Clark, *Perspectives*). Perkin offers a very perceptive commentary on the vagaries of the university's long history within the British context. For anyone interested in the mess surrounding the non-establishment of a Catholic university in Ireland according to the Newman Idea, see Louis McRedmond, *Thrown among Strangers—John Henry Newman in Ireland* (Dublin: Veritas, 1991). Newman could not abide Irish food; the bishops could not abide his Idea.

Chapter Two: The Faculty *Is* the University

William Rainey Harper's always interesting views on his new University of Chicago and the whole "research" movement are well detailed in Wegener, *Liberal Education*. Emerson's comment about the University of Rochester "improvising like a picnic" may have deeper, broader, and more permanent import than he intended. Research mega-universities do seem to have improvised with some of the abandon of a Sunday picnic. The University of Rochester actually followed a very different path toward its position in the AAU crowd of research universities and, as such, may be more internally managed than most. But that is another treatise—and the subject of all too many speeches while I had the privilege of presiding at the U of R.

Chapter Three: Tenure Is a Necessary Condition of Academic Freedom

For the founding documents of AAUP, see Richard Hofstadter and Walter Metzger, *The Development of Academic Freedom in the United States* (New York: Columbia University Press, 1955). Fred Crosson's most interesting article on academic freedom and institutional homogenization is in Theodore M. Hesburgh, ed., *The Challenge and Promise of a Catholic University* (Notre Dame: University of Notre Dame Press, 1994). As usual and always, *The Chronicle of Higher Education* is a source for documentation on items such as the Angela Davis case, the Charles Curran case at Catholic University, and all sorts of commentary continuously on the pros and cons of tenure.

Chapter Four: Universities Are Neutral on Moral Value/Universities Teach Moral Value

The comment on Nathaniel Eaton, from Harvard, comes from Lawrence A. Cremin, *American Education: The Colonial Experience 1607–1783* (New York: Harper Torchbook, 1970). This is also the source of information about Mrs. Eaton's cooking alluded to later in the text: "Meatless meals, which featured sour bread and dry pudding." The quotation from Charles Seymour of Yale is found in Marsden, *Soul.*

Chapter Five: The Liberal Arts Curriculum Aims at Distribution/Diversity

In *Education and Identity* (San Francisco: Jossey Bass, 1969), Arthur Chickering goes on to describe "horse and buggy" education as well as "junkyard" education—his preferred mode.

The section dealing with Bryn Mawr and the definition of "diversity" appeared in a chapter of a previous work—George Dennis O'Brien, *What to Expect from College* (New York: St. Martin's Press, 1991)—and is printed here with permission. I am hard pressed to point to a prime source for the various deconstructionist, multicultural, politically correct movements rumbling across the American collegiate scene. I assume that the general notion behind these movements is familiar enough from the popular press and the multiple complaints lodged against PC urges.

Chapter Six: Teaching Is the Primary Task of Higher Education

My information regarding Uri Treisman comes from personal conversation and from documents prepared by the Charles A. Dana Foundation, which presented him with an award for outstanding educational innovation. My former colleagues at the Simon School may be nonplussed by my expressed admiration for the care with which they constructed their curriculum. (All is forgiven!) One of my more depressing moments in office was a breakfast with the chair of the curriculum committee from the Simon School and his opposite number from the Arts and Science College. The latter listened patiently to the description of the Simon School plan of study but replied that this would not do for arts and science because *there was no aim* for undergraduate arts and science education. This claim is true if one concentrates only on disciplinary *content*—obviously, physicists know things that economists do not, and vice versa. However, there are certain broad skills of clarity of expression, problem solving, and such that might well connect across disciplines and give overall shape and direction to the curriculum. Finally, admitting no aim would suggest that there can be no overall dialogue between the disciplines. (Fortunately, curriculum planning did not end with that breakfast.)

Chapter Seven: The Problem with Higher Education Is the Administration

Since the Yale University incident cited, a new administration seems to have had more luck in seeking some budgetary restriction. Perhaps one president (at minimum) must be immolated before serious budget action can be undertaken. The classic (and ironic) study of higher education as an MBO non–case in point: Michael D. Cohen and James G. March, *Leadership and Ambiguity: The American College President,* 2d ed. (Boston: Harvard Business School Press, 1986).

Chapter Eight: Low-Cost Public Education Benefits the Least Advantaged

I would like to have clearly authenticated figures on the family income differential between SUNY and the private colleges and universities of New York. Indirect evidence of the inverse discrepancy has been generated from time to time by the Commission on Independent Colleges and Universities in New York. The comparison quoted by the state senator was purported to be from the New York State Department of Education, which, he said, was reluctant to make the figures public. I am convinced that such a discrepancy does exist, however, given the factors that are driving choice as well as examples elsewhere, for example, Puerto Rico and the World Bank study: International Bank for Reconstruction and Development, *Higher Education: The Lessons of Experience* (Washington, D.C.: The World Bank, 1994). The specific quotation on wealth transfer from poor to rich comes from British researcher Gareth Williams in Clark, *Perspectives.*

Chapter Nine: The University Is the Axial Institution of Modern Society

Professor McCauley's quotation appeared originally in the journal *Liberal Education* 68 (spring 1982). We exchanged opinions in that publication regarding the efficacy of his argument. I have not changed my mind as a result of our interchange. I believe that the statement about Kant's correspondent was told to me by one of my Kantian instructors, the late Professor Warner Wick. I have not found the quotation; if no such quotation exists in Kant's letters, I reserve the right to assign the source of misinformation elsewhere (to some philosophical enemy rather than to one of my revered friends and mentors). The point is clearly Kantian. A footnote in a late edition of *The Critique of Practical Reason* reads:

> A reviewer who wanted to find fault with this work has hit the truth better, perhaps, than he thought, when he says that no new principle of morality is set forth, only a *new formula*. But who would think of introducing a new principle of morality, and making himself, as it were the first discoverer of it, just as if all the world before him were ignorant what duty was or had been in thoroughgoing error.

Chapter Ten: Synthetic Morality

There is a fair amount of philosophical comment in this chapter on the nature of moral discourse. I am heartened by the fact that similar arguments, with considerably greater depth and sophistication than here appropriate, can be found in Alisdair MacIntyre, *Whose Justice, Which Rationality* (Notre Dame: University of Notre Dame Press, 1988), and also in his Gifford Lectures, *Three Versions of Moral Enquiry: Encyclopedia, Genealogy, and Tradition* (Notre Dame: University of Notre Dame Press, 1990). Equally valuable is Charles Taylor, *Sources of the Self: The Making of Modern Identity* (Cambridge: Harvard University Press, 1989). Both MacIntyre and Taylor are keen on the indispensability of history and tradition for grounding moral discourse; they are thus equally opposed to the magisterial presentation of a "transcendental morality" by John Rawls, *A Theory of Justice* (Cambridge: Harvard University Press, 1971). Further development of my argument would differentiate in more depth and detail the difference between traditions in art and morality, but I believe that the text makes a strong prima facie case for moral traditioning using the analogy with artistic development.

Chapter Eleven: Ultimate Synthesis—Money, Mission, and Management

For the discussion of mission-with-content, see Burton R. Clark, *The Distinctive College: Antioch, Reed, Swarthmore* (Chicago: Aldine, 1970).

It is not insignificant that my graduate education was at the University of Chicago during a time when the glow of Robert Hutchins remained a presence. He himself had departed for the Ford Foundation and then on to the Center for the Study of Democratic Institutions (El Parthenon, as he referred to that idealistic thinkery). The Hutchins "glow" could be regarded as persistent light of educational vision or residual heat generated by stringent criticism of his views, but the Hutchins "plan" was everywhere in evidence. The first university protest I ever witnessed, complete with placards, chants, a cordon of students, and the lot, was a student protest *against* the introduction of electives into the fixed curriculum of the Hutchins College. I believe that Hutchins's ideas for the university remain of significant value and might well be restudied for their financial implications as much as their philosophical justifications.

Several years ago I was reviewing a biography of Hutchins. Carrying the book to an AAU meeting, I was confronted by a prominent Ivy League president who tapped on the volume and said, "There was a troublemaker!" Indeed—a tragic troublemaker. That Hutchins's views on higher education were not more widely debated, modified, and incorporated may be seen as a small-scale American tragedy. What prevented sensible adoption and adaptation were two salient features: Hutchins's personality and a supposed allegiance to Thomistic synthesis. Hutchins was nothing if not arrogant in the presentation of his educational gospel. (I invited him to speak at Princeton while I was there. He had not been on the Princeton campus in thirty years, but it took him only three minutes to gratuitously affront the locals.) If personal high-handedness was not enough, flirting with Thomism seemed even worse. The Thomism of the day appeared to both its defenders and its detractors as the be-all and end-all of all philosophy. Hutchins's plan took on the aura of dogmatic deduction, which would be quite sufficient to cause its rejection by the broader academic community. I am not sure whether Hutchins himself regarded Thomas as the last word in metaphysics. He did not have that deep a philosophic bent; he just liked good debate. Alisdair MacIntyre's current revisionist St. Thomas (see *Three Versions*) presents him as the paradigm of an open-ended "craft" tradition of philosophizing—anything but dogmatic. Had that been the prevailing view of Thomas, perhaps the Hutchins plan would have had broader currency.

Whatever one might think of the specifics of Hutchins's collegiate curriculum, it had the distinct advantage of highly self-conscious planning, moral direction, and cumulative learning—all virtues substantially lost in the "do your own disciplinary thing" philosophy that currently prevails in higher education. I would especially applaud "cumulative learning." When the research revolution began its takeover of higher education, Jesuit educators were in steadfast opposition. The elective system, which permitted wide course choice and fostered the new urge for disciplinary specialization, violated the essential principle of the traditional Jesuit *ratio studiorum*. The *ratio* was based on the notion that course material had to be sequenced, building toward some overall view of the nature of knowledge, ethics, and life. Now the Jesuits had their own idea of what this cumulative learning might look like, and one is allowed to disagree with the synthesis. The Hutchins College had its own *ratio*, culminating in the final year's legendary O.M.P. (Organization, Methods, and Principles of the "sciences") course. One might quibble and quarrel with the S.J.s or the O.M.P., but attempting an overview seems fully commensurate to the depth and power and scope of the higher learning. It is surely the road to wisdom.

Index